The Big Talk

Talking to Your Child about Sex and Dating

Laurie Langford

John Wiley & Sons, Inc.

New York • Chichester • Weinheim • Brisbane • Singapore • Toronto

This publication is designed to provide accurate and authoritative information in
regard to the subject matter covered. It is sold with the understanding that the
publisher is not engaged in rendering professional services. If professional advice or
other expert assistance is required, the services of a competent professional person
should be sought.

The list on pages 114 to 116 is taken from *Focus on the Family,* January 1977. It is
part of a forthcoming book by Dayle Allen Schockley. Used with permission

The story on pages 195 to 197 is taken from *She Calls Me Daddy* by Robert
Wolgemuth and published by Focus on the Family. Copyright © by Robert D.
Wolgemuth. All rights reserved. International copyright secured. Used by permission.

Library of Congress Cataloging-in-Publication Data:

Langford, Laurie.
    The Big Talk: Talking to your child about sex and dating / Laurie Langford.
        p.   cm.
        Includes index.
        ISBN: 978-1-62045-709-2
        1. Sex instruction.   2. Sexual ethics.   3. Sexual abstinence.
    4. Parenting.   5. Parent and teenager.   I. Title.
    HQ57.L33   1998
    649'.65—dc21   98-10052

Printed in the United States of America

10 9 8 7 6 5 4 3 2 1

Contents

Introduction

Did your parents give you a complete and useful sex education? Most people respond to that question with "Yeah, *right!* The word *sex* wasn't even mentioned!" About one-third of fifteen-year-old girls and boys say *neither* parent has talked to them about sex, nor does communication appear to improve as they get older. As a result, most children learn about sex from their peers, school, or the media (that's a scary thought). Teenagers usually begin learning what they need to know *after* they have become sexually active, if they learn at all.

The "big talk" used to mean Mom or Dad sat you down for one brief discussion about the birds and the bees. The conversation may have included information on anatomy issues such as menstruation and other physical changes. Almost no one remembers exactly what was said, and it rarely made a difference in their lives.

Today, the big talk usually consists of a warning to be "careful," to wait until you're "ready," or to be "safe." It seems that many people have thrown up their arms in despair, resigning themselves to the idea that teenagers are going to be sexual and that the best we can do is teach them how to be safe and responsible. But how safe and responsible is it for a teenager to have sex, even if he or she does use contraception?

Well, I have a few ideas that I think you will find even more helpful as you have the big talk with your child.

I am not a therapist, nor do I claim to be an expert on raising children. The information that I share with you is not based on psychology or years spent obtaining a degree. I write from my own personal experience. Contained in the following pages is *everything I wish I had learned throughout my childhood and teen years about sex and dating.* Like many of you, I learned everything I now know the hard way—through trial and error. At fourteen I ran away from home, where I received my own version of sex education (not one I would recommend for your child!). I supported myself primarily by playing pool for money, which meant that most of my youth was spent in pool halls and bars. Like every teenager, I thought I knew everything, and I insisted on learning just about everything through painful experience. Living at home was difficult at best. My mother was killed in an auto accident when I was two years old. My father was an alcoholic. This situation, in addition to other problems, prevented my father and stepmother from teaching me valuable life skills. Having the big talk was out of the question. We were dealing with basic survival. During my teen years as well as throughout my twenties, I dated a lot and found myself in relationships, but I didn't have the tools I needed to make them work. I am now thirty-three years old. The past eighteen years have been my training ground for writing this book. Fortunately, I learned from my mistakes. I am now passing on to others what I have learned, including helping parents to teach their kids how to avoid many of the things I experienced. It took me far too long to learn the information I've tried to convey in this book. I was fortunate in that I craved knowledge, and I had a deep longing to learn how to build a relationship and avoid casual sexual relationships. Your child, provided you begin having the big talk now, won't have to learn everything the hard way.

My life experiences led me to write my first book, *If It's Love You Want, Why Settle for (Just) Sex?* (Prima, 1996). During seminars I gave on the subject, I was often asked by parents, "How can I teach my child these principles before it's too late?" I knew this information could greatly benefit parents, who are more concerned (and in many cases more confused) than ever before, about what to teach their kids on this subject.

Talking about sex with your child is no easy task. I know, because I've spoken to many parents who have told me that this is one of the most uncomfortable aspects of parenting. You don't know what to say or when to say it, your child may be too embarrassed to discuss the subject, and the right time never seems to present itself. I will suggest ways to overcome these obstacles. The first step is to determine what you're going to teach.

You will find *The Big Talk* different from other books on the subject. Most books are filled with facts, figures, and pictures of body parts. The focus is primarily on anatomical changes during puberty, with a clinical, dry tone. Most authors leave out information on how to date and build a relationship based on love and commitment. Advice on exactly what to say and how to say it is usually not included. While I believe that information on anatomy is important, it certainly wasn't what I desperately needed to know when I was a child and teenager.

What kind of information is *crucial* for your child to know? For me it was the age at which it was appropriate to become sexual, how to say no to sex without scaring the boy away or hurting his feelings, what sex is really all about and how it changes a relationship, how to behave on a date, what boys find particularly appealing in a girl, and information about love. Boys have their own set of concerns: Should I make a sexual advance, and if so, when? Will I be seen as a wimp if I don't? Do girls like it when you pressure them? How do I ask a girl out? How should I handle rejection?

This is the kind of information you will find in the following pages. I will share some of my own childhood experiences throughout the book, as well as the stories of the dozens of parents and teens I've spoken to (their names will be changed). (To avoid redundancy, the words *he* and *she* have been used alternately in each chapter of the book. Almost all of the information applies to both sexes, however.) While everyone's childhood and teenage years are different, the information we all need to learn is essentially the same. Your own personal experiences can be your greatest assets in teaching your child about sex and dating. As one mother wisely said, "My mistakes can be my child's lessons."

Be Prepared

Most parents know they have to have the big talk, but they procrastinate. "Our lives are so full, who has the time?" one woman said. "I have no idea what to say!" another mother told me. "I guess I secretly hope that my child will just figure it all out so that I won't have to deal with the embarrassment of discussing it" is how one single father put it.

The good news is that having the big talk isn't as complex as it seems. And it isn't just one talk. The big talk is a series of talks that you will have over the course of your child's life. Children don't need long, drawn-out dialogues about every minute detail on sex. They need only a few simple, basic principles explained to them and then consistently reinforced throughout their upbringing.

The goal is to help your child learn the skills and tools necessary to avoid having one-night stands, mediocre relationships that lead to despair and unfulfillment—and all the other physical, spiritual, emotional, and mental harm that can come from having casual sex—and to give her the tools she'll need to build a healthy, loving relationship that lasts. This isn't accomplished in one conversation. Make sex, love, and dating open topics in your home by talking opening and honestly about them on a regular basis. If you don't, you may run into problems when you do discuss the subject. Shane, nineteen, would have welcomed discussions about sex if they had been a consistent part of his childhood. "My mom took me through the clinical rundown, then my dad took me for a drive to visit relatives who lived about three hours away. He said, 'Son, do you know what moral cleanliness means?' I felt trapped. Here we were, in the car alone for three hours. I was mortified. It was just so *intimate*. If we had been more open and intimate at other times, it would have seemed more casual and comfortable. But it was this one big, uncomfortable talk, and then that was it. He never talked about it again!"

When you know what you're going to say, and how you're going to convey that information, you will actually become passionate about educating your child. At that point, all you need is some time with your child. Getting her to participate is another story. But ideas on how to create open communication are given in chapter 1. If you begin having these conversations when your child is younger, you'll have a much easier time talking to her about this subject when she reaches her teens. Having these talks will help your child develop control over her own life. As your child reaches her teens, you'll be able to let go of the reins somewhat because high standards will already have been established. Actual dialogues are presented in each chapter, so you'll know exactly what to say and how to say it. You will find that many of the "talks" overlap, and some of the discussions are mentioned more than once but are expressed in a slightly different way. This is because kids forget information that's given to them in one brief conversation. They need to hear the same ideas again and again in order to fully internalize the information.

Read through *The Big Talk* and discuss it with your spouse. If you are divorced, discuss the contents of the book with your ex-spouse and determine what information you should convey to your child. For your child's sake, the two of you should do your best to present a unified front. Also, gather brochures and pamphlets from various organizations, and go to the library and bookstores to get copies of books on the subjects of parenting, sex, dating, self-esteem, and love. Attend the sex-ed class being held at your child's school, and obtain a copy of the curriculum or workbook she will be using. Many parents trust that educators will give their children valuable information but are later appalled at what is actually being taught.

In *The Arizona Republic*, the author, Michael Chiusano, wrote about a first grader who came home and told his father that women could change themselves into men and men into women. It seems that the child's teacher was offering detailed information about the sex-change process. Another school, in Newton, Massachusetts, gave seventh graders "graphic descriptions of oral and anal sex." Chiusano wrote: "Across the country, bizarre and intrusive programs are part of everyday business in public (and private) schools, a world virtually at war with the everyday values of parents." Parents are not notified in advance about what will be taught. Be proactive and find out for yourself what is being taught *before* your child is exposed to information that may conflict with your own values. The fact that kids are hearing about these things in grade school is all the more reason to start educating your child early.

There is so much information your child will receive on a daily basis that may contradict what you believe. In order for you to combat this flow of damaging and life-threatening information, you need to consistently teach higher principles in your own home.

Be Confident

Many parents I spoke with made comments like "I wouldn't dare say that to my kid!" or "My son would never go for that!" But remember, *you* are the parent—the one who sets the rules, the adult. If you've lost control, get it back! Have a family meeting and announce that some serious changes are going to be made, new rules are going to be established (your child can help determine some of the rules), and that there will be consequences for those who fail to follow these rules. It's a fair system because everyone will know what's expected as well as the consequences of not complying. You will determine which rules to establish as you read through this book. One mother who did this said, "This way your kids can't get mad at *you*, because you're just enforcing the rule that has been established in your home. You just keep pointing out that it's the *law* that says this is the way it is!"

Teenagers will whine, pout, get angry, refuse to talk to you, and use a thousand other tactics to try to get you to compromise and bend the rules. But for the good of your child, you have to stand firm and not cave in. Explain that the rule is in place to *protect* her, not to make her miserable. Most teenagers will appreciate having clear guidelines to follow. One teen girl admitted, "A lot of parents let their kids do whatever they want. Even though it's a pain sometimes, in the long run I like that my parents have rules."

Also, exude confidence as you present the ideas in this book. One fifteen-year-old boy said, "I don't like talking about sex with my dad because he gets all nervous." Talk matter-of-factly about the subject. Appear casual, confident, and prepared. This will make your child feel more comfortable about the process.

Having the talks that relate to teenagers can be difficult, because when kids reach their teens they usually want to pull further away from their parents. They want to spend more time with their friends. Make being at home with the family and talking about meaningful issues attractive by adding fun and creating a sense of harmony in your home. Your child should know that participating is mandatory. When an adolescent says, "I don't want to talk about this stuff with you!" you can respond with, "I'm sorry you feel that way because we're going to have a lot of these kinds of talks." Discussing important, meaningful issues should become a part of your family culture.

Teach Abstinence

The Big Talk will show you how to teach your child to abstain from sex until *marriage* based on practical reasons that this is the best choice. Chapter 6 explores other options, such as waiting until she reaches adulthood and is in a committed, loving relationship or is engaged to be married. I feel passionate about teaching abstinence until marriage because of my own personal experiences, as well as because I've seen the devastation that can come with premarital sex in the teenagers and single adults I've spoken to. But you will have to explore the options for yourself and determine exactly what values you want to impart to your child based on your own religious and moral beliefs. The information in chapter 6 will help you clarify your own beliefs on this matter.

Your child needs to learn early that it is possible to wait until marriage, that even though it may seem as if everyone else is doing "it," she doesn't have to. She needs to be able to clearly articulate what her sexual standards are ("I am waiting until marriage"), and to know how to respond to sexual advances. She needs to understand that she is in charge of her body, and that no one can make her do something she doesn't choose to do. And she needs to know how to relate to the opposite sex, so that she can have positive dating experiences.

Methods of Teaching

The next step is determining *how* you will convey the information. Within each chapter you will find several "talks" to have with your child at various times in her childhood. You choose the time and place, preferably when you can be alone with your child without interruptions. Because the big talk involves having many conversations over a long period of time, you will have to be creative about coming up with private moments. You might want to take your child out to her favorite restaurant, go for a drive, or stay up late some evenings when you can talk privately. You can also establish a weekly family night where the entire family meets to discuss various topics. (This will be covered in more detail in chapter 1.) Some of the discussions can be initiated more spontaneously—for example, as you're watching a movie at home, or when you're talking about a friend or family member who just found out that she's pregnant. There are always opportunities that allow you to talk about the subject without its appearing to be planned or contrived.

Each chapter also contains metaphors, games, role-playing exercises, and hypothetical examples for you to use as teaching tools. You can prepare your child for one-on-one talks by saying, "Next Tuesday night I'd like for us to spend some time together talking about some important issues. I thought we would go out to dinner—just the two of us." If your idea meets with resistance, stand firm. Say, "I thought you would enjoy hanging out with your mom for a change! Listen, this is really important. Besides, we'll have fun. I'm looking forward to spending some time together!" Don't let last-minute things get in the way of your time together. Once a commitment has been made, both of you need to honor that commitment and get together no matter what, barring a real emergency. Let your child know that these discussions are going to be a regular part of her life. Assure her that it won't be too painful, that you want to *discuss* issues, not preach to her, and that you will always try to include some kind of fun. You probably won't encounter this much resistance if you're talking to a younger child. It's a bit more challenging when you begin having the big talk with a teenager, though. Although it might seem more comfortable for mothers to talk to their daughters, and for fathers to talk to their sons, there's no reason it can't work the other way around. In fact, sometimes it's very effective to do it this way, depending on the kind of rapport you have with your child.

The Big Talk is a book of practical information. The message isn't religious per se, but it can work in harmony with whatever your religious beliefs may be. Of course, it is better to begin teaching moral values early, but it's never too late to introduce the principles that are outlined in this book. Discussions that pertain to younger children have to do with the body: teaching your child to care for her body, discussing body parts, and introducing the concepts of sacredness and modesty. Between the ages of eight and twelve, you will go into more detail about sex and reproduction, puberty and establishing sexual standards. With teenagers you'll discuss how to deal with sexual advances and issues relating to dating, love, and relationships. Some parents feel that a child who is between the ages of eight and twelve is too young to learn about sex, whereas others think that if you wait until the child is thirteen or fourteen, it may be too late. You'll have to decide for yourself when you want to have some of these discussions with your child, but I do make specific suggestions for the age at which each talk should occur.

The book has been organized into four parts: "Getting Started," "Setting Sexual Standards," "Handling Sexual Pressures," and "Establishing Healthy Relationships." Relationship issues are covered last because I believe kids should determine their sexual standards first. Learning how to develop a healthy relationship will make more sense once your child knows how she should handle the sexual aspect of a relationship. I have found that sexual advances usually surface before relationship issues do.

Please don't procrastinate! Studies show that kids *want* their parents to talk to them about sex. Most teenagers know that they have too little information and knowledge about sex and dating, even though they don't like to admit this fact. But young people do want to learn and, believe it or not, most adolescents still think that their parents are the most reliable source for helpful information. In fact, most adolescents agree with their parents' views on many issues: education, family, being responsible, and so on. They may not verbalize their agreement, but they do share many of the same values.

Sometimes it takes a while for teenagers to realize that, just maybe, parents know what they're talking about. But don't give up. As Mark Twain said, "When I was eighteen I thought my father didn't know a thing. At twenty-one I was amazed at how much he learned in three short years!"

These crucial years ahead can be painful and confusing for your child. Or they can be uplifting, wonderful, and inspirational, as you go about the business of preparing her for a life of love and happiness. May this book act as your guide in providing your child with a solid foundation of wisdom about sex, dating, and love that will serve her throughout her life.

❖ I ❖

Getting Started

❖ 1 ❖

Creating Open Communication

The ultimate goal of having *the big talk* is to *reach* your child. You want your words to touch your child's heart, and inspire him to incorporate the values you teach into his own life. You want him to *want* to follow the advice you give, and to develop his own values. This can be accomplished as your child internalizes the information you share. But how you convey the information will make all the difference.

According to a study conducted by Boyd C. Rollins and Darwin L. Thomas ("Parental Support, Power, and Control Techniques in the Socialization of Children," 1979), there are important distinctions between the *power* of parents (your ability to force compliance even if your child disagrees) and parental *control attempts*. Control attempts are described as either *coercive* (a dictatorial approach with severe consequences) or *inductive* (based on explanations and reasoning). The study shows that parental coercion is most likely to be effective in the short term, but induction is most likely to result in the child's adopting the parents' standards and living in accordance with them in the future.

You don't want your child to comply with your advice only because you insist. You want him to actually believe in the wisdom of those values as a result of considering the consequences or benefits of the choices he has made. This won't be easy to do, considering that kids (and particularly teenagers) are often preoccupied and at times uncommunicative, but it can be done. Don't buy into the idea that kids don't listen to their parents. Many teens whom I spoke with said, "I'd feel weird talking to my parents about that stuff at first, but eventually I'd get into it."

No matter how poor your communication or relationship with your child may be right now, there is so much you can do to improve it. As you read through the following chapters, you will see that a lot

3

of communication will take place. You will have many conversations with your child about various aspects of sex and dating. But you will be able to do this only if you already have an open, trusting relationship with your child. One way to accomplish this is by adding *emotion* to your discussions. Rae, seventeen, said, "My parents never talk about their feelings. They only tell me what to do." Saying "I want to talk about this because I love you and want the best for you" is more effective than saying "You know I don't approve of what you're doing."

It's very sad, but my father's hopes and dreams for me were very different from what he conveyed to me when I was young. It's only been over the past few years that I have fully understood what my dad really wants for me and how he truly feels. He's always saying things like "Laurie, I want you to experience the joy of having your own family. That's where it's at—that's where you'll find true happiness and meaning in your life." When my dad talks to me in this way—with fatherly love and concern—I am moved. There is a connection that occurs between us because I know that he cares, and because I know that he doesn't want me to be alone, to not experience true, lasting love. In moments like these, I am open to discussing my fears, doubts, and hopes with my dad. And I do, which allows him to share his wisdom with me.

Unfortunately, my father and I couldn't communicate when I was growing up. I realize that he did the best he could under the circumstances. But so much more learning could have taken place if we had been able to have these heart-to-heart talks then. Don't wait until your child is all grown up to tell him how you really feel, and to express what you really want for him. Let him know now. He just might listen.

When talking to your child, share your *intentions* in addition to offering information. Your child may not always know that you might be afraid for his welfare, or that you want only the best for him, or that you want him to be more confident and secure with himself. He may only hear you going on and on about what he *should* do or criticizing him about what he's doing wrong. Former Surgeon General Everett Koop, who was a pediatrician, was asked if he had one thing to say to parents, what would it be? His answer: "Make yourself available for dialogue with your children, because they desperately want to know how you feel about them."

When our words are carefully chosen, then backed up with love, sincerity, compassion, and genuine concern, we can have a huge impact. Sigmund Freud said, "Words have a magical power. They can bring either the greatest happiness or deepest despair; they can transfer knowledge from teacher to student; words enable the orator to sway his audience and dictate its decision. Words are capable of arousing the strongest emotions and prompting all men's actions."

If you already have good, open communication with your child, that's great! You'll have a much easier time talking with him. But depending on the relationship you currently have with your child, you may need to gently break down any walls that have been constructed. This is particularly true if you're dealing with a teenager and you haven't had intimate discussions with him up to this point. Kids under the age of twelve are usually open and curious and therefore less inhibited when it comes to discussing just about any subject.

Start with a Clean Slate

Imagine how different your relationship might have been had your parent (the one you had a difficult time talking with) come to you with a humble heart and a loving spirit, and said, "Honey, I just want you to know that I love you with all my heart. I know I haven't always been the best parent. I haven't always listened to you or shown interest in your feelings, but I want to start over. More than anything, I would like to begin today to build a better, closer relationship with you. Life is too short, and you'll be out on your own before long. I don't want there to be any walls between us. Are you willing to try, too?"

I can't imagine a child not responding to this sincere plea. If you feel that you and your child have a wall between you, try this approach. If your child doesn't respond as you would like, then the wall between you is perhaps thicker than you thought. This means you need to be even more persistent and patient in trying to break through. But human nature is generally open to this kind of sincerity and humility. If there are walls and bad feelings, try this approach before you attempt to have the big talk.

The Six Building Blocks of Good Communication

The following "building blocks of good communication" were gleaned from conversations I've had with teenagers. In reflecting on my own childhood, I realized that these principles weren't a part of my relationship with my father and stepmother, which is largely why we couldn't talk openly about meaningful aspects of life. They are Trust, Respect, Honesty, Love, Understanding, and Family Identity. Without a foundation of these qualities in your relationship with your child, having the big talk will be difficult at best. You can achieve good, open communication if you consistently follow these guidelines.

Trust

Teenagers mentioned *trust* as being their biggest concern when it comes to relating to their parents. You child won't be open and honest with you if he doesn't feel safe doing so. Try to do the following:

Keep Confidences

What a great feeling it is to have at least one person with whom we can share our innermost thoughts and feelings. Every child needs this kind of connection, and who fills this role better than a mother or a father? If parents blab every tidbit of information that is shared with them, it soon becomes clear that they can't be trusted and mum's the word. Always keep your child's personal life private from outside friends and extended family, but let the child know that sometimes you have to discuss personal issues with your spouse. Vow to develop a deep and meaningful relationship that is created by keeping confidences.

Trust Your Child until You Have a Reason to Do Otherwise

Sometimes communication is severed before you even get started. This can happen if your child feels that you don't trust him to begin with. One seventeen-year-old boy told me, "My mom always thinks I'm doing something wrong. But the funny thing is, she never *asks* me what's really going on, she just assumes the worst."

One teenage girl, who was going through a rebellious time, told me that her mother said, "So, who'd you shack up with last night?" This girl grew up believing she was cheap because that's how her mother viewed her. This mother had some cause to think her daughter wasn't making wise choices, but she showed distrust before even having a heart-to-heart discussion. Your child may destroy trust with his behavior and then have to earn your trust back, but being trustful until you have reason to believe otherwise will open up communication tenfold. Question your child to obtain the facts before offering advice or stipulating consequences for what you think is bad behavior. Also, *threats* destroy open communication and imply that you don't trust your child. If you find yourself saying, "If I ever catch you doing this . . . . !," spend more time developing a trusting, open relationship with your child.

Trust doesn't mean letting your adolescent stay out all night, or allowing him to be in dangerous situations, but it does mean showing faith in his ability to make wise choices until he gives you reason to rethink that position.

FULFILL PROMISES

Many teenagers feel they can't trust their parents to be there for them or to come through for them in times of need. You are committed to your child, and you realize that this is a lifetime relationship—one of the most important relationships you will ever have. But does your child know this? Keeping your word is one link in building an incredible bond that is based on trust.

Respect

Many teenagers complain that their parents don't give them credit for being thoughtful, intelligent people with valid ideas and the ability to make meaningful contributions. This can cause a child to shut down and avoid expressing himself to a parent. Showing your child that you respect him just might inspire him to respect you, and if your child feels respected by you he'll behave in ways that will ensure that respect. Here are some ways to do this:

LISTEN TO YOUR CHILD

Make it known that your child's thoughts, feelings, and opinions are relevant and important to you. Robert, sixteen, said, "If I actually had a parent who would talk to me as kind of a friend and really listened to me—especially when I start giving my opinion—that would be so great!" Patrice, fourteen, said, "My mom is always ready to give me advice, but sometimes all I want is for her to listen and let me get it all out."

Sometimes it's wise to bite your tongue, at least for a while, and allow your child the opportunity to express himself. Reflect on what your child tells you before offering your own insights. Aside from encouraging your child to open up, this allows you to think things through and better understand how *he* thinks.

Earn Your Child's Respect

Charlie Rose was interviewing Mira Sorvino, the Academy Award–winning actress. He asked her what it was like working for Robert Redford, one of the biggest names in Hollywood. Her answer was very interesting. She said, "I have so much respect for him, I just wanted to do a good job. I didn't want to let him down." You can foster this same attitude toward you in your child.

When I asked one mother how she managed to raise such well-behaved children, she had this to say, "Physically, children, and especially teenagers, are able to do whatever they want. But if you have their respect they do what you ask of them out of respect and love for you."

The Cravens, the parents of four teenagers, told me likewise: "We believe that the respect our children have for us is largely because of the sacrifices we have made for them over the years. We have stayed up half the night with school projects that had to get done; we have gone into debt in order to provide special equipment or things that our kids have needed; we have spent countless hours talking until the wee hours, counseling or consoling a brokenhearted child. It is very difficult to hurt or rebel against someone who has laid down their life for you. It has just always been a part of our family culture to be kind to others, to serve, and to love those around us. This has become our children's way as well."

A male friend of mine talked with me about his upbringing. "When I was young, I vowed to wait until I was married to have sex," he said. "Partly because I felt that was the right way, but also because I didn't want to hurt my mother's feelings. In our home, I don't ever remember walking out the door without getting a kiss. My parents were so loving to us that we felt compelled to act honorably, for them if nothing else."

Look Your Child in the Eyes When You Speak to Him

Studies have shown that when a parent looks into the eyes of the child he or she is addressing, something magical happens. Children experience a greater feeling of peace. They gain a deeper sense of trust and connection to the parent. This takes practice, partly because in our society we aren't exactly trained to do this. It is an intimate, emotional experience to look someone in the eyes for more than a couple of seconds at a time, but every child needs to be able to make that connection.

GIVE YOUR CHILD A CERTAIN AMOUNT OF SPACE

Parents don't own their children. Children are a wonderful blessing, and parents have a responsibility to nurture and teach them, but the children don't belong to their parents as if they were a possession. Parenting is more of a stewardship; you have these wonderful little people for a time, but they come with their own personalities and missions, and eventually they must go out and fulfill their own purpose in life. They need a certain amount of space to make their own choices. Teenagers usually let their parents know when they need more breathing room. Respect your adolescent's need for more freedom. Give him more independence little by little, and as he proves to be a responsible person.

Honesty

It's almost impossible to really help your child and teach him what he needs to know if you can't even get to the truth of how he honestly feels and what he's going through. But before you expect him to be honest with you, you have to be honest with him. Try the following:

BE REAL

Kids complain that their parents can't have a normal conversation about sex and dating. Teens say that their parents get nervous, uptight, "weird," as though they were hiding something or holding back information. This gives the impression that sex is a forbidden subject rather than a normal part of life. Many teenagers claim that their parents avoid having deep, meaningful conversations about important issues, or that when their parents do initiate intimate discussions they seem to have an agenda. These teens say they don't feel they can trust their parents to offer them a comprehensive sex education, only a biased perspective. It's okay to present only the values you would like your child to adopt, but you can also discuss opposing views or what's going on in society. Begin now by letting down whatever barriers you yourself may have constructed and talk naturally with your child about the subjects that matter most in his life.

BE TRUTHFUL

Adolescents are pretty savvy. They know when they're being talked down to, conned, or if something is being sugarcoated by adults. Many adolescents say that they don't turn to their parents because they don't think they'll get the whole truth. Be honest with your child about what is really going on, not only to give him a complete education but to cultivate an open, trusting relationship. You can preface or end honest answers with "This is what some people believe . . . but in our family we believe differently, and this is why. . . ."

DON'T PREACH

Nothing will destroy communication faster than being preachy. Regardless of how right you feel you are, sermonizing is ineffective in getting your child to make wise choices. It *is* effective in constructing walls that may never come down. Kids want to feel that a discussion is a two-way street—you talk, then they talk—and that together you will analyze, discuss, offer opinions, debate. Teenagers want to know *why* things are the way they are. They want to know that you are willing to discuss all aspects of a situation and provide them with *choices,* not just your *law.* (This doesn't apply to rules you have established in your home, although kids want the freedom to discuss their views regarding the rules.)

Keely, sixteen, told me something that I frequently hear from teenagers: "Sex is very embarrassing to talk about with parents. Most of what I've learned, I've learned through friends. I pretty much know the basics, and I'll learn from people. I don't go to my parents because they always go off on a tangent about what I'm doing wrong." You will want to assure your child that he can come to you without being afraid of your reaction, and that you will discuss the issues together.

Love

If your child feels loved, accepted, and appreciated, he will be more likely to listen and participate in discussions about important subjects. Try the following:

Be Affectionate

Zig Ziglar, the best-selling author of *Raising Positive Kids in a Negative World* (Oliver Nelson Books, 1985), once said, "Love is the highest, purest, most precious of all spiritual things. It will draw out from men their magnificent potential." Being affectionate is one important way of showing your child that you love him. A pat on the back, a kiss on the cheek, a big hug, and especially a warm "I love you!" sprinkled throughout the week have therapeutic effects on us all. Your child will feel special, loved, cherished, cared about. This will have a ripple effect in his day-to-day living. As he hears these words or feels your loving touch, he can then go out into the world with a radiance that he may not have experienced before. He will stand taller and smile a little brighter. He will draw to him higher-quality people, and he will be more emotionally capable of building healthy relationships.

In his book *Children of Character* (Canter & Associates, 1997), Steven Carr Reuben, Ph.D., writes: "Benjamin West, one of the first Americans to win recognition as an artist, used to tell about a childhood incident in which he painted a portrait of his sister on the kitchen floor. When his mother came home, before directing him to clean up the mess, she looked at him and exclaimed, 'What a beautiful picture you have made of your sister!' Then she bent down and kissed him. 'With that kiss,' West later recalled, 'I became a painter.'" You never know the full impact love and affection will have on your child.

Show Acceptance and Appreciation

Goethe said, "The way you see people and the way you treat them is what they become." Nothing will encourage open and honest conversation more than showing genuine acceptance and appreciation for your child as he is *right now*. He may make poor choices or have lousy friends or dress in outrageous clothes, but these things don't make up *all* of who he is. Search for those gems within his character. Find ways to accept the things you cannot change about him. Verbally express your appreciation for what you admire in him. If you do, you'll see amazing improvement in all other areas of your relationship. You will see your child behaving more responsibly, you'll experience kinder behavior from him, and you will see a more confident child. The idea is to work with the traits your child possesses rather than trying to make him something he's not. As the humorist

Robert Henry said, "People do not live by bread alone. They need buttering up once in a while."

BUILD YOUR CHILD'S CONFIDENCE

In order to say no to sexual advances, date quality people, and have a healthy dating life, teens need to have self-confidence. Julene, the mother of five children, said, "The best thing a parent can do is watch very closely what happens on a daily basis with their children. For example, if you notice that your child feels inferior to others, you begin to work on that. Perhaps you notice things happening between this child and his siblings. Sometimes siblings can try to tear each other down as a way to boost their own egos. I tell my kids that we want to always be *builders,* not *destroyers.* I had to ask my little daughter the other day, 'Do you think that was a building type of comment you made to your brother, or something that would destroy the way he feels about himself?' Kids do respond when they're approached in a loving way that points out the effect of what they are doing."

Talbot, the father of three teens, said: "Confidence seems to come by learning how to be independent. We have a rule that at the age of twelve our kids have to be self-supporting, other than housing and food. We own a farm, so they are able to do extra work on the farm to earn money. They buy their own school clothes and pay for their entertainment. We have only seen excellent benefits and rewards for doing this. Our children feel very confident and proud that they are able to provide for themselves."

Juliana, the mother of two children, said: "The greatest opportunity a parent has to build a child's self-esteem and let him know of his worth is when the child is misbehaving. That moment is crucial because if he has misbehaved, and yet we still show him that we love him, the message he gets is powerful. He thinks, 'Oh, Mom loves me even though I've done something wrong—I must be a pretty good person.' Whereas if you don't convey this, he thinks, 'Mom must not love me—maybe she would only love me if I were perfect. I must not be a very good person.'"

Amelia, the mother of four children, said: "The key is to talk *kindly* to our kids, to never make them feel that we are attacking them. Trust is what we're striving for here—love is the only way we will ever get there. Kids need to know that you are on their side. Verbal abuse is the first thing to destroy progress. Parents start yelling at their kids, then criticizing. This is all abusive behavior, and it destroys any chance of building trust."

Samson, the father of five children, said: "During dinner we encourage our kids to talk about their strengths and what they like to do. Sometimes we have siblings mention what they love best about each other, which always makes for a fun time. Kids can complete sentences that you create, such as, I am . . . I like to . . . My best trait is . . . My sister and I are alike/different in the following ways. . . ."

Remind your child often that he is an important part of your family, that he is a worthy participant in the world around him, and that he has a lot to offer. Convey to him that he is loved regardless of how smart or talented or successful he is. Express your belief that he is attractive, unique, and special. Make it crystal-clear that you are committed to supporting him.

Understanding

In creating open communication, you and your child will want to understand each other's perspective and feelings. Try the following:

TRY TO UNDERSTAND YOUR CHILD'S PERSPECTIVE

Have you ever been in a relationship with someone who may have been nice in many ways but failed to show interest in your innermost thoughts and feelings? We all have very deep feelings and opinions about things. We all have dreams and aspirations that often transcend what others around us are aware that we have. The problem is, we may never have been asked about these things. Who wants to share his views with an uninterested audience? Even more true, who wants to share his innermost thoughts with someone who might criticize or condemn him?

Your child has very specific thoughts, opinions, and feelings about practically every subject. If he hasn't thought about a particular subject before, once it is brought to his attention he will begin to form his own views on the matter. More often than not, kids keep these views to themselves. Your child longs to share his views, but he will do so only if he believes they will be met with acceptance, appreciation, and enthusiasm.

LET YOUR CHILD KNOW WHAT YOU EXPECT

Explain to your child what is expected of him. Rules need to be clearly spelled out, and your child needs to understand why each rule is important. When you set the rules of the household, you protect yourself from being the bad guy. When a rule is broken, the child must face the consequences, which have already been established. You say, "I'm so sorry that you chose to break that rule." You can actually sympathize with your child over his poor choice, and the fact that he will have to suffer the consequences.

Make it clear to him what his job is: to be a good student; to show up for classes and other activities; to be responsible; to do his chores around the house; to attend church or temple; to serve others; to prepare for adulthood and his own future family; and to have fun along the way.

Don't Protect Your Child from Taking Responsibility for His Actions

On the news more and more, I see parents who would rather find a way to save their guilty children than allow them to learn from their mistakes and ultimately become better human beings. One woman, whose son had just been caught on video torturing people with pellet guns and other forms of abuse, pleaded with the authorities not to punish him. "He's a good boy! He never hurt anyone," she said. This was even after she saw the videotape herself.

On the news I learned about a young boy named Jeremy, who had written his name on the city sidewalk several times, costing the city some money. The city sued the family. The mother was appalled. Instead of using the opportunity to teach her son a valuable lesson, she tried to justify his actions.

Far too many parents say, "That's how teenagers are!" The truth is, teenagers can be obnoxious, unruly, and undisciplined *if we allow them to be*. But most teenagers are not this way. I find most teens to be very thoughtful, respectful, and bright. When your child makes a mistake, assist him in learning the lesson. Tim Storey, a wonderful motivational speaker, once said, "Out of your *tests,* you get *testimonies.* And out of your *messes,* you get *messages.*" But this happens only if children are held responsible for their mistakes.

Family Identity

You can improve communication with your child as you spend more time with him and create activities and rituals that are unique to your family. Kids tend to rebel less if they feel invested in the family. This means that your child has to put something into the family, and be a part of it. Kids who have a strong family identity end up respecting their parents more than their peers, because that's where they find love and fulfillment. Try the following:

DO SPECIAL THINGS WITH EACH CHILD

Kids need one-on-one time with their parents. One family makes a monthly date with its children. One month, Dad takes his daughter out and Mom takes her son. The next month they switch. You can teach social skills, manners, chivalry, and communication skills—all to prepare your child for dating the opposite sex. The best part is that your child will love having you all to himself for a night.

Here are a few real-life examples of ways in which parents have made their kids feel special and loved:

David: "One of my fondest memories is when my dad took me to the office with him when I was just a young boy. I just hung out while he worked, talked on the phone, and held meetings. I learned a lot. The best part was just feeling important enough to my dad for him to take me with him."

Michael: "When I was little I remember finding a fun little spot to play: underneath a big desk we had in our den. One time my mom crawled underneath the desk to be with me. We just sat there and talked. Of all my childhood memories, this is my favorite."

Kendra: "My mom knows that chocolate cake is my favorite. One time we were fighting. But when I came home from school there was a chocolate cake just for me, with 'Happy Cake Day Kendra!' That made my day."

Charlene: "My nine-year-old son and I had a nightly routine where we would talk about our feelings when I tucked him into bed. After a while I sort of forgot about it, until one night my son said, 'Mom, let's talk about our feelings!' I had no idea how much the ritual meant to him."

The Abbotts: "We know that our daughter appreciates us for standing up for her when she was taunted by other kids at school. We eventually took her out of the school and taught her at home for a while. She just couldn't believe that we would go to the extra trouble for her. Out of that experience we learned something very valuable: that our convenience is not more important than her well-being. Pulling her out of school was a big deal—a real sacrifice for us. But it was worth it, because our daughter is doing great now."

Through my conversations with kids, I have found that it is the *little* things that parents do that make the difference—a word of encouragement, a loving touch, showing up at a game or a performance. These are the things that stand out in a child's memory.

SHARE YOUR OWN EXPERIENCES

Conversations I have with adults usually begin with "I wish my parents had taught me . . ." They then list all the things they learned many years later, in their twenties, thirties, or forties. It's easier for us to reflect on our experiences years later and honestly admit the areas where we sorely lacked wisdom. We have already been through the fire.

In her book *The Measure of Our Success* (Harper Perennial, 1992), Marian Wright Edelman writes: "It is the responsibility of every adult—especially parents, educators, and religious leaders—to make sure that children hear what we have learned from the lessons of life and to hear over and over that we love them and that they are not alone."

Practically every experience you have had in your own life can be used as a teaching tool for your child. It isn't that you need to share all of these experiences with your child, and go over every embarrassing detail. You can, however, pass on the moral of the story or the principle that you learned as a result of the experience. You may not feel that you are bursting with profound insights and valuable lessons, but you are. Think about your own experiences and discover the truths that you can impart to your child.

Hannah, sixteen, said, "I like it when my mom tells me about when she was a young girl. She does that more now that I'm a little older. It makes me realize that she wasn't perfect, either—that she's done things."

You have to be careful in sharing your own experiences with your child. Some teenagers claim that they feel less guilty when they make mistakes if they know their parents made the same mistakes when they were younger. One eighteen-year-old girl said, "I see that my parents had a few sexual relationships before they were married, yet they turned out okay. So I figure what's the big deal?" If you do share experiences with your child, be sure to add the emotional or spiritual pain that may have accompanied the decisions you made, and the wisdom you gained.

HOLD WEEKLY FAMILY NIGHT DISCUSSIONS

Establish one night per week when you spend time together as a family. This will create a perfect opportunity for you to teach your child valuable principles, and to just have fun as a family. The meeting could be held on a weeknight or on the weekend, whichever works best for your family. Have pizza or enjoy a favorite dessert as you talk. This will give your child more of an incentive to be there and to participate.

No one else should be allowed to attend, except on rare occasions. You don't want your child's friends to inhibit or alter the intimacy you share as a family. Each week presents a new topic to discuss. Eventually you will repeat certain topics in order to reinforce ideas and bring out new insights.

You and/or your spouse should conduct the evening, but everyone participates in the discussion. All ideas and comments are welcomed; no one is to be made to feel stupid or inferior, and all questions are excellent questions. Be careful not to lecture. Remember, the goal is to educate by discussing issues and helping your child to reach his own conclusions, but your child won't want to continue in the process if he feels that he's listening to a sermon.

Announce what the topic will be for the evening. For example, you might discuss "Dating Guidelines" or "Determining Your Sexual Standards" or "How to Get a Date" or "How to Deal with Sexual Advances." Some nights you might choose topics that aren't related to sex or dating, such as "How to Be a Happy Person" or "How to Develop Friendships." Remember to stay focused on the topic for that week. Many of the topics will overlap, but you don't want to attempt to cover several topics in detail at one sitting. You want to convey small chunks of information that your child can easily digest. If your child asks a question that might take you in a different direction, you can always give a short answer and then say, 'That would be an excellent topic for next week!' That way your child has something to look forward to and you keep the discussion focused.

FILL UP YOUR CHILD'S LIFE WITH FAMILY TIME

Establish activities and characteristics that are unique to your family. This can be done through family traditions, regular chores, birth stories, special ways of sharing holidays, family projects, field trips, and family vacations.

The Smyths, the parents of sixteen children (yes, sixteen!) said, "One of the best things we have ever done is have a family devotional every day. Sometimes we have it in the morning, and other times at night. There were times when we had to get up at 5:30 A.M. in order for everyone to be able to participate, but the effort has really paid off. We start with a prayer, then we read a few Scriptures, and we appoint one family member as the 'captain,' which means they have to share their testimony of our faith—what they believe in strongly and how this has benefited their life. Of course, it hasn't always been easy to maintain this ritual, but when we have been consistent this has done more to strengthen our family and build individual self-esteem than anything else we've done."

The Taylors spend lots of family time together by having dinner every evening at the same time and allowing each member of the family to choose his or her favorite dish one night out of the week. They also go camping and fishing during the summer months, and sledding in the winter. These are some of their best memories.

How to Begin a Conversation

One thing I consistently hear from parents is "How do I start the conversation? It's so awkward!" I've provided specific dialogues in each chapter of this book. You may not want to repeat them word-for-word, but they may save you the frustration of having to figure out what to say. Here are some actual dialogues you might like to consider in getting your own conversations started:

"I'd like for us to have a talk about sex. Now, I know this may be uncomfortable for you (as you child rolls his eyes), but it is such an important part of life, and as your parent it's my job to make sure you have all the right information. You may already know a lot, and you may even be able to teach me something! But I want us to have an open, two-way discussion about it. I'm not going to preach—I just want to share some thoughts with you."

"As a kid, my parents never talked to me about sex and dating. I want it to be different with us. There is so much to understand, and I see it as my job to talk to you about all facets of life—including sexuality and building relationships. You're going to have your own ideas and insights, and I want you to feel free to share them as well."

"We're going to have a series of talks about all kinds of things: sex, dating, the opposite sex, love. Sometimes they'll be casual, but other times they'll be more structured. For the first one, why don't we order a pizza? I'll pay, and you just promise to show up and participate! Deal?"

"Sex is a fascinating subject, and in our family it's an open topic. Over the course of your childhood and teen years, we're going to cover a lot of information that will make your life much easier! You'll be so far ahead of most people your age, because most families don't talk about these issues."

As you talk about intimate subjects with an adolescent, he will typically respond with one- or two-syllable answers—Yes. No. Okay. Sure. Duh. I dunno—but over time you'll break down the barriers and get him talking. Give lots of encouragement. Say things like "Oh, come on, it will be fun!" and, "It won't be so bad! In fact, sex is most people's favorite subject!" Come up with your own ways to lighten the mood and help him to feel comfortable.

Sometimes you can "interview" your child in a nonthreatening way to find out what he already knows. You could ask, "What do you think of someone who has premarital sex?" Or, "You know, a lot of television ads are suggesting that people should practice safe sex. What are your thoughts on that?" At first your child may wonder why you're asking the question, and he may even be suspicious that you have an agenda. But if you let him know that you're just curious about what he thinks, and then allow him to express his thoughts without criticism, he'll feel safe talking about these issues at other times. If as a result of asking these questions, you find that your child is off base, you'll know which areas you need to work on. If he seems receptive, share your thoughts on the issue. If he isn't receptive, you can always bring up the subject later in order to teach the principle or values you would like him to adopt.

There is so much you can do to get your child to listen and participate in discussions that will prepare him for dating and building a relationship with the opposite sex. He will listen, and the information will sink in. Make it clear that his entire education, including his *sex* education, is a top priority in your life.

❖ 2 ❖

"You Are the Landlord of Your Own Body"

Rosemary, the mother of two daughters, told me, "More than anything else, I wish my mom had taught me that my body belongs to me, and that it's special. When I reached my teens I got involved with boys, just like most of my girlfriends. We thought it was cool. We never once thought that by sharing our bodies with these boys who didn't love us we were doing something damaging to ourselves. But now, all these years later, I know that what happened had a negative impact on me."

The most common statement made by adult women I spoke with was "I wish I had learned to honor my body more." These woman have had enough experience in the dating world to know that the reason they became intimate with many of the men in their lives was that they didn't value themselves (this includes body and spirit) enough not to.

I also wasn't taught how to view my body. Prior to going through puberty, I needed to know that caring for my body is my responsibility, and that it is special. As a teenager, I discovered that my newly developed body elicited a lot of attention from the opposite sex. This revelation was exciting to me, but I didn't understand the implications of the attention or what to do about it. Because of my low self-esteem and lack of education about these things, I viewed the attention as positive, and I began to see my body as a tool that I could use to get the love and attention I so desperately wanted and needed.

Teenagers often make decisions on impulse based on strong emotions, peer pressure, or the desire for immediate gratification. Rarely if ever do they think, "Doing this would be violating my body." Teenagers often think they are invincible.

Many of the talks you will find in this chapter are designed for younger children, but the concepts apply to all ages. They will help you teach your child that her body is sacred, that it is of great value, and that she is responsible for caring for, protecting, and maintaining her body for the rest of her life. I'll also discuss ways to protect your child from sexual abuse.

The Rights and Responsibilities of Ownership

When we are young we need to understand that we are responsible for our body's care and protection. We are the sole owners and caretakers of our bodies. This means that we have the *right* as well as the *responsibility* to say no to anything that might be hurtful or damaging.

The Landlord Metaphor

The landlord metaphor is a great way to help your child understand that she is both responsible for and in charge of her body. Take her through each of the following questions. At first your child may need help coming up with the answers, but if you start having this discussion when she is about eight or nine years old and continue to discuss the concept periodically throughout her childhood and adolescence, it will help her to internalize and remember the concept. Ask:

Q: What is a landlord?

A: The owner of an apartment building, a house, or an office building.

Q: What are the landlord's responsibilities?

A: To take good care of the building, to handle repairs and maintenance, to collect the rent, to make sure he finds good tenants, to run credit checks on possible tenants.

Q: What happens if the landlord neglects or takes his responsibilities lightly?

A: He could lose his investment, his property could be seriously damaged, he might get bad tenants who take advantage of him.

Q: How does this apply to you and your body?

A: I am the landlord of my body.

Q: And what are your responsibilities as the landlord?

A: To take good care of and maintain my body, not to let others take advantage of me, to associate only with people of character, to get to know a person well before getting seriously involved.

Q: How long does this job last?

A: For the rest of my life.

When your child approaches puberty, you could explain that some people might think that her body is "public property" or *their* property—and they may try to touch, use, or take advantage of her body. Let her know that no one has the right to do this. Impress upon her that her body is sacred and special, and that she is to be modest and private in order to protect herself.

Seeing the Body as Sacred

I never considered the idea that my body is sacred, but I can imagine how different my life would have been if my parents had raised me according to this principle. This belief would have created in me a desire to treat my body with tenderness, care, and concern. I am not saying that I should have worshiped my body, but I should have been taught to see it as an important vessel that houses my spirit and carries me through life. Perhaps I would have recognized much of the attention I received as a teenager for what it truly was: an attempt to exploit my body for selfish reasons. As a young girl, I was very trusting. I didn't have the ability to discern a person's true intentions. I don't think you should frighten your child or give her the impression that all boys are out to use her, but I think every young girl should be prepared for the potential realities. Practically every young girl will notice that, as her body begins to develop, she becomes the object of attention from the opposite sex. She needs to understand this attention and know what to do with it.

In future talks you will go into more detail about setting specific sexual standards, but when your child is about eight years old you could say, "We believe that our bodies are sacred. We have taught you to look both ways before crossing the street, to care for your teeth and hair, to eat healthful foods, and to get plenty of rest. We also believe in taking care of our bodies spiritually. Part of what this means is that we don't allow others to touch us inappropriately." You might then share additional ways in which your daughter can care for herself spiritually based on your own spiritual beliefs.

Many religious parents teach their children to be "chaste." This term, which hasn't been very popular since the sixties, may conjure up visions of piousness and Victorian-like prudishness. But the word *chaste* simply means to be morally pure in thought and conduct—to be decent, modest, and virtuous. Most parents want this for their children, regardless of their religious orientation. The word *pure* means to be free of adulterants or impurities—to be full-strength, clean, complete, containing nothing inappropriate. If you don't feel comfortable using the word *chaste,* discuss the concept of being pure or virtuous. A metaphor for this principle involves a glass of water.

The Glass of Water Metaphor

During family night, present your child with a clear glass of water. Here is a potential dialogue you could have with her. You may need to help your child with the answers. You may not want to have this discussion with a child who has been sexually abused, because you could end up giving her the impression that she isn't pure.

> Q: Do you see how clear and clean the water in this glass is? There are no impurities—nothing is clouding the water. Let's see what happens when we spice it up a little by adding various items from our spice rack. We'll pour in a little chili powder, some ground cloves, maybe some ground ginger. How does the water look now?

> A: Murky. Clouded.

> Q: Right. The water is no longer pure and clean. Now pretend this glass of water is your body. What does this experiment tell you?

> A: To not pollute my body with things that aren't healthy.

> Q: Yes. Your body is sacred—it needs to be kept clean and pure in order to continue to run smoothly. Not only do you want to eat healthful foods, get plenty of rest, and exercise, you also want to protect your body from all outside influences that could create murkiness. Sometimes people think they need

a little spice in their lives, but this can backfire and pollute their system spiritually, emotionally, and physically.

If your child is taught to take special care of her body when she's young, she'll be more likely to make healthful decisions when she's older. If she believes that her body is sacred, chances are she'll be less likely to engage in casual sexual behavior and/or exploit someone else as she matures.

Vanessa was very careful to teach each of her children how they should view their bodies. "We have always taught our children that they should have reverence toward all parts of their bodies—that each part is unique and has a function that is beneficial to them. We tell them they should never do anything that is degrading to any of these parts, and that if we keep them clean these organs and parts can bring us great joy, pleasure, and will enable us to give and receive love. Certain parts are created as a coupling device, so that a married couple can be brought together as one to reproduce, but not only for that purpose." This conversation can take place when your child is about eight or nine, depending on her maturity level.

The Body Is Beautiful and of Great Value

Most teenagers experience feelings of insecurity. You want to help your child develop a positive view of her body. Kids usually operate from a limited perspective, one that parents can shed light on. Teenagers aren't going to get the kind of encouragement they need at school from their peers; that's where they feel pressure to compete.

As is true of most teenage girls, I loathed my looks. I felt that my chin was too long, my teeth were crooked (I had a space between the two front ones), my skin was too fair (I couldn't get a tan if my life depended on it), and my body was far too skinny. This negative attitude was based on my own perceptions of what was beautiful. It had everything to do with boys. It seemed to me that boys were attracted only to short, blond girls with bronze tans who knew how to dance. Late at night, in my big bed with the antique frame, I dreamed of being someone else . . . someone much more petite and perky: a cheerleader, the most popular girl in the school, with boys waiting for me at the end of every class.

I often wonder how different my self-concept would have been if I had consistently heard that beauty isn't about being blond or short or tan or anything like that. Or that a charming personality and beautiful character go a lot farther than good looks. I didn't notice all of the girls who were plain, or even unattractive according to the world's standards, who had adoring boyfriends. I didn't realize that we all have certain aspects that are appealing. I also didn't truly understand that I would change a lot over the next couple of years. I really think I should have been prepared for the insecurities that are so common among teens before I reached my teens. If, just prior to puberty, you can explain to your child some of the feelings many teenagers experience, she will already know what to expect and she might not have as much of a struggle with these feelings of insecurity. She'll think, Oh, my mom already explained to me that we're all beautiful in our own way and that I shouldn't worry about these things.

In teaching your child to accept her physical appearance, you could say, "Kids sometimes make the mistake of trying so hard to fit in and be liked that they try to be like everyone else, or at least like the popular kids. But you'll be so much happier if you know what your assets are and you accept your limitations. You have qualities and attributes that belong only to you. By happy about that! Confidence is so much more attractive to others than a lack of self-acceptance. Don't try to be like everyone else—just be you. Be proud that you're growing and changing. Everyone goes through this."

Explain to your child that everyone has worries: most teenagers get acne; some girls are obsessed with their breast size; boys are concerned about the size of their penis; and everyone worries about whether they're good-looking enough. But in the end none of those things really matter. What does matter is who you are on the inside. Remind your child that she is a unique person with special talents and traits that are uniquely hers. Encourage her to cultivate those aspects of herself with passion! People will sit up and take notice no matter how she looks. And if they don't notice her now, they probably will later.

Aileen, the mother of fourteen-year-old Teresa, said, "My daughter thinks she's ugly right now because of her height and weight. I tell her, 'Maybe you're not as gorgeous or as thin as some of these girls right now, but your time will come.' Then I point out her beautiful aspects. She has gorgeous, long legs. I tell her how much her body is changing, and how pretty her skin is. It makes her feel good." I like the fact that this mother was honest with her daughter about not being as attractive as the other girls right now. Kids know the truth, and they don't want you to pity them. Aileen was honest yet encouraging.

Being Familiar with How Your Body Works

Children need to know about their bodies and how they work. Irving Klitsner, M.D., founder and former director of the Teen and Young Adult Health Center in southern California, says, "Parents need to talk about the anatomy from the time children are born. If your child asks questions, answer her with simple, short answers that can satisfy her curiosity at that moment. If your child asks what a penis is for, you don't necessarily need to go into detail about the entire reproduction process. The child probably isn't emotionally ready to handle that information, nor does she usually want to know too much. It's much more important that you build the foundation for an open, honest relationship between you and your child that will help make future talks easier and more effective."

When your child is very young she is with you almost continuously, so you have many opportunities to teach her the various parts of the body and their functions. During bathtime, while dressing and undressing, or while playing together, you can teach her what she needs to know. Introduce your child to the concept of sacredness and self-respect. Discuss all body parts as though they are all equally important. You could say, "These are your hands, which will help you write and pick things up, and shake hands . . . and these are your legs, which will help you run and walk . . . and this is your penis, which is very important so that you can go to the bathroom. . . ." The point is to make "private parts" a normal part of your conversation rather than giving your child the impression that they are bad or dirty. It's also a good idea to explain to your child that some people use derogatory, or "bad," words to describe body parts and functions but that this isn't appropriate because our bodies are sacred.

Sometimes a three-, four-, or five-year-old will ask questions about her body, such as "Why don't I have a penis?" Just answer your child's questions honestly and nonchalantly. You could say, "Because you are a girl, and girls have vaginas. Only boys have penises." Some experts suggest that you describe all of the sexual organs—for example, you could talk about the vulva, vagina, labia, and clitoris, and the penis, testicles, and scrotum. This might be a good idea when the child is seven or eight years old, or when your child becomes curious.

Valuing Privacy

Children don't automatically know what should be kept private, whether it be information about their bodies or details about the family. Have a brief conversation about this so that your child will know what is appropriate.

You could say, "Some things are very personal, and they should be kept private. For instance, we keep our bodies private by wearing clothes. We don't show our bodies to other people, except Mom and Dad and sometimes the doctor. We should also keep private those things that happen in our family that are private. Certain things should just be kept between us [You might share a couple of examples at this point.]. Also, it isn't always a good idea to share personal experiences or thoughts you may have with just anyone. You don't necessarily know how others may react, or what they may do with that information. People don't need to know everything that's going on in your life."

Being Modest

Modesty is not something that holds much clout in our society these days. I find it very amusing to watch reruns of *American Bandstand*, and then compare them with today's version. You definitely see a lot more skin in the '90s episodes!

Unfortunately, many parents aren't convinced that modesty is important. For some, the word is difficult to define. Buddy, the father of sixteen-year-old Gaylin, told me that his daughter likes to wear short, tight skirts and other provocative clothing: "She likes to wear short skirts and tight pants. It's cute. They look appealing on her." I asked if he worried about how boys would behave around her based on how she dresses. "I don't think it matters how they respond," he said. "They can do whatever they want, but it's what she does that is important." I agree to a point. But there is a real danger in giving others the wrong impression, attracting the wrong kinds of boys, and basically asking for trouble. Girls can be attractive without being sexy.

Sydney, the mother of a fourteen-year-old daughter, has a different view: "People say, 'Whoa! How can you let your daughter wear that short skirt with those platform shoes? But I think she needs to get it out of her system. She needs to be beautiful in her eyes, and she thinks she looks good. So who cares?"

Her daughter does have a need to believe that she is beautiful, but there are so many positive ways in which that message can be shared! Her daughter will have a much better chance of seeing herself as attractive if she dresses modestly, because with modesty she'll develop self-respect and elicit the appropriate appreciation from others. Her natural, wholesome appearance will attract people of a similar vein—those who value modesty and their bodies as something that is private and special. What better way for Sydney to teach her daughter how beautiful she really is than by teaching her to be modest! She could say, "When you wear clothes that are more modest—meaning they aren't too short or too tight or revealing—you look the prettiest I've ever seen you. You know why? Because you look like a sweet, wholesome, healthy girl who truly cares about herself and about the image she projects. You then appear to be a girl who has self-respect and sees herself as special. Then you can relax and enjoy yourself when you go out rather than being concerned with what others think or having to fight off boys who have only one thing in mind."

Contrary to what many girls believe, boys really don't appreciate girls who dress too provocatively. Fifteen-year-old Jesse said, "Girls are too aggressive these days. They dress too sexy. One girl in biology class wears really tight shirts. I don't mind—I mean, it's pretty cool, but it can be too revealing." Explain to your daughter that the attention created by sexy clothing is not the kind of attention that will ultimately make her feel valued and loved.

When you talk to your daughter about being modest, be careful to consider her feelings. I remember buying a new pair of shorts for the summer and showing them to an aunt I was visiting. They were bright red and had drawstrings on each side that could be tied in a bow. She looked at the shorts with a disapproving expression and said, "Obviously you can make them real sexy by pulling the strings tighter." Her comment cut to the core. She was right—I had purposely bought the shorts because they were sexy. But I didn't know *why* I felt a need to dress this way. I now know that my behavior was due to a need for attention, to be loved, and to a lack of self-worth. If you think this is the case with your child, spend more time building her self-esteem and spend more one-on-one time with her. Often adults react to the inappropriate behavior with disdain rather than trying to understand *why* the child feels the need to behave this way. You can't expect a child to automatically know what is appropriate, particularly if you've never talked to her about these issues.

Perhaps a more positive way of handling this type of situation is to express your love and acceptance while still offering wisdom. You can tell your daughter that she is attractive, and that you appreciate her sense of style, but she should know that she doesn't have to dress sexy in order to get boys interested in her. Make it clear that what truly causes a boy to fall head over heels for a girl is her *virtue.*

Explain to your child that she has a body—and a soul. She can draw attention to her *body* by the way she dresses, or she can draw attention to her *soul* through her personality and her thoughts. Ask her which she prefers to have the opposite sex pay more attention to. Tell her that she can always get someone to notice her body, but to get this person interested in the *inner* her is a whole other matter. Point out all of her positive personality and character traits that others will appreciate.

Respecting Other People's Bodies

Instructing children in how to care for and protect their own bodies isn't enough; we also need to teach them to be respectful of others' bodies.

Have a conversation similar to this with your child. "Just as we have taught you to take care of *your* body and not abuse it in any way, it is just as important not to violate *another* person's body. Their bodies are just as sacred as yours." This will begin the process of teaching your child how to reconcile her sexual impulses with integrity.

Protecting Your Child from Sexual Abuse

More important than talking to your small child is watching over her and protecting her from dangerous situations. As one mother said, "Today a mother needs to be a mother hawk. So many things are going on today that weren't as prevalent several years ago. We don't even allow sleepovers anymore because of the potential dangers. You don't want to show suspicion or create paranoia with your children by being obsessed with these concerns, but always be on the lookout."

Mary Kay Lehto, a licensed clinical social worker says, "It's important that you raise a child with *spunk,* who is cooperative with you but is also able to speak her mind. In sexual-abuse cases, the child is tricked. But if the child learns to be confident in saying 'Hey! Stop that!' she can learn how to stand up for herself when something strange happens."

Mary Kay Lehto went on to explain some of the situations she deals with on a daily basis: "It's very common for a parent to call our office about certain behavior she sees in her child and ask, 'Is this anything I should worry about?' It's typical for children ages four to six to want to explore each other's bodies and play out sex games, but when it involves behaviors such as humping, oral sex, or inserting objects, you should be concerned. Then it's best to get professional advice." Here are several tips on how to protect your child:

- Keep the door open when small children are playing.
- Supervise children while they're playing; it doesn't take long for things to happen.
- Know the children your child plays with.
- If you find your child playing sex games, talk to her about what's appropriate. Point out that we keep our clothes on, for example, and that we don't touch others in that way.
- Redirect your child by saying, "Please put your clothes on and let's find another game to play."
- Casually ask questions: What game were you playing? What made you think of that? Where did you hear that idea?
- Watch for red flags: touching the genitals of others, forced exposure of others' genitals, sexually explicit conversations with another child of a significant age difference, chronic interest with exposing or peeping, simulating intercourse with dolls, animals, peers.
- Talk to the parents of the other child involved.
- Go with your instincts—it's better to be safe than sorry.
- Don't overreact or make too much of the situation, particularly if your child is exploring her own body; this is normal.

One mother I know was concerned when a nephew came to visit. He had brought along with him a male friend, who gave this mother a "funny feeling." She didn't have much information to base her concerns on, but going on intuition she kept a closer eye on her five-year-old daughter. She never allowed her daughter to be alone with this boy, and she made sure that her little girl slept in the room upstairs rather than downstairs where the boys slept. It would have been easy to write off her suspicions, or to get too caught up in whatever she was doing to pay such careful attention, but this mother recognized that she had a responsibility to protect her child. Fortunately, nothing negative occurred in this situation. Perhaps nothing would have happened regardless of this mother's concerns, but she did her part in protecting her child from potential dangers.

Your child needs to feel that she is precious to you and that never in a million years would you allow danger or harm to come to her. Whether it is allowing her to date someone who is too old for her, allowing her to stay out too late, or being observant as to the environment and influences she is surrounded with, you need to constantly have your finger on the pulse. Sandi told her children, "Remember, you can always leave. No matter where you are or what time it is, we will come and get you." This makes a child feel safe and loved, which will give her more confidence in life.

You also want to be very observant and really listen to what your child might be trying to tell you. Vicki, thirty-nine, shared this experience: "When I was sixteen, I went on a second date with a guy who was about four years older than I was. He was all over me on the first date. I just remember that I didn't know how to say no! When he came to get me I told my mom to come out and tell him that I had to be home early. My mother didn't do this automatically, which has always stuck with me. In a way I felt unprotected, like she wasn't looking out for me." After your child returns from a date, you can ask her if she had a good time, and if her date treated her respectfully. Sometimes teenagers wait to be asked before divulging information.

Don't Allow Your Child to Be "Sexualized"

Many experts say that exposing a small child to graphic sexual pictures, movies, language, and even being naked in front of her as she gets older can prematurely awaken the child's sexuality. One woman I spoke with has a five-year-old daughter. The daughter came into the room where we were talking and began rolling around on the floor near us. She was naked, exposing herself as she rolled around. Her mother made no effort to stop her or to tell her to get dressed. In fact, as her daughter came over and kissed her neck, this mother said, "This little one is so sensual!" Her daughter seemed to delight in her comment and appeared to be a little seductress. This mother, like so many concerned parents today, didn't want to create insecurity and fear in her child. She didn't want her daughter to grow up with any "hang-ups." But by endorsing sensual behavior in her child at such a young age, she may have paved the way for bigger problems in the future than she had anticipated. If the concepts of sacredness, modesty, and privacy are taught from the beginning, future problems can be minimized.

If you make sex, or sexually titillating topics, too much of a big deal in your home, you could run into problems. A social worker I spoke with said that many of the families he encounters spend too much time quizzing their small children on whether their private areas have been touched. Stormy, the divorced mother of a four-year-old, quizzed her daughter every time she came home from spending the weekend with her father. She asked, "Did Daddy touch your private parts?" After saying no the first few times that she was asked the question, this little girl eventually said, "Yes, Daddy touched my bum, and he's not supposed to do that." The authorities were called, which ignited an investigation and resulted in more questioning directed at the little girl. They discovered that the father did nothing wrong. Stormy's daughter was traumatized and sexualized by the questioning. She is now petrified at the thought that someone might try to touch her.

Also, cherish your child's innocence. At age eleven, Miriam received her first subscription to *Cosmopolitan*. To this day she remembers one of the first articles she read, which said that if you want your lover to think you're thinner than you are, you should buy panties that are extra small and hang them in the bathroom in plain view. Miriam's mother also bought her a diaphragm at thirteen. Miriam wasn't even sexually active at that point, but her mother felt she had a *right* to her own sexuality when she felt ready to experiment. She honestly felt that she was doing right by her daughter. Miriam was sexualized at a tender age by these blatant invitations to experiment sexually. "The message I kept getting was to have sex, to try out these things I was reading about, and to use my body to entice men," she told me. It's no surprise that Miriam ended up being promiscuous.

Kenny watched James Bond movies as a boy and got the impression that the greater the number of sexual partners you have, the more of a hero you are. He observed that James Bond usually had about six different sexual partners per movie. These are the messages you will want to protect your child from whenever possible. When and if your child is exposed to these things, be sure to share your views by saying something like "We don't believe it's right to be with so many people in that way. Sex is sacred and is meant to be shared with one person—the one you love and are committed to."

You can establish rules that place certain magazines—even teen magazines—and R-rated movies off-limits; television programs, too, should meet your approval. Brenda, the mother of three daughters, said, "My twelve-year-old loves the teen magazines. I used to subscribe to them, but after reading what's in these magazines I decided to cancel the subscriptions. But it didn't work. She buys them on her own." You can make a strong statement that these types of magazines are off-limits at *all* times, no matter where the child is. Then explain why you feel so strongly about this. Help her to see your logic. She may say, "Mom, it's no big deal! I already know those things, and they aren't going to make me do anything crazy!" Follow her comment up with, "I understand, but as your parent it's my job to make sure you don't spend your time reading material that isn't morally or spiritually beneficial. I expect you to trust my judgment on this. I would be hurt and disappointed to know that you went against this rule in our family. When you become an adult you can read whatever magazine you want, but by then you'll probably have lost interest in things that aren't uplifting."

Another mother said, "If you try to restrict kids from doing too many things, they rebel. My daughter would probably go see an R-rated movie behind my back." Your child can do things without your consent, but that shouldn't deter you from establishing rules and explaining why the rules are in place. As you show her that you trust her, if and when she does go against your rules, guilt and remorse will usually lead her back eventually.

I called the number for Movie Phone recently, and as I listened to the recording about upcoming movies I heard this statement: "We strongly encourage you not to bring children under the age of three to PG or R-rated films." The age of *three*? What about the age of eight, ten, fifteen? Even some PG or PG-13 films aren't appropriate for kids to watch. R-rated films are chock-full of sexual experiences and innuendo, violence, and language that is clearly not a positive influence for children of any age. Three years old and younger may be the only time some of these sexual messages *aren't* picked up by a child, although they shouldn't be exposed to these films, either.

Be Vigilant with the Internet

Four million people are on the Internet daily. The Internet is an interconnected system of computers. It was originally started by a coalition of government educational institutions and private industry. It was publicly funded, and the purpose was to move research around quickly and easily. The infrastructure grew like a weed from there.

This growth was just a natural progression. For example, schools wanted to make this information available to their students. As a result, more and more people became linked together. The problem is, there is no central control or central source of funding. You can't control the Internet, because it's international. Basically, anyone who has a computer can access whatever information is available.

There are Web sites that a user can tap into and gain access to whatever information is available. Some are visually oriented sites. For example, *Penthouse* has a Web site. Anyone can go to the magazine's Web site and tap into what's there. Usually this information is a sample of what's offered in the magazine because it's a form of advertising.

The Internet also contains news groups and chat sessions that you should know about. These aren't visual; they're more like having a pen pal or carrying on a phone conversation with someone. Some of these chat programs are fine, but there's always a possibility of danger. Many of the programs are sexual in nature, and sometimes kids become titillated by these "taboo" liaisons. They can turn into an addictive situation, and more often than not, people end up meeting someone who makes it possible for them to live out their fantasies.

The other danger is that if your child participates in a chat session or a game program that is positive and isn't related to anything sexual or pornographic, you never know who might connect with her in the guise of a normal person. This person could lure a naive child by saying something like "Hey, I know a lot about computers—maybe we should get together and I'll let you check out all of my programs and I'll teach you everything I know." The next thing you know, your child is mixed up with someone dangerous. There have been cases where sexual predators sent out e-mails to kids, pretending to be kids themselves.

Fortunately, there are ways you can monitor and protect your child from these potential dangers. If you want to eliminate certain Web sites from your child's computer, you can do so. Find someone who knows how to program the computer in this way if you're not familiar with the procedure yourself. You can buy software that blocks access: Cybersitter, Netnanny, Cyber Nanny. To obtain additional information about software packages, call Surfwatch Software, a product group of Spyglass, Inc. (800) 458-6600. Also, there is a rating system that can prevent your child from gaining access to certain Web sites. It is similar to the V-chip used for television. This system allows you to censor what your child can access. Some computers have this system built-in. You create a password and set the level of content that you want your child to see. When the user attempts to access a site that is outside the rating level you have chosen, the system won't allow her to do so. The system is based on language, nudity, sex, and violence. One problem is that although the rating system exists now, it hasn't been adopted by every user. But what you can do is prevent access to sites that aren't rated. The risk here, of course, is that you may eliminate some positive sites that you or your child may want to access. Other programs allow you to keep a log. If you're away for the day, for example, when you return home you can see which sites were accessed. This can help you monitor the situation. But there is still a possibility that your child will get information that you don't approve of.

The fact is, the Internet can be a wonderful educational tool. You don't want to create fear regarding the Internet, or titillation by making it too mysterious. But you do need to be watchful. Talk to your child about the Internet, and establish rules for its use in your home.

By discussing the concepts in this chapter with your child, you will ensure that she develops a healthy, positive attitude toward her body. She will know how she is to view her body, care for it, protect it, and maintain it throughout her life. These talks about the body will set the tone for future talks about the mechanics of sex.

❖ 3 ❖

Sex and Reproduction

All of the smaller talks that make up the big talk will teach your child about sex. But you'll want to have a discussion that specifically covers what sexual intercourse, or making love, is. Discussing reproduction and the physical aspects of sex is probably the most uncomfortable part of having the big talk for most parents. It can be unnerving for parents and children, particularly teenagers, to discuss something so intimate and private. This is why it's best to have this discussion when your child is between eight and twelve years old. Typically, this is the age when children begin hearing about sex through their friends, the media, and in some cases, their teachers. If you can explain the process and attach important moral values to the subject before your child hears conflicting ideas from these outside sources, you will create a foundation on which to build future talks. Your child will be able to distinguish between the information she hears from others and what you have already explained to her. She'll already know the truth. Also, she will feel good about the fact that you let her in on something that is obviously new and exciting. She will feel that you trust her with grown-up information that many of her peers may not be privy to.

You will have to decide for yourself how much detail you would like to share with your child, and at what age. But in keeping with the idea that sexuality is an open, normal topic for discussion in your home, it's best to approach this aspect of the big talk as nonchalantly as possible while still giving your child valuable information.

What to Discuss and When

In the previous chapter, we discussed information that you will convey to your child about her body: that her body is sacred, that she is to care for her body and not allow others to touch her inappropriately, the importance of modesty and privacy, and so on. Ideally, you will have these discussions with your child when she is very young. If you've already made it a natural part of your family life to talk about these issues, you'll have a much easier time discussing what sexual intercourse is all about.

Children under the age of eight or nine do not need to know details about sexual intercourse. They aren't emotionally ready to handle this information; nor do they usually want to know too much. If you wait until your child is a teenager to discuss sex, however, you could also run into problems: it often becomes more difficult to talk to teenagers about such an intimate and possibly embarrassing topic; teenagers often feel they already know everything they need to know; and sometimes they have already formed their own opinions about the subject, which makes it more difficult for you to make an impression. But just prior to preadolescence, most children are curious and open to learning from their parents. This is the right time to talk about sex, although you will still need to consider your child's emotional development. Some kids need to know the facts at eight or nine years of age, whereas it might be more appropriate for other children to learn these things at ten or eleven. Every child should know this information by the time they reach puberty, because this is when sexual hormones kick in and they will begin to hear about sex from other sources.

Younger Children (Ages Three through Seven)

Younger children will often ask questions such as How are babies made? or Where did I come from? There's no reason to bring up the subject unless your child asks, and then keep your answers short, giving her only as much information as she is able to handle at one time. Some children will want more information, while others tend to get bored and distracted. Kids are rarely coy about how they really feel. If they don't want to talk, they'll let you know. Keep it light. If your child is under eight and she wants to know more details than you feel she's ready for, you might say, "That is an excellent question! We plan to talk to you about that when you're a little older. It's such a special conversation that we want to make sure you're ready for it."

Sometimes a small child will ask about the affection you and your spouse share. One family I spoke with used this response: "Mommies and daddies are affectionate with each other because they love each other. It feels good to hold each other and to be close. Someday when you grow up and get married, you can experience this, too!"

Doug Goldsmith, Ph.D., executive director of the Children's Center in Salt Lake City, says, "When a younger child asks specific questions, it's helpful for parents to find out why the child is asking the question. For example, if a child asks, 'What do moms and dads do to make a baby?' the parent could ask, 'What made you bring that up?' or, 'Well, what do you think happens?' This helps the parent explore what is going on in the mind of the child."

When and if your child asks where babies come from, you can talk about her own birth in order to make it more personal. You could explain that she was in a special place near Mommy's tummy called the uterus, that she was just teeny, and that she grew over a period of nine months, until she became a normal-size baby. Tell her how excited you were when she was born. You can explain that she came out of an opening between Mom's legs called the vagina. You can be more specific about how the egg and sperm connect and how she developed into a baby if you like, but this brief explanation should satisfy her curiosity for now. Answer any questions she might have, but be careful not to give more information than is necessary. The point is to answer questions truthfully, using correct terminology and giving your child information that won't mislead her or cause her to worry.

One little girl thought babies were made by magic. Some children believe the stork brings babies. Others think we grow like plants or hatch from eggs. One little boy was told that the father plants a seed inside the mom and a baby grows. He wondered whether they used a shovel! While you don't want to bombard your child with facts that are too advanced for her mind to comprehend (particularly about intercourse), there's no reason why you can't explain where the baby is in the mother's tummy, how it develops, and how it comes into the world.

Vicky Burgess, Ph.D., a clinical psychologist and a licensed marriage and family therapist, says, "Ask your child what she wants to know, then take her down the path based on where she is in terms of her level of interest."

Children in Grade School (Ages Eight through Twelve)

It is at this stage that you will discuss the mechanics of sex. Be careful not to overwhelm your child. Many teenagers told me that their parents gave them no warning as to what they would be discussing and then very matter-of-factly laid out all the facts. They said they were shocked and, in some cases, disgusted with the information. Be sure to explain that sex is an incredible experience within the right context, and that although it may seem weird or disgusting right now, she won't feel that way as she gets older.

You could say, "When you were younger you asked us how babies were made. We gave you a simple answer about being in Mom's tummy, but we want to elaborate on that now that you're older. You'll probably hear a lot about this at school, through friends, movies, and television. We want you to know the truth.

"When two people love each other and are committed to each other, they make love. Other terms for this are to have sex or have sexual intercourse. They actually become one. [Explain the process in your own words.] This is the most amazing, incredible experience two people can share. Making love creates an emotional bond between a couple and deepens their love for each other. This experience can also create a baby if the couple isn't using birth control. Sperm from the man's body connects with an egg from the woman's body, then it fertilizes and creates life. [It's helpful to use books with pictures to illustrate this.]

"Some people don't believe it's important to save this experience for marriage, but we hold sex in a much higher regard. It's not something that should be experienced outside of that commitment. It's too powerful and special."

Encourage your child to ask questions, and let her know that she can ask you anything. Make a point of emphasizing the idea that this is an incredible, positive part of life.

Evelyn, the mother of twin sons, told me how, at age eleven, she learned about sex. She should have learned about sex earlier because kids at school were talking about the subject. "My older sister asked me one day if I knew how babies were made. I said, 'No, that's disgusting!' But then I admitted that someone at school had told me, but I didn't even want to mention it because it was so shocking to me. My sister prodded until I told her and my mother. They both laughed and said, 'Yes, that's right!'

"I think it would have been better if my mother had started a little bit younger with me, breaking into the idea slowly, in different situations. Then I might not have been so shocked when kids at school started talking. I felt betrayed in a way, like my own family kept these important secrets from me. Having them laugh about the situation didn't help. I also think that my mother should have talked to me privately about it. Having an older, teasing sister doesn't make the learning process any more pleasant."

Instead of reinforcing how special the sexual experience is, Evelyn's mother ignored her comment about its being "disgusting." She could have said, "Making love is a profound and emotionally bonding experience. It isn't disgusting at all. When two people deeply love each other and are committed to sharing their lives together, making love is one way for them to share that love with each other. It brings them closer together. And, of course, out of that experience a baby can be made. There is no more incredible experience than that! If you have any questions about this, please feel free to come to me. I'll share more with you over time."

Teenagers (Ages Thirteen and Up)

If you haven't already discussed exactly how sex works by the time your child reaches her teens, initiate a conversation. Don't wait for her to bring up the subject—most teenagers don't ask their parents questions about sex. If you had these discussions with your child when she was younger, find the time to review some of the ideas to reinforce what you've already discussed.

More of what teenagers need to know will be covered later. They need to be clear about their standards, how to respond to sexual advances, and how to deal with their own sexual impulses.

Dos and Don'ts in Discussing Sex and Reproduction

The following list of dos and don'ts evolved from conversations I've had with psychologists, educators, social workers, and parents. They can serve as guidelines in answering your child's questions regarding sex and reproduction.

Don't:

- Give too much detail too soon. Most professionals agree that giving a small child too much information can overwhelm her and create problems later.
- Make sex or sexual issues the main focus of conversation in your home.
- Use cute or made-up names for body parts or in describing sex and reproduction.
- Overreact if you find your child playing out sex games. These are very common experiences for small children. Just calmly teach

your child what is appropriate behavior. If the behavior is more serious, consult a professional.

Do:

- Answer all questions openly and honestly.
- Teach your child to say "no" to things that are harmful or dangerous.
- Teach what is appropriate behavior regarding being undressed in front of others, touching, and conversation with others.
- Use correct terminology for sexual organs and practices.
- Attach your moral values to discussions about sex and reproduction (only moms and dads do this, the concept of sacredness, the importance of privacy and modesty, consideration for the feelings of others).
- Encourage your child to ask questions.
- Show enthusiasm and appreciation for your child's curiosity.

What the Term *Sexuality* Really Means

It's important for your child to know what the term *sexuality* really means. She will encounter information from friends, magazines, television programs, and so on that may be incorrect or misleading. Knowing this, as well as facts about reproduction, is just as important as all the other aspects of an education. Most of what kids need to learn about the physical aspects of sex and reproduction they will learn at school, but you will still want to discuss the subjects at home, too. When you talk about sex with your child when she is between the ages of eight and twelve, you can elaborate by explaining what the term *sexuality* means.

Most people think the term *sexuality* strictly means sexual intercourse. But that is just one part of what it means. Your child needs to understand the bigger picture and the correct meaning of the word. To start the conversation you could say, "I think you will find this very interesting. I didn't learn until much later in life that there are three areas of definition for the word *sexuality*: gender, orientation, and intercourse. *Sexuality* means a lot of things—it isn't just making love."

Then share the following ideas with your child in your own words:

GENDER

Gender has to do with being male or female. When someone asks what sex a person is, that's the same as gender. It's also the way we conduct ourselves, our mannerisms, the role we assume, how we dress, and so on.

ORIENTATION

Whether a person believes she is heterosexual, bisexual, or homosexual determines her sexual orientation. (We will discuss homosexuality later in this chapter.) You should explain what homosexuality means and share your views on the subject.

INTERCOURSE

This is the actual act of having sex.

If you wait to have this discussion with a teenager, you'll probably hear, "Mom, I already know all this stuff from school!" You could say, "Oh? What have you learned?" Find out if she really does know. If you get the clear signal that she has had enough, let it go for now. You can end the conversation with "We'll talk more another time."

Should You Go into Detail about What Sex Is Like and How It Works?

Some parents don't feel comfortable discussing the actual act of sex with their children. One mother said, "There's no reason to go into detail about that—my kids will figure it out when the time is right!" Another mother said, "In our family, we don't feel it's right to dissect and discuss in great detail something that is so special. We don't want to make it *common* by talking about it as though it were no different from any other topic." Many parents are afraid that if they talk about sexual intercourse they might encourage their child to have sex. But according to Doug Goldsmith this isn't the case. "Some parents believe that if they don't talk about sex openly, their kids won't do it. But often the reverse is true—if you *don't* talk about sex, kids will sometimes do it, largely because they are so curious. If parents are more open about the subject, kids often lose their intense obsession with sex because their parents already shed light on the subject." Other families discuss sex at great length—at the dinner table or anywhere and at any time. You have to decide what you feel is best, given your religious or moral values. But even if you don't broach the subject yourself, at some point the question of how sexual intercourse works will probably come up. Don't avoid the subject—just be honest. This is your opportunity to teach your child moral values. Tell your child exactly how the process works and explain that it's natural and good under the right circumstances. You can express your views without acting as though the topic were taboo. Don't confuse your child or avoid telling her exactly what happens when two people make love. When she's older and she experiences sex for the first time, she'll be grateful.

May Kay Lehto, a licensed clinical social worker, says, "One subject that should be addressed if you're talking about sexual intercourse with teens is the fact that girls naturally become lubricated when they are sexually aroused. This can happen even when they're only making out. I've had many girls tell me that they were shocked, disgusted, and completely unaware that this happens. I think that both sexes should be forewarned of this. You could say, 'This is what the body does, and don't let it frighten you.'" You may not feel a need to discuss this kind of thing with your child now, but most teenagers do make out, and knowing about this biological occurrence could be beneficial to them.

When one young boy asked his mother what sex is like, and how one knows what to do, he received this clever answer: "Oh, honey, I don't want to rob you of the wonderful adventure of discovery. Mother Nature will take over and you'll know just what to do." This was an excellent way to keep the mystery alive for him and at the same time ease his fears. When your child is older and possibly engaged to be married, you can go into more detail.

The truth is, your child can figure out the reproduction process and how sexual intercourse works on her own, either through life experience or sex-ed classes at school. But if you discuss these topics in your home, you can attach important moral values that will help your child make thoughtful decisions in her own life.

If Your Child Is Engaged to Be Married

Prepare your engaged child for a healthy sex life. I've heard countless stories of married couples who had horrible experiences simply because they weren't aware of some basic aspects of sexuality. The idea that couples can explore and figure it out together sounds great, but it doesn't always work that way. In fact, studies show that the two primary causes of divorce are problems relating to money and sex. The primary reason parents avoid giving direction is that it's uncomfortable for them to talk about these things.

One parent expressed this view: "I think it's important to allow your son or daughter to experience their own quest rather than just giving them *your* answers. Their experiences may be different, and that's okay. If you give too much information and too many specifics, it can taint their own process of discovery." I agree. Many adults, however, say they would have been grateful for a few specific suggestions.

Roger, a forty-one-year-old divorced father of four, said, "I always thought the clitoris was on the *inside* of a woman. For years I tried to find it, which I'm sure was a mystery to the women I've been with. Once I finally figured out where it really is, I thought, Why didn't someone teach me this?"

Find the right moment—either when your child asks specific questions or when she is engaged to be married and is therefore preparing to be sexual. Give her a few basic ideas on how to make intercourse enjoyable for her and her partner. Young adults should be warned that having sex for the first time or two can be uncomfortable but that the discomfort ends and it soon becomes enjoyable. In addition, fathers can say to their sons, "Son, I have learned a lot over the years about how to be a considerate lover, and I thought I'd share some insights with you. You know, some women never have an orgasm simply because neither partner knows how to make it happen. Lots of women pretend to have orgasms because they want their husbands to feel they're pleasing them. But this is so unnecessary! Most women have orgasms from clitoral stimulation, not just penetration. [Explain where the clitoris is.] You have to practice, and sometimes be very patient. You can ask your mate what pleases her. Also, a woman usually wants to cuddle and be close afterward. This is very important to her, whereas a man sometimes just wants to go to sleep. Be sensitive to her needs." You can get more specific based on your own experiences, but this is the basic idea.

Mothers can say to their daughters: "When you get married you'll be able to enjoy being intimate with your husband, and it'll be great. I want to share a few things with you that I've learned over the years and that I believe will help you to enjoy it even more. We don't achieve orgasm in the same way men do, and sometimes it's not so easy for us.

But it is possible for us to have them regularly, and it's a shame to deny ourselves this pleasure simply because we don't understand how it works. A few women are able to have an orgasm with penetration, but most women can only have them through stimulating the clitoris. [Explain where the clitoris is.] The combination of stimulating the clitoris *and* penetration is extremely pleasurable, and if it's done for a long enough period of time it will bring you to orgasm. You have to practice this until you get the rhythm down. Experts say that plenty of foreplay—touching, kissing, and stimulation of the clitoris ahead of time—can make a huge difference in having a positive sexual experience."

How the opposite gender's body operates, especially sexually, is important information. Creating a satisfying sex life is obviously an individual matter. What feels good to one person may be a complete turn-off to another. But sharing the following information can help anyone gain a more positive sexual experience. Share this with your engaged child. A considerate lover:

- Is sensitive to the other person's needs; unselfish and interested in pleasing her.
- Is uninhibited; able to relax.
- Enjoys sex.
- Is not too directive; allows the experience to unfold naturally.
- Is in tune with her partner; able to read him.

Your adult child will engage in a conversation about this topic if you make her comfortable. If you have many talks about sexuality over time, it will make this one easier. Twenty-year-old Julia was recently married. She told me, "On my wedding day my mother asked me if there was anything I wanted to know about sex. I was a virgin. I told her no, that I'd figure it out. I was curious about a few things, but my mother had never discussed these things with me before, so it was just too uncomfortable."

Another daughter engaged to be married—and also a virgin—asked her mother, "What if my husband wants to make love and I don't?" Her mother gave her what I think is a very wise answer: "One of the greatest joys of marriage is to give, even at times when you don't feel like giving. The fact is, there may be times when you *can't* give, due to illness or whatever reason, so it's wise to give when you can. The exciting part is, when you are unselfish it usually turns out to be great! There is such a sweet feeling between husband and wife—an emotional bonding that takes place. And this union needs to be renewed continually."

Obviously a wife is not required to say yes every time her husband expresses a desire to have sex. But the spirit of what this mother was teaching is very noble, and I'm sure it will go a long way toward creating a more beautiful marriage for this young woman. You can share the same concept with your son.

Homosexuality

When you discuss what sexual *orientation* means, you can also talk about homosexuality. This is a complex issue. You may be completely turned off by the idea of homosexuality, you may see homosexuality as a serious sin that needs to be overcome, or you may not see it as a problem. Regardless of your religious or moral beliefs, however, the subject of homosexuality needs to be discussed. Explain to your child what homosexuality is. It could be that your child feels that she is gay, and undoubtedly she will meet someone who is gay at some point in her life. Your child needs to know what your views on homosexuality are, and how she should treat people who are gay. You'll also want to think about what you will do if your child is gay.

If You Suspect That Your Child Is Gay

If you *suspect* that your child is gay you'll want to deal with the situation as soon as possible. You don't want to ignore the signals and end up finding out the truth when she's thirty years old. And, despite your suspicions, your child may not be gay. If you feel that homosexuality is a sin, or you would simply prefer that your child weren't gay, there are ways of handling the situation without destroying the relationship you have with her.

Doug Goldsmith says, "I have seen many cases where a young child [who may or may not end up being gay] has gender-identity issues and the parents want me to fix the problem. But homosexuality is not a psychiatric illness that can be treated. Parents need to grapple with their own fears, ideally with a therapist, and then provide unconditional love to their child."

As you discuss sexual orientation, ask your child what she thinks about the idea of homosexuality. Make her feel safe about discussing the issue. If she has had homosexual thoughts or feelings, you want her to be open with you.

If you are having all of the smaller talks that make up the big talk, you're more likely to have gained insight into the issues your child is dealing with.

If Your Child Announces That She Is Gay

If your adolescent announces that she is gay, first determine whether she really believes she's homosexual or she's just going through a phase. Does she believe she was born this way? Does she want to change, or is she comfortable with this orientation? You want to find out how she feels about the situation because chances are she gave considerable thought to it before coming to you. Find out how she came to this conclusion. Sometimes kids think they are gay simply because they had a sexual fantasy that included someone of the same sex or because they had a crush on a same-sex friend or kids at school called them gay. This doesn't necessarily mean a person is homosexual.

If your adolescent believes that she was born gay and has come to accept this about herself and is asking you to accept it as well, you could say (adjust the wording to fit your own belief system), "This has come as a big surprise to us, as you can imagine. We do appreciate your honesty and willingness to come to us. We don't believe homosexuality is a natural way for couples to relate to each other. We've always taught you that men and women belong together as man and wife so they can create a family. We don't fully understand homosexuality. We don't understand why some people seem to be born with these feelings. We do know that you are our daughter and we love you no matter what. You deserve our love and support, even if we don't completely agree with this lifestyle. We are here for you." If you aren't comfortable with the idea of your adult daughter and her partner sleeping together in your home, tell her so, but also say that you would like to meet her partner. You may not like this idea, but the hurt and damage that can occur by not at least being friendly could be worse.

You may not be this calm and collected at first, but try. It takes time to get used to the idea, but what choice do you have? Your adolescent may realize down the road that this lifestyle isn't for her, but that may never happen. You may want to mention that many people who are homosexual don't participate in homosexual sex. They choose to abstain for various reasons. Don't try to force your child to adopt these ideas, but it's important that she know how others sometimes deal with the situation. If you are sensitive to the feelings of your teenager, and you preface your ideas with reassurances of your love and support, the discussion will be more positive.

Sadly, there is a growing number of suicides among gay teenagers because they are unable to cope with the knowledge of their homosexuality and they often receive no support from their families. Many of these men and woman experience tremendous inner turmoil. They are often confused and tormented by feelings they don't understand. You can provide your teenager with the unconditional love that she needs.

Vicky Burgess says, "Society is *tolerating* gayness more now than in the past, but people aren't *accepting* of it. It's okay not to like the idea of homosexuality, but it's important that we not hurt others who might be gay. If parents make snide remarks or participate in gay-bashing behavior, teenagers follow suit. They may not realize it, but their comments could be made to someone who has a son, brother, or sister who is gay. Teenagers need to learn not to be insensitive to people who are different from them."

Regardless of your child's sexual orientation, you still need to have all of the talks outlined in this book. Your adolescent still needs to know how to respond to sexual advances, the importance of not exploiting others, that sex and our bodies are sacred and our bodies are not intended for casual sexual experiences, and how to establish love and commitment.

Love is the goal here—real love that lasts, along with family, harmony, health. These are the things you want for your child. I believe *The Big Talk* can help you guide your child to these goals. You can do this! Don't leave your child's sex education up to the government, the schools, the media, or life experiences. One day your child will thank you for your concern and effort in teaching her about the things that matter most in life.

❖ 4 ❖

Changes During
Puberty

Your child will go through a major transition in life during puberty, both physically and emotionally. He needs to know what
to expect, and how he can make the process smoother—ideally, *before* he reaches puberty. This is the one aspect of the big talk that I do
remember my stepmother having with me. She told me what to do
when I began menstruating. I think it's important to go beyond the
physical changes and discuss feelings of attraction for the opposite
sex, feelings of insecurity, and sexual impulses, all of which are intensified during puberty.

Puberty: What Is It?

Puberty is the process of reaching sexual maturity. It usually begins
anywhere between the ages of nine and thirteen. Most girls begin puberty approximately two years before boys. Puberty is a time when
sex hormones are released in the body. The male sex hormones are
called androgens. The most important of the androgens is testoster-
one. These hormones trigger the physical changes, such as a boy's
voice deepening, hair growth, and so on. For girls, the sex hormones
are called estrogen, and they trigger breast development, menstruation, hair growth, and other changes. These hormones also bring about
sexual feelings and attraction for the opposite sex.

As your child approaches puberty, you may notice he no longer
feels comfortable being naked in front of you or his siblings; he may
want more privacy. This is normal, so be careful not to inhibit
your child or make him feel guilty about his newfound feelings.
There are specific changes that occur in girls, and others that are pe-
culiar to boys. We'll discuss the most common ones throughout
this chapter.

Discussing Physical Changes

Dr. Irving Klitsner says, "There are different stages of adolescence: ages ten through thirteen—early adolescence; ages thirteen through fifteen—middle adolescence; and ages sixteen and up—late adolescence. Parents should talk to their preteen-agers between the ages of nine and ten. In some cases, between the ages of twelve and thirteen, depending on the child. You want to talk to them before the physical changes take place."

To begin the conversation about the physical changes that occur during puberty, you could say, "Your body is showing signs of changing. You're growing up! Let's talk about the changes that are right around the corner for you. I don't want you to be surprised or frustrated by the process."

The most common concern for teenagers going through puberty is: Am I normal? What they are really asking is: Am I average? Reassure your child that he is normal, and that although we all come in different shapes and sizes, he's right on schedule and not to worry. Remind him that other kids are worrying so much about their own development that they scarcely notice those around them.

Your Daughter's Body

A girl's body matures long before she matures emotionally. Your daughter will worry about breast size, whether she's pretty enough, skin problems, being awkward or lanky or overweight, and when she'll start her period. Explain to her the changes she will experience: she will grow physically, and fill out in the hips and breasts; body hair will grow; and she will begin menstruating. Suggest that she take a shower every day, use deodorant, and take special care of her skin to prevent acne because of the sweat glands that will develop inside her. You can also talk about shaving her legs and underarms, but warn her to be careful to prevent cuts and scars.

Go into detail about the breasts first, since this is usually the first change she'll experience. Explain that her breasts will become tender and begin to grow, and that when this happens you'll take her to get a bra. Make a particular point of discussing the fact that although society often makes a big deal of breast size, she needs to accept whatever size she ends up being. Being comfortable and confident about your body is so much more attractive than coming across as insecure and embarrassed about your figure.

Show your daughter how to give herself a breast exam every month, and explain the importance of doing this faithfully to make sure she doesn't have any lumps. During her period she may feel a few bumps that won't be there when she isn't menstruating, but these are normal. She should be able to tell when an abnormal lump is present. She should let you know immediately if she finds one. Don't forget to ask her if she has any questions.

TALKING ABOUT MENSTRUATION

Many women said that getting their period was a scary time. Let her know that this is an exciting time because she is going from being a little girl to becoming a woman. She should know that this is a positive thing, not dirty or negative.

You could say, "The fact that you're menstruating means that you could actually get pregnant. You'll get your period once a month, and it will last anywhere from four to seven days. Most women menstruate regularly, about the same time every month. But other women are irregular—they may get their period every four to six weeks or so, and that's okay. Your flow will probably be lighter initially than you expected, but that could change."

Give her some pads so that when the time comes she'll be prepared. She can also use tampons if they are comfortable for her. You can show her how to use them, or she can follow the directions on the box. Be sure to advise her to change her pad or tampon frequently, and not to flush it down the toilet. Some girls experience cramping, or headaches, before or during their periods. If your daughter is uncomfortable, there are herbs and other remedies that alleviate cramps. She should know that she can still exercise, swim (if she uses tampons, not pads), or do just about anything during her period.

Be careful not to assume that your daughter already knows what she's doing. Leanne, the mother of two daughters, said, "I told my daughter Ramsy about having a period and what to do. She just said, 'Mom, I already know this!' She had learned it all in school and she seemed annoyed that I brought it up. But then as we talked further, she said things that weren't quite right. For example, she thought that once you started menstruating you just bled all the time, forever. Thankfully, that's not the case! Anyway, I decided right then that I wouldn't let things slide just because my kids tell me they already know."

Many teenagers don't understand the correlation between getting their period and being able to get pregnant. When fifteen-year-old

Astrid announced that she was pregnant, her parents were shocked. "My mom said, 'I thought you knew how to take care of yourself!' But every time she said be careful I said, Yeah, Yeah! The problem was I didn't know what to ask. I felt dumb. And I didn't know that I could get pregnant at fifteen." This should be taught to both sexes.

Taking Charge of Her Health

Instruct your daughter in how to make her own doctors' appointments as she gets a little older (seventeen or older). Discuss how often she should have a physical exam. Go over the various kinds of doctors she may need to see over the course of her life: general practitioner, optometrist/ophthamologist, orthodontist, dentist, gynecologist, and so on. She should establish a relationship with a doctor who understands children, adolescents, and young adults. She should feel comfortable with the doctor in order to consult the doctor about serious medical needs. This primary care physician may be a pediatrician, an internist, a family practitioner, or in some cases, a gynecologist. If a girl is not sexually active, she may not need to have a Pap smear until age nineteen or twenty. If she is sexually active, an exam is required once a year. If she has had medical problems in the past, such as a sexually transmitted disease, or other problems with her reproductive system, she should see her doctor every six months. It's a good idea to prepare her for her first pelvic exam and Pap smear by explaining the procedure. Remind your teenager that her health is a priority, and that she needs to be responsible in caring for herself.

Your Son's Body

Boys struggle with puberty just as much as girls do. They worry about when their facial and chest hair will grow, when their voices will change (and when they do start changing, they hope the crackling stops soon!), that their biceps, chest, and legs will become more muscular, and that they'll grow taller. They worry that they aren't good-looking enough, or that they aren't developing as quickly or as obviously as their peers. It's a scary time!

Talk about the physical changes your son will experience: His body will grow everywhere—in stature, muscles, penis, and testicles. His voice will change. Body hair will grow. His blood pressure will change, as will his heart rate. His appetite will increase, and so will his activity level. Talk to him about potential wet dreams, or nocturnal emissions, and unexpected erections. He needs to know that these things are normal and that he shouldn't be alarmed by them. Some boys, however, never experience wet dreams. He also needs to know the importance of good hygiene (daily showers, deodorant, skin care). Dad can show him how to shave. You can also talk about the fact that boys are often concerned about penis size, and that this really doesn't matter. Help your son to feel confident about his body.

Discussing Other Changes

In addition to talking about the physical changes that will take place, you'll want to discuss the emotional ones, such as feelings of attraction to the opposite sex and sexual impulses.

Attraction to the Opposite Sex

I am always fascinated when I watch documentaries of famous rock bands. The girls in the audience are screaming, fainting, and completely losing control over the band members. It reminds me of when I was a teenager, and the feelings I experienced in the presence of someone I found really cute. The emotions are intensified during adolescence. Your child may develop crushes, or what is known as puppy love. Don't be too alarmed if this happens. It's normal, and it doesn't necessarily mean that the feelings will lead to something serious. Preteens and young teenagers usually move through these phases rather quickly. Future talks about love and intimacy will help you sort through these feelings with an older teenager. For now, you could say something like this: "Another aspect of puberty is that you'll start to feel attracted to the opposite sex. This is a natural part of growing up. Remember when you didn't like girls? Well, as you go through puberty that will change. You might even find yourself feeling nervous around some girls. Over time, you'll become more confident, and we'll have other talks about how to relate to girls and how to date. I just want you to know about the changes you're going to experience, and that they're normal. You're wonderful and I'm really proud of you."

Feelings of Insecurity

Many kids feel insecure during puberty. They are attempting to fit in and find themselves. Most teens feel gawky, ugly, inadequate in comparison to their peers, and particularly uncomfortable around the opposite sex. Much of this insecurity comes from coping with the physical changes, particularly if your teen is teased by siblings or peers. You can ease his fears and concerns by explaining that we all go through this, and we all move on to adulthood eventually.

Also, talk to the entire family about the importance of not hurting someone's feelings as he goes through puberty. Teasing is particularly common among peers. Siblings tease about facial hair, a changing voice, developing breasts, and interest in the opposite sex. This can damage the adolescent's self-esteem and intensify feelings of insecurity. Explain that these changes are a normal part of growing up and shouldn't be ridiculed.

Sexual Impulses

The hormones that create sexual feelings are very powerful. In preparing your child for these changes, you could say, "As you go through the physical changes that come with puberty, you'll also experience lots of crazy emotions. This is because there's an increase in the hormones that are running through your body. What's happening is a very real, biological occurrence. Knowing that will help a lot as you go through it. Sometimes you might have strong sexual feelings, and you won't understand why. Just expect these emotions, and understand that you don't have to act on them. They will pass." We will discuss ways to deal with these feelings in future talks. Right now, you're just preparing your child in advance for what to expect.

Give Your Child a Break During This Time

Your child is experiencing a lot at this time in his life. Be sympathetic toward him as he goes through puberty. Don't expect his behavior to always be consistent. Your child might be more moody than usual, or somewhat antisocial. But this usually passes. Remember all of the frustrating emotions you experienced as a teenager?

Boys will have to deal with locker rooms full of other boys who compare one another's physical features and make jokes. Girls have to deal with whether they are the most beautiful or the most popular in the class. Kids can be cruel, and your child could be faced with snide remarks, judgmental glares, and snickers behind his back. Your child needs admiration and encouragement now more than ever. Find traits you admire in your child and make it a habit to build him up whenever possible. Whenever he solves a problem, completes a task, does something unselfish, looks particularly attractive, gets a good grade (or tries hard), give him lots of praise. You may be the only person who does supply him with this much-needed encouragement.

Puberty is also a time of experimentation. Teenagers are trying to figure out who they are and where they fit in. Let your adolescent know that you are available as a sounding board, a resource center, and a shoulder to cry on when needed. But instead of just telling him this, make it obvious through your actions. Going through puberty isn't easy for anyone, even if you do have *The Big Talk* on hand. But if your child is prepared and has been given ways to cope with the intense changes, he will at least have an easier time making the transition.

❖ 5 ❖

Sex Is *Not* Just Physical

S ometimes it seems that everywhere you turn you see ads about sex: how to have safe sex, the importance of condoms, how to protect yourself from getting AIDS, and so on. Our society seems completely focused on the *physical* aspects of sex. Rather than being pro-active and teaching kids how to abstain, and believing in their ability to abstain, it seems that many have thrown in the towel, saying, "You're obviously going to have sex, so here's how to protect yourself." The emotional and relational side of having sex seems to be ignored. The fact that sex alters our emotions and seriously affects the nature of a relationship is left out of the equation. Yet the emotional aspect is the most important thing for your child to understand.

It's true that hurt emotions can't kill you, but based on my conversations with women, the threat of contracting a disease had little impact on their sexual behavior. It was the pain and heartache of going from one sexual partner to the next over the years that motivated them to make a change in their behavior. This was true for me as well. Knowing that I could have contracted a disease never influenced me or my behavior. But learning whether the person I was with didn't truly love me, or was just using me, got my attention. I figured a disease was a physical malady that a simple visit to a doctor could cure (this was pre-AIDS, of course), but the other issue affected my heart and the way I felt about myself as a person. I had to live with that pain. Undoubtedly teenagers already know that they can use a condom to reduce their chances of getting a disease. What they may not know is the powerful effect sex can have on the emotions. This is particularly true of girls.

Many teenage boys have told me that the threat of getting a disease has little effect on their sexuality as well. One boy told me, "If I get AIDS I guess it's my time to go." But when I talked to him about the emotional pain and heartache that he might create for a girl, he seemed to show remorse.

If children think that all they need to be concerned with are the physical consequences of having unprotected sex, they develop the belief that sex is solely a physical experience designed to provide pleasure. To counter this societal message, you can teach your child that sex is sacred, that it has an enormous effect on our emotions, and that it has meaning beyond being a pleasurable experience. If you explain these points to your child when he is between the ages of eight and twelve (when you discuss the mechanics of sex), he will probably maintain the same view when he reaches his teens. The concepts will be firmly embedded. As you discuss these issues, you can also explain that in the right context sex is a wonderful, positive part of our lives. (In chapters 6 and 7, "the right context" will be explored.) You touched on this subject when you talked about the mechanics of sex, but you can reinforce the idea again.

A brochure published by Education, Training, and Research Associates (ETR), one of the largest publishers of health-education issues in the United States, notes: "Teenagers have most of the 'facts.' They usually know how male and female bodies work, and that sexual intercourse can lead to pregnancy. Teens want help with questions about values, relationships, love, and how sex fits into a young adult's life. They want to know how to behave." Educating your child about these issues is what *The Big Talk* is all about.

Sex as a Wonderful, Powerful, and Positive Part of Life

One of the most important things you can teach your child is that sexual intercourse is the most beautiful experience that two people can share. It would be a disservice to give your child the impression that sex is dirty, sinful, or burdensome. Most parents don't intentionally communicate this idea, but it often happens as a result of not talking about the subject openly. Kids also get this message from friends and the media. Young people often use slang words to describe sex, and movies often portray sex as a casual experience.

Make a point of telling your child that sex is a wonderful thing and that it's nothing to be embarrassed about. You can have this discussion in conjunction with your conversation about sex and reproduction, or at a later time. You could say, "I want you to know that at the right time in your life sex will be fantastic, special, sacred, fun, pleasurable, and powerful. It is not dirty, embarrassing, or bad in any way. Some people joke about sex or use slang words for it, but we see sex as a beautiful, wonderful part of the life that a husband and wife share. We hope that when you grow up you'll have the same views."

Kids are very curious about sex—and not just the dry facts about contraception, sexually transmitted diseases (STDs), and clinical details of human sexuality. They want to know what sex is like, how it feels, and how to do it even if they have no intention of doing it now. Be sure to address the issues that interest your child as well as giving him values that will guide him as he makes his own decisions regarding sex and dating.

Discussing the Emotional Effects of Sex

We will cover how to help your child establish sexual standards in chapter 7. But first, talk to your child about the fact that sex is more than just a physical experience. Some of the discussions in this chapter as well as the ones in the previous two chapters can be lumped together in one discussion. But you may want to break them down. You don't want to overwhelm your child by giving him too much information at one time. Each discussion makes a specific point, and you want him to remember these points. Initiate a conversation about your child's sex-ed class. Ask him what he's learning. Unless he's too embarrassed, he'll probably mention the physical realities of sex. Then you might say, "Isn't it interesting that in our society everyone talks primarily about the physical part of sexuality? Yet it's the *emotional* part that is most important! Once you become sexual with a person, the relationship is never the same. Far too often, one person believes that having sex signifies love and commitment, while the other does not. Often the girl bonds emotionally, but the boy doesn't. This certainly makes for a rocky relationship, and someone usually ends up hurt."

Point out to your child that even if one partner doesn't bond emotionally he is still likely to find a loveless, sexually based relationship just as unfulfilling. After all, who wants to feel like the bad guy? And no one enjoys being confused and frustrated when the other person starts behaving differently after becoming sexual.

Listen to what your child has to say. Ask him about his friends—both male and female—who are sexually active. Use their relationships as examples of how a relationship can get complicated after becoming sexual. Keep the conversation focused on the idea that it's a *relationship* he eventually wants to build, not just a *sexual experience.* Tell him, "The point is, we all want to love and to be loved. We want to build a relationship that is solid and lasting. But having sex too soon often ruins the chances of true love ever fully developing. Having safe sex doesn't protect us from the emotional bond of sex. It also isn't a surefire way to be completely safe from disease and pregnancy." Explain that the only way to guard against bonding emotionally with the wrong person, or even with the right person too soon, is to understand the *emotional* ramifications of having sex and then to avoid having sex too soon. The wheels in his mind will be turning, and even though he may not agree with you or comprehend all that you're saying, important seeds will have been planted.

I realized soon after losing my virginity that sex doesn't affect all of us in the same way. Some people—usually men—seem to be able to separate love from sex. They have an uncanny ability to view it as a physical act alone, not necessarily a physical expression of love. I, on the other hand, felt more deeply attached on an emotional level, and I've noticed that many other women react as I did. No one explained this to me ahead of time; nor did anyone prepare me for the devastation that inevitably comes when feelings aren't mutual and commitment hasn't been established, especially after you've shared such an intimate experience with someone. Even the experience itself didn't teach me this—not at first, anyway. I somehow felt the need to justify the result, or to blame it on the man and his inability to love. I simply didn't understand what was happening—I had no idea that having sex too soon was the real problem. Eventually I just detached myself from the experience, as so many young girls are doing today, and I learned to separate the physical act from my emotions.

This pattern of having sex without love, of becoming detached from our feelings, of not making decisions based on established sexual standards, is sadly very common among today's teens. The pattern continues through adulthood, almost unconsciously, until one day at thirty, forty, or whenever we get tired of the pattern, we say, "Wow! I've been intimate with people I really didn't know very well, or love, or who were completely wrong for me!" Teenagers who aren't clear about their standards and how to deal with sexual advances may be destined to repeat this pattern unless they are taught these things consistently from a reasonably early age.

Sandra, fifteen, became emotionally bonded by having sex. She later discovered that the boy really didn't care about her. Sandra was too young even to have been dating (sixteen is a good age to begin dating), let alone to have been having sex. But once she did have sex with this boy, she bonded and therefore was more willing to accept his behavior, which became increasingly more abusive. She told me, "At first my boyfriend was nice to me. We would have sex at his house sometimes. But on the phone he started to be mean to me. I guess I liked him too much, because I took a lot from him. He'd joke around and call me a bitch, and he'd say 'I gotta go' just to hear me say 'No! Don't go.' "

Boys also have negative experiences when they have sex without love. Colton, seventeen, said, "I lost my virginity in the tenth grade. I like the girl, but not a lot. I felt disgusted with myself. I jumped up and said I gotta go—I can't do this. After that, I didn't want to be around her." The same thing happened to him a year later, but with a different girl. "I was more physically attracted to this girl than anything else," he said. "But those same disgusting feelings came up when we started having sex. I felt gross." Colton has no idea why he felt the way he did. He was looking at sex as a physical expression that had nothing to do with love and commitment. He needs to have an adult, preferably one of his parents, explain these feelings to him and help him to avoid these situations in the future. You don't have to wait until your child is in a situation like this before you discuss solutions. You can equip him with what he needs to know so that he won't be faced with these problems. You can discuss these realities with him in an appropriate way before he reaches his teens.

If you continue to have the big talk with your child over the course of his childhood, and you're involved in his life, you avoid being completely unaware of these devastating situations. Both Sandra and Colton come from very good families in which they have loving parents and a stable home life. The frightening thing is that their parents don't know what's really going on with them, which prevents them from being of any real help to their children. These kids are on their own—they're having to learn about this aspect of life as I did: through painful experience. It doesn't have to be that way.

Oxytocin—The "Bonding Hormone"

As you discuss the emotional effects of sex with your child, you may want to inform him about a hormone called oxytocin. According to researchers at Boston City Hospital and at Northwestern University

Medical School, as well as a Stanford University study, oxytocin may be the reason girls—and sometimes boys—feel emotionally attached to their partner as a result of sexual activity. Oxytocin is produced by sexual arousal. Once you begin having sexual intercourse oxytocin is released throughout your body, and it creates an overwhelming feeling of connection and nurturance. This is the same hormone that is released in a mother who nurses her baby. The hormone gives her powerful feelings of love and tenderness toward her baby. Males, too, have oxytocin released in their bodies, but the amount is much less. For this reason, they may not experience the same intensity of feeling. This is why some boys and men are able to separate sex from love.

Oxytocin may explain why many girls—and women—remain in unhealthy, sexually based relationships. The emotional attachment that comes from sex is very powerful. Your child should understand this before she finds herself becoming emotionally attached to the wrong person (or causes someone else to become attached to him) and at the wrong time.

To begin the discussion, you could ask your child, "Do you know *why* sex changes everything and causes some people, particularly girls, to bond emotionally?" In talking to your daughter you could say, "When a woman has sex, a hormone called oxytocin is released in her body. This hormone causes her to bond emotionally with her partner. She experiences deep feelings of love and connection to him. Men don't have the same amount of oxytocin in their bodies, so they don't always feel the same emotional connection. That's why it's so important for a woman to protect herself emotionally by not having sex with a man who doesn't love her to begin with and who isn't committed to her. It's too risky to bond to someone who may not feel the same way. That's why it's wise to wait until marriage. Then you know that your partner loves you. At that point, making love will be so much more special and meaningful. Your relationship will be based on love, commitment, trust, and respect. This is what I want for you, because you deserve the very best!"

For boys, you can share a slight variation of the same perspective: "Because of oxytocin [explain what it is], you want to be careful that you don't cause a girl to bond emotionally to you if you have no intentions of building a life with her. And even though boys may not feel as emotionally attached when they have sex, they usually don't feel good about the experience, either. This is why waiting until marriage is the best choice. At that point, you're both already in love and committed. In our society, many guys have no regard for the fact that women become more attached once they've had sex. They think only of their own needs and desires. But you're a man of integrity. I know that you wouldn't want to hurt someone."

Knowing about this hormone can alter the way your child views sex. It can also affect how he conducts himself. If he knows that having sex isn't just a physical experience but that emotions are dramatically altered, with expectations then surfacing, he's more likely to postpone sex until he's committed, engaged, or married.

Discussing the Social Consequences of Sex

The social consequences that come with being sexually active as a teenager can be devastating. Fifteen-year-old Carni had sex with a boy who then told all his friends about the experience. Her reputation was seriously damaged for the rest of the school year. Many girls said they were ignored or shunned by boys after becoming sexually involved with them. Boys experience this as well. The following story is heartbreaking, and although it may be an isolated incident, many girls find themselves in similarly painful situations. "After I started having sex with my boyfriend the cool girls decided they didn't like me," said sixteen-year-old Dakota. "I hung out with a girl who wasn't sure if she was a lesbian or not—so the cool girls spread the rumor around that they weren't sure if I was a lesbian or a slut. Then one boy said he had a video with me having sex with him. You couldn't see the girl's face, so some people believed him and thought it was me. It really hurt me that people would believe these things." Can you imagine the amount of inner turmoil this young girl has to deal with every day? Dakota's mother is completely unaware of her daughter's plight because they don't have open, honest communication. You can talk to your daughter about these realities and ask her if any of her friends have had a similar experience. Her response will give you insight into what *she* may be dealing with. It's amazing how much teenagers will share with you if you just ask.

Attaching Meaning to Sexuality

In order to teach you child about sex, you will want to help him understand what it means to have sex. If there is no meaning behind the act, then what is it, and why do we do it? We have already touched on this in previous discussions, but it's good to reinforce the ideas.

You need to help your child develop his own inner belief system about what the act of sex means for him, even if he doesn't plan to experience it right now.

A twelve-year-old boy and an eleven-year-old girl were hanging out together one day and the subject of sex came up. The girl said, "Oh, my mom told me all about that." Curiously, the boy asked, "Oh, yeah? What did she tell you?" The girl answered, "She told me, 'You get used to it!'"

You don't want your child to form the wrong views! Ask him, "Why do you think people have sex?" Wait for answers and discuss the ones your child comes up with. Discuss how some people choose to have sex because it feels good, or because it's the thing to do, or because they think they may lose the person if they don't, or to make a baby. Express your own views of sexuality. One mother said this to her daughter: "We believe that two people should make love because they love each other and are married. Sex is a wonderful way to draw closer to your partner—and, of course, to create life when the time is right for that." Ask your child why he thinks some people are okay with having sex if they are only dating and aren't necessarily in love. He may say, "I don't know" or "I guess they think there's nothing wrong with it if that's what they want." You can clarify by saying, "It seems as though many people think sex is just a part of a relationship—it's part of the equation. But it doesn't have to be. There is no rule that says you have to have sex if you're dating someone. In fact, sex can ruin what could be a solid, lasting relationship."

Many teenagers see sex as Andrea's friends do. She told me, "Sex just isn't a big deal to any of my friends. I mean, I'm the only virgin in my group. My friends respect me for wanting to wait, but they don't see sex as something special or anything. Most of them lost their virginity at fourteen or fifteen, so now they just don't think it means anything." Tap into your own child's mind to determine if this is how he feels. If so, set him straight. You can explain that it's never too late to start over (to re-virginate, as you'll see in chapter 9), and that sex still has special meaning, regardless of whether you have already experienced it with someone.

Janae, who's sixteen, lost her virginity at age 14. The boy was seventeen. "He kept asking me if I was okay with it," she said. "He even let me think about it for a while, but I honestly couldn't think of any reason to not do it." Janae's family never discussed the deeper meaning of sex with her; nor did they give her concrete reasons to wait. To Janae sex was something obscure, without meaning or purpose. It was just something she did because it was asked of her. The sexual pressure she received was stronger than her standards. The crux of the problem, however, was that she hadn't established any standards. Your daughter must be able to clearly articulate why she is abstaining and the reasons should extend beyond concerns about pregnancy and disease.

Sex as Sacred

Do we as a society portray anything as "sacred"? The term usually suggests an attachment to religious meaning. The concept obviously applies to most religious ideas, but must one be religious to regard something as sacred? Some definitions of *sacred* are (from the *American Heritage Dictionary*) "worthy of respect; venerable; made or declared holy." The word *holy* is defined as "belonging to, derived from, or associated with a divine power; living according to a strict or highly moral system; regarded or deserving special respect or reverence."

We all have our own convictions or beliefs about what may or may not be holy or sacred. Discussing the concept with your child is an important part of having the big talk. In chapter 2, we discussed the body as being sacred. You can now discuss the idea that sex is also sacred. You could say, "Most human beings believe that life itself is sacred. We know that life is not something to be taken lightly. We go to great lengths to save a human life when death is knocking at the door, and we celebrate new life with a special reverence and joy that exalts almost any other experience.

"If life is sacred, then the act that creates life must also be sacred. The power and awesomeness of sex make it worthy of being elevated to a higher plane—to that of a loving, sacred act. Sex can bring another human being into existence, and can create a bond between two people that is more powerful and intimate than any other."

Imagine how different our society would be if at a young age we were taught that sex is sacred. Let's fact it, society doesn't exactly paint a picture of sacredness when it comes to sex. Television programs and motion pictures depict sex as an insignificant experience. In the film *The Flintstones*, Halle Berry's character, the sexy secretary to Fred Flintstone, says seductively to Fred, "Please feel free to *use* me however you see fit!" And this is supposed to be a film for the entire family!

The popular game show *Singled Out* has college-age contestants who are asked questions. One question was "What's a better reason to break up: Won't put out or Giving it to someone else?" In the background, you can see the audience jumping around, laughing, and acting as though these are just normal, everyday questions.

In the sitcom *The Fresh Prince of Bel Air,* Carlton loses his virginity with a woman he just met. Then he finds out that she's married. He thought they had something special. When he confronts her, she replies, "Carlton, it was just one night!"

A teen magazine sported this blurb: "Boy Sluts: Why Guys Cheat!" This is not just an American phenomenon. In England, popular teen magazines flaunt the following blurbs on their covers: "Girls Who Sell Sex for Designer Clothes," "Give Good Love and Get Him Hooked," "Get Loved Up," and "I Slept with 40 Boys in 3 Months."

You know the problems—they're fully displayed on television, in magazines, music videos, motion pictures, musical lyrics, and practically everywhere you turn. It is overwhelming, and while you may not be able to change what is going on around you, you can make sure that important principles, such as the idea that sex is sacred, are observed in your own home. You can also have an impact on your own home by carefully monitoring the movies, television programs, and magazines your child is exposed to.

It's best to avoid watching movies and television shows that portray sex as common, but obviously this isn't always possible. When there is a scene on television in which two unmarried people who just met have sex, take the opportunity to say, "Did you notice that not only was that couple not married but they didn't even discuss their feelings for each other or the nature of their relationship before becoming intimate? We don't believe that's a healthy way to behave. We see sex as something much more sacred. If sex were sacred to them, they wouldn't have been willing to be intimate with each other under those circumstances." It isn't enough to just state your views; you've got to help your child understand *why* you believe as you do.

Young children may not be mature enough to fully comprehend the meaning of *sacredness,* nor would you want to talk specifically about sex, but they will pick up on the attitude and spirit you attach to words. You can make *sacredness* a household word in your home. Talk about things that are sacred: your family, your love for each other, God, anything that you feel should receive special reverence or respect. If your child sees or hears a derogatory comment about something you hold sacred, teach him the views you embrace as a family. You could say, "We don't believe in talking about those things in such a crass or disrespectful way—these things are special to us."

Sixteen-year-old Jerome came home from school one day and said to his mother, "A slut at school wanted to get busy with me, but I told her no." Jerome's mother was relieved, and said, "That's great! You may have caught a disease."

This mother missed a perfect opportunity to teach her son the concept of seeing sex as sacred, and to give him additional reasons not to have sex, aside from the danger of contracting a disease. Jerome also needs to learn to view girls in a more positive light. She could have said, "You know, Jerome, I'm really proud of you for not succumbing to her sexual advances. That shows real integrity and moral strength. But let's talk about this girl. You should never call anyone a slut. It seems to me that girls who are promiscuous are this way because they desperately want to be loved and accepted. In many cases, they don't know any other way to behave. Isn't that sad? She may be a very sweet girl who simply has a lot of problems. It's unfair and harsh to put a label such as 'slut' on her. Don't you agree? Now, let's talk about *why* you said no." She could then discuss the reasons for waiting, and the fact that sex is sacred—which would certainly make it clear that using such terms as "getting busy" is inappropriate.

Your child should have a clear understanding of the meaning you attach to human sexuality. There should be no ambiguity about it: Sex is something to be elevated, not denigrated. It is awesome and special, not dirty or common. It is something that is *set apart* for an important purpose that has deep meaning. It is not an ordinary, casual experience.

End the discussion with a challenge: "We hope that you will always view sex as sacred and special. We trust that you will always strive to make healthy, positive decisions when it comes to your own sexuality. I'm glad you're so open and willing to discuss this topic, and I hope you'll come to me if you ever feel confused about this."

Once your child has a strong belief that sex is sacred and isn't just a physical experience, it will be much easier to help him establish unequivocal sexual standards, such as the commitment to wait until marriage. He will see the value in waiting because he will understand that sex is a meaningful and profound experience.

❖ **II** ❖

Setting Sexual
Standards

The Benefits of Teaching Abstinence

M ost parents agree that teenagers are too young to have sex. Many say they would prefer that their kids waited until marriage to have sex, but they usually follow that statement up with "But I realize that's pretty unrealistic these days." In fact, most parents don't even discuss abstinence until marriage with their kids because they see it as a pipe dream. "Nobody waits anymore! How can I expect my kid to wait when the whole world is having premarital sex?" one mother said.

In this chapter we will discuss some of the common admonitions parents give their children, and we will cover more specific, beneficial ways for you to help your child develop solid moral values. We will also discuss practical ways to teach abstinence until marriage, as well as explore other options, such as waiting at least until your child is in a committed relationship or is engaged to be married. I will make a strong case for abstinence until *marriage,* because I know from my own personal experiences, and that of many others, that abstaining until marriage is the safest, wisest choice. Obviously, you must decide what standards you want to teach your child. You may decide to teach one standard, or you might want to present the pros and cons of various options to your child in order to come up with the one that best suits your family's values.

Is Abstinence Until Marriage Unrealistic?

Abstinence until marriage may seem like an archaic concept, given the fact that most people don't wait. But the fact is, it is a viable, obtainable goal for anyone. Regardless of your own feelings on the subject, abstinence until marriage is an option that should be presented to every child, whether or not she chooses to wait. If only one teenager waits until marriage to have sex in these modern times, then it is possible for *anyone*. And there are many teenagers and single adults who have chosen to wait. It may be more difficult for some given the social climate, and particularly those who have been sexual in the past, but it is possible. But we can't expect teenagers to embrace the idea of waiting if their parents don't even believe in the possibility.

We do live in a very sexually focused world, in which children and teenagers are surrounded by sexual messages and constant enticements to be sexual. It's also true that most older teenagers are having or have had sex: 53 percent of girls ages fifteen to nineteen are sexually active. But these statistics don't have to include *your* son or daughter. After all, let's not forget the 47 percent of teenagers who *aren't* having sex!

Some parents feel that teenagers are going to have sex—period. Brad thinks it's impossible for teenage boys not to have sex. "If a girl is there, and he likes her, he's going to go for it," he said. If this father were to have the big talk with his son, he would discuss the consequences of being physically intimate—for his son *and* his son's partner. He would help him see things from the girl's perspective. This father's limited view sets his son up to be sexually active even before he explores other options—unless his son decides to abstain on his own, which is unlikely. Because of his own belief system, this man could actually increase his son's chances of being sexually active, or even promiscuous. What he needs to do is talk to his son about the pros and cons of having sex at different stages of a relationship and help him form his own standards.

Although I've heard many heartbreaking stories, I also know many adolescents who are successfully choosing to wait until they are married before they have sex. They have clear reasons for doing so, and they live up to their moral standards in spite of what is happening all around them. These kids aren't the nerds of the school, or social outcasts. Many are religious, but they aren't seen as religious fanatics. In fact, many people have no idea that these kids are waiting until marriage because they keep their values private. They just quietly, yet consistently, live true to their beliefs. We don't hear much about these kids.

Abstinence until marriage isn't just for the religious, the prudish, the unattractive, the asexual, or even non-adults. This choice is for anyone who wants more from a relationship—more love, commitment, self-respect, and long-term fulfillment rather than short-term gratification. If you personally feel that abstinence until marriage is the best choice, and it's something you would like to teach your child, maintain your integrity by passionately teaching this standard. You may have doubts in the possibility of your child's embracing this standard, but your child will respect your unwillingness to compromise by teaching a different standard.

Common Admonitions Parents Give Their Children

Parents who don't see abstinence until marriage as a realistic option, or who don't teach specifically when it's okay to have sex, usually tell their teenagers to "be careful" or to "be responsible" or that they should be "in love." Some parents attach an age to being ready. "I encourage my daughter to wait at least until she finishes high school" was one mother's advice. When a fifteen-year-old boy asked his sex-ed teacher when it's okay to have sex, she said, "When you can leave the lights on and not be embarrassed, and you think you're in love and aren't being forced to do it, you're ready."

Telling a child to wait until she's "in love" or "ready" or "older" or "responsible" or "safe" leaves too many questions unanswered. It's like telling a child who wants to drive a car, "All you have to do is wear a set belt and have a license. Oh, and don't forget to be careful!" To leave out the fact that there are laws that must be followed, along with all the other aspects of driving a car, would be sending your child on a dangerous ride. She would be grossly unprepared and vulnerable to many potentially damaging forces. And she may never recover from these experiences. She could figure it out on her own—after all, driving a car isn't all that difficult. But it's a big risk. She may make some serious mistakes before finally "getting it." And we all know that sexual relationships are much more complicated than driving a car.

Let's go over some of these admonitions. What does "ready" mean? At fourteen, I thought I was mature enough to do just about anything. I was "ready" whenever I wanted something badly enough. In the heat of the moment, teens rarely think, "Am I ready for this?" And even if they do, their hormones say, "Yes, I am!"

What does "safe" mean? Does it mean using a condom every time? And are you going to trust that your child knows the difference between a latex condom and a sheepskin one? Will you trust that he will use it properly and consistently? Are you prepared to show him? And

what about the fact that condoms aren't 100 percent effective in preventing pregnancy and disease?

What does "being in love" mean? Do teenagers know when they're
in love, or how to create love? How are they to distinguish between
love and lust? What about being "responsible"? Does this strictly mean
protecting themselves physically by using a condom? Do teens know
that responsibility also lies in considering the other person's feelings
and expectations?

Age has very little to do with whether a person is "mature" enough
to make healthy decisions about her sexuality. We assume that when
a person reaches adulthood she is old enough to make her own decisions regarding her sexuality. They should know better. While that
may be true to a point, the fact is we all know single people in their
twenties, thirties, or forties who haven't figured out what their sexual
standards are; nor do they know how to avoid having sex too soon.
In fact, a study conducted by the Alan Guttmacher Institute shows
that it is *adult* women, not teenagers, who account for the highest
number of unintended pregnancies, abortions, and nonmarital births
every year.

Gaining knowledge, wisdom, and practice in implementing
our standards as we reach emotional maturity is what makes us quali-
fied to make healthy choices. So just because a child is approaching nineteen, twenty, or whatever age we deem to be "old enough
to know," we shouldn't assume that she's well equipped to make
sound decisions about her sexuality. The information in *The Big
Talk* will aid you in helping your child develop more specific
standards.

Some of these hazy admonitions are given because many parents
don't see the seriousness of teens having sex. Or they feel that if their
teenager isn't sexually active at this point in time there's nothing they
can do *now* to prevent future problems from surfacing. Lucinda, the
mother of a fifteen-year-old daughter, said, "I don't worry about something that isn't happening now. I have no idea where my daughter will
be from week to week in terms of her emotional development. So I
take life day by day."

Living one day at a time is great, but when it comes to establishing sexual values, parents and teenagers need to plan ahead. You have
to help your child project into the future—from the moment a sexual
advance takes place to the day she gets married. You don't know
when that day will come, but she needs to know how to handle these
situations before they creep up on her.

Parents Who Are Opposed to Teaching Abstinence until Marriage

As I mentioned earlier, many parents secretly wish their children would wait, but there are also many parents who are uncertain that waiting until marriage is the best choice and many others who are strongly opposed to the idea. Arthur, a single father of fifteen-year-old Sadie, said, "I feel that a good marriage is based on compatibility, and sex is a very important area to check out first. In fact, I think they should live together." As we talked further, Arthur said something that revealed a completely different attitude. He said, "As Sadie and I were watching television the other night she turned to me and said, 'I'm going to wait until I'm married to have sex.' I told her I thought that was a good idea, and I hope she maintains that thought." I reminded Arthur that he was contradicting himself. He had previously told me that he wouldn't want his daughter to wait until marriage. "Oh," he said. "Well, I guess what I mean is that I don't think it's a good idea for *me* to wait until marriage. I would say that waiting until getting engaged would be better."

Arthur wants the best for his daughter, but he is confused about the sexual standards he would like his daughter to adopt. I asked him if he planned to have a talk with Sadie, to teach her that waiting until she becomes engaged is a better choice. He said that he didn't want to shatter her dreams and lower her standards. He figured that would happen naturally in time. And he's probably right. Without a parent to encourage her to set high standards, Sadie probably won't be able to follow through, given the outside influences she's bound to encounter.

I mentioned to Arthur that it won't be easy for Sadie to maintain her current standards. "Oh, I know," he exclaimed. "She'll come across boys who will do whatever it takes to get her clothes off!"

"So, who's going to teach her how to implement these high standards in her life?" I asked. "Who's going to show her step-by-step how to say no to a sexual advance, which is sure to come her way if it hasn't already happened?"

His response was "Well, if she comes to me, I would be happy to answer her questions." Unfortunately, that day may never come.

Maria, the mother of a thirteen-year-old son, said, "I don't advocate abstinence until marriage. I think it's great for some people, but I don't believe it's natural. Waiting for so long is too tough, anyway." An entire life of celibacy could be considered unnatural, but abstaining until marriage does not pose a threat to a person's overall health. Considering that abstinence until marriage can prevent a person from contracting a life-threatening disease, it seems that it is the healthiest choice. Abstaining from sex is tough, but it's not impossible. Maria told me that her son has already made up his mind that he's not going to wait until marriage. I wonder if her son came to this conclusion based on pondering the pros and cons of having premarital sex or because of his *mother's* orientation.

Sixteen-year-old Cameron was given this counsel by his father: "It's best to wait, but I wouldn't mind if you didn't." Yet when I spoke to Cameron's father he shared a different message with me— one of concern and love for his children. "I want my children to be happy," he said. "I don't want them to be promiscuous like I was. I wish they would find someone special and just settle down with them rather than going through a whole slew of people." Sharing this honest, heartfelt view with Cameron would have had a much more powerful impact on him than the father's original statement. Cameron already knew that his father had been promiscuous based on past conversations. But what he didn't know was how unfulfilling those experiences were for his father. If you tell your child it's best to wait but then discount the gravity of the decision or negate the plausibility of its happening, and you don't show him *how* to wait, then how can that child be expected to avoid going from partner to partner?

Other parents feel that sex is something that should happen more spontaneously, as long as both parties act responsibly. Many parents feel that a few innocent sexual experiences are harmless for a teenager. Sometimes kids are capable of moving on after a sexual encounter without incurring too many emotional repercussions. But far too often someone gets hurt. And what seems like an innocent occurrence turns into a long-term pattern full of pain and heartache. Karen, twenty-one, shared her experience with me: "Once you have a sexual experience, however innocent it may seem, it has a snowball effect. When I was fourteen the neighbor boy talked me into having oral sex with him. That was my first sexual experience. Eventually, I had sex with that boy. I know now that for him it was about conquering another girl. I gained about thirty pounds after that. I became fat and ugly. Through therapy I learned that gaining weight was a protection mechanism. I didn't know how to protect myself verbally, and I lacked self-esteem and inner confidence. I subconsciously created a wall of protection (layers of fat) around myself. But the weight didn't do the job. I became promiscuous over the next several years. I didn't know how to have a relationship, so I had sex."

Parents Who Feel Hypocritical Telling Their Kids to Wait

Many parents see their own hypocrisy as a stumbling block to teaching their children abstinence until marriage. "I don't tell my daughter she should wait until marriage, because I'm not married and I'm having sex with my live-in boyfriend. It would be ludicrous!" said the mother of a fourteen-year-old girl. This mother has two choices: She can change her current status with her boyfriend in order to set a better example for her daughter (by ending it, or by marriage), or she can explain that although she is living by different standards her daughter doesn't have to do the same. She can let her daughter know that there are drawbacks to living together, and that she wants more for her.

Hypocrisy is the biggest turnoff to kids. "Do what I say, not what I do" builds walls between you and your child. These are issues you will have to explore for yourself as you read through the discussions in this book. If your standards for yourself are completely different from the standards you want for your child, reconsider your own values. A single parent who counsels his or her child to wait until marriage, yet has a partner spend the night, has a conflict of values. Your child will definitely pick up on it. Children will typically form their own values based on your actions, not your words. But the price you pay in living a lifestyle that may be acceptable for *you* is that you may be setting a terrible example for your child. In *Raising Positive Kids in a Negative World,* Zig Ziglar says, "Parents, if you will set the example, you won't have to set the rules."

Some parents justify their own behavior rather than make adjustments for the welfare of their kids. "I'm single, and my girls have watched me be less careful in sexual relationships than I would want them to be," one mother said. "They see the double standard, but they can learn. They know I'm not perfect." Kids can learn from observing less than moral behavior in their parents, but this behavior is more likely to have a negative effect than a positive one.

Some parents are still dealing with guilt and remorse over their own mistakes. One mother said, "My daughters know that their father and I didn't wait, so I never felt right telling them they should wait. I did tell them to wait until they care about the person." This mother avoided teaching a higher standard, not because she didn't believe in this higher standard but because of her own guilt.

What you have done in your past should have no bearing on what you teach today. You could say, "That's right, I had premarital sex—and that's precisely why I'm teaching you to wait until marriage. I know from experience that having sex outside of marriage isn't the best choice. I want better for you. You can go out and make the same mistakes I did, but why do that when you can learn from my mistakes and listen to the wisdom I've gained as a result of making those mistakes?"

Promiscuity—How Many Sexual Partners in a Lifetime Are Okay?

The danger of teenagers having premarital sex is that they could end up living a life of promiscuity. Promiscuity isn't usually about *sex*, as many folks would like to believe. Sexual impulses may be strong, especially for an adolescent going through puberty, but strong sexual urges aren't the most common reason that teenagers go from one sexual partner to the next. The problem stems from the emotions, diminished spiritual wellness, and a lack of purpose. The focus needs to be on building a child's self-esteem, and giving her the love and emotional security she needs to make healthy and confident decisions about her sexuality, not on bombarding her with dry, clinical facts about condoms, STDs, and plumbing facts.

Most parents admit that they don't want their children to be promiscuous, but they often don't equate a few sexual experiences with being promiscuous. Most people aren't even certain how to define the word. According to the *American Heritage Dictionary,* the definition of promiscuous is: "Confused. Lacking standards of selection; indiscriminate. Indiscriminate in sexual relations. Casual; random." If you and your child have the big talk, and your child internalizes the information, she will gain her own convictions and learn how to be selective and discriminate.

Those who are or have been promiscuous rarely see themselves as being promiscuous. One father boasted that he had had approximately forty sexual partners over the course of his life. "I never picked up some stranger in a bar and took her home," he said. "These were all friends or love relationships. They were women I knew and with whom I was honest about the relationship we shared." This father may have been discriminate in his mind, but his relationships were casual. Encouraging your child to wait until marriage can help her avoid this pattern.

Forty may seem like a large number to you. But what about ten? Twelve? Twenty-five? How many sexual partners would you want for your son or daughter? And would it make a difference if he or she were seventeen or twenty-seven?

Today we have terms that soften the idea of promiscuity, such as "serial monogamy," or we excuse the behavior by saying, "Oh, that was the times—everyone was doing it." Today we say, "Everyone is having sex in high school—that's just the way it is." Sex has become an expected and acceptable part of practically every dating relationship. Having several sexual partners, therefore, does not seem out of the ordinary or inappropriate. But is this really okay for *your* son or daughter?

When I asked Barney these questions, he said, "My son Mark isn't going to be a promiscuous person. He's a sensitive, compassionate boy. I hope he has fewer than six partners up until the time he marries. He may even be able to figure out if he's with the right woman after only two or three sexual partners."

Barney is a kind, loving father. But he hasn't thought to teach Mark that these "sexual partners" are girls who may not want to be stepping-stones on his way to finding the love of his life. Having sex with someone shouldn't be a means of determining whether that person is "marriage material." Children need to be taught that sex is something to be shared between two people who *already* love each other and are committed to the relationship. Making love is a very special way of expressing and sharing that love with each other, not a way to determine if someone is right for you.

Why Teens Have Sex

It's important to understand why teens choose to have sex (and often end up being promiscuous) rather than just resigning ourselves to their sexual activity. Teenagers have sex for many of the same reasons single adults do. They share similar feelings of loneliness, fear, and insecurity. Teenagers want to be loved and accepted. Additional reasons teens have sex include wanting to fit in or please the other person, not knowing how to say no to sexual advances, feeling they have to say yes, strong sexual desires that were awakened as a result of making out, or wanting to rebel. As I mentioned earlier, being sexually active as a teenager often results from emotional and spiritual emptiness and a lack of purpose.

If you were promiscuous as a teenager or a young adult, ask yourself why you think this was the case: Were you trying to get the love you weren't getting at home? Did you long to fit in and belong to someone? Did you think it would bring you greater confidence or fulfillment? Was it strictly because of a desire to gratify sexual feelings? These are the same issues your child may be struggling with. These are the issues that need to be addressed more so than the promiscuous behavior itself.

Sometimes having one or two sexual experiences cures teens of their curiosity. Sometimes a sexual experience proves to the adolescent that she isn't ready for sexual relationships. But more often than not, one experience leads to another, until the teenager establishes a pattern of having sex without love.

Some parents believe sexual promiscuity for teens is inevitable, as does this mother of a fifteen-year-old son. "Teenagers are going to have sex, and they're going to have more than just a couple of sexual partners," she said. "That's the world we live in today." But, as Connie Marshner, an author, was quoted by *USA Today* as saying, "Teenage promiscuity isn't inevitable. . . . We're talking about adolescent humans with dignity and self-control, not adolescent horses and dogs."

Appropriate behavior tends to come naturally to those who have a strong sense of self, and who feel loved by their parents and extended family. Teenagers who are clear about their sexual standards, and therefore know *why* they would choose to have sex rather than falling victim to circumstance, know how to deal with sexual advances. They have been prepared beforehand. Dissatisfying, stagnating, sexual relationships that don't work do not have to be a part of your child's life—not as a teenager or as an adult. Not if you deal with that potential reality *now!* Rather than surrender to the idea of promiscuity among teens, we should try to understand why our children are choosing to be sexual and then find ways to fill the void in their lives. If we go to the root of the problem, we can find solutions.

Your child learns how to avoid being promiscuous or falling into a series of sexual relationships over the course of many years as she determines her sexual standards, practices ways to respond to sexual advances, and avoids dangerous situations. You help her maintain these commitments by giving her love, praise, encouragement, strict guidelines to follow, and a loving home environment where she feels safe and protected. This may sound like an oversimplified solution, but it can be done—and besides, what have you got to lose?

THE RESULTS OF CASUAL, SEXUAL RELATIONSHIPS

In the course of speaking with dozens of teenagers who have been sexual with one or many partners, I've noticed a pattern. There was a definite sadness in many of these teenagers' voices—a hollow sound that stems from a resignation of the spirit. It's as though many of these kids reached a point where they knew they weren't going to figure it out, that life isn't such a picnic, and that they really are alone in the truest sense of the word. I found this to be true for both boys and girls, but there was a deeper sense of hopelessness among girls. After having a few meaningless sexual encounters that they initially thought had potential, a part of these girls dies. Their lights don't shine—they are dulled. They don't exude youthful enthusiasm. They sleep more than is necessary, they seem disinterested in life, they wear darker colors in clothes and makeup. They take fewer positive risks because of self-doubt. I often wonder how these teenagers will ever be able to build a healthy, strong relationship when the time for marriage approaches. It seems inevitable that these kids will experience the same struggles that I endured.

On the other hand, girls and boys I've spoken with who hold on to their virginity (or who re-virginate, as discussed in chapter 9), who have established standards and for the most part remain true to them, do not exude these negative attitudes and behaviors. They seem relatively happy—you can hear it in their voices and see it in their faces. This makes perfect sense when you consider the fact that they aren't worried about getting pregnant or getting someone else pregnant. They don't obsess to the same degree about a love interest, because they aren't as physically and emotionally invested. These kids haven't used or been used by others—not to the same degree, anyway, as teenagers who are sexually active. I noticed that they laugh more easily. They're more comfortable in their own skin. Your child can experience the same confidence as you help her to establish clear standards.

Teaching Abstinence

More and more people are seeing the necessity of teaching abstinence—at least until teens become adults and enter into a serious, committed relationship but ideally until they marry—as evidenced by *The Statement on AIDS Education,* by William J. Bennett and C. Everett Koop, M.D. They were quoted as saying:

> Young people must be told the truth—that the best way to avoid AIDS is to refrain from sexual activity until as adults they are ready to establish a mutually faithful monogamous relationship. Since sex education courses should in any case teach children why they should refrain from engaging in sexual intercourse, AIDS education should confirm the message that should already be there in the sex education curriculum. AIDS education (as part of sex education in general) should uphold monogamy in marriage as a desirable and worthy thing.
>
> AIDS education guided by these principles can help protect our children from this terrible disease. But an AIDS education that accepts children's sexual activity as inevitable and focuses only on "safe sex" will be at best ineffectual, at worst itself a cause of serious harm. Young people should be taught that the best precaution is abstinence until it is possible to establish a mutually faithful monogamous relationship.
>
> With regard to AIDS, science and morality teach the same lesson. The Surgeon General's Report on AIDS makes it clear that the best way to avoid AIDS is a mutually faithful monogamous sexual relationship. Until it is possible to establish and maintain such a relationship, abstinence is safest.

The Big Talk's approach to teaching abstinence is to be specific: "It's best to wait until you're married [or in a committed, loving relationship with marriage as the goal, depending on your belief system], and this is why. . . ." The idea is to help your child establish a definite time as to when it's okay for her to be sexual, and to teach her how love and commitment are established—in other words, to set a standard. (I'll discuss possible standards in greater detail in chapter 7.) You help her to see how sex fits into her life.

A commitment to abstinence comes from a deep, well-thought-out decision to wait based on analyzing the consequences and benefits of the choices available. Your child's decision to wait must be backed up with confidence and enthusiasm. This attitude is grounded in a real understanding of the rewards of waiting, such as a healthy, lasting relationship, peace, happiness, health, and a positive self-image. Teenagers will obtain this kind of detailed information only from concerned and informed parents. Don't rely solely on abstinence-based curriculums taught in schools. The information covered may not be detailed enough and usually doesn't include values. In addition, you have no way of knowing how much of this information your child has absorbed.

When *you* get clear about the standards you want to teach, and then present them to your child with the what, why, when, and how, she will have something solid to grasp—a firm foundation on which to base future decisions. She may choose to live by a different set of standards now or later, but it won't be because of your ambiguity or failure to present all the necessary information, such as the consequences of not waiting *and* the benefits of waiting.

There is no guarantee that your child will heed your counsel or even listen, for that matter. But in presenting her with clear choices and standards you can feel good about the fact that you did your part. You cared enough to give your child the wisdom and guidance she needs to avoid having casual, sexual relationships. In the next chapter, we'll discuss specific ways to help your child develop her own sexual standards.

❖ 7 ❖

Establishing Standards

The most important aspect of the big talk is to help your child establish solid sexual standards before he even begins dating. This means that your child knows, and is able to clearly articulate, exactly when it's okay for him to be sexual, including how far he'll go with other sexual activity. It isn't enough for you to dictate *your* beliefs—your teenager must embrace his own moral standards based on the information and guidance you give him. You *aid* your teen in forming his own value system, but ultimately the choice is his. Your child needs to truly believe in the standards he sets. This will occur as you explain why it's important to have standards, and as you discuss the consequences of having sex at various stages in a relationship, as well as the benefits of waiting. Your child can then make a personal pledge to abstinence based on the standard he chooses.

Why Setting Standards Is Important

Having specific standards is important for many reasons, particularly to avoid situations like the following: "Mature women don't act this way," he said to me with a bored look as he rolled his eyes. "They are more *free*, and less hung-up. This is high school stuff," he continued. I sat there, trying to gather my thoughts to come up with a response. I wanted to say that I wasn't even *in* high school yet, but I didn't want to draw more attention to my age. That might really turn him off, I thought. I could think of nothing intelligent to say.

At fourteen, I was described as "fourteen going on forty" and "a force to be reckoned with." So why was it that I felt completely powerless and at a loss for words? His words wounded me. The last thing I wanted to be, especially in his eyes, was *immature*. I knew I had to act fast if I wanted to keep this exciting, sophisticated man interested in me. I remember thinking, *I want to please him. I want to show him that I can do it—I can be amazingly mature, incredible, and free!*

Proving myself worthy wasn't as fulfilling as I had imagined. My free-spirited ways seemed to affect this man only for the moment. Soon after our time together he disappeared. No flowers, no tender words of love, no talk of the future. Despite the fact that I was too young to even consider love and marriage, being sexually involved made me *feel* that I should. There was a feeling of emptiness that would go away only if I blocked out any acknowledgment of my feelings. A fortress was built that separated my heart from my head.

This little vignette from my own life is echoed by many teenage girls and even some boys today. How many sexually active teenagers do you know who are in healthy, loving, solid relationships that have a future? Sometimes teenagers do find themselves in relationships that appear to be healthy and solid, but these relationships rarely last or lead to marriage.

What stands out for me as I reflect on this scene is not so much the immoral behavior on the part of this man, although he clearly was wrong. Nor is it that my parents should have kept a closer watch over me, although that, too, is true. The truth about my experience is this: 1) I didn't know that *I* was solely responsible for setting my own standards. 2) I didn't know that I had the *right* to set my own standards. And 3) I didn't know *what* my standards were. I didn't understand that having sex wasn't the answer. Giving your child this wisdom and confidence is what *The Big Talk* is all about.

If I had known these three simple points it wouldn't have mattered how cunning this man was, or where my parents were; I would have known what to do. But, like so many girls, boys, men, and women today, I was confused and unsure of how to direct my own life. This is largely why having clear standards is so important. I should have known (with the help of my parents) what my standards were by the time I was twelve years old.

Instilling solid moral standards in your child takes time and effort. It's a lifetime endeavor. If you say, "No sex before marriage—period," your child may hear you but choose to live his life differently based on his own set of values and those of his peers. Mary Kay Lehto says, "If you teach your child that your way is the *only* way, he'll be reluctant to come to you should he do something different. Many teenagers rebel if they feel forced to adopt their parents' beliefs. It's very difficult for a child to openly say 'I don't buy that' if he thinks his parents will come down on him for doing so."

If you help your child establish his own standards based on valid, practical information, while revealing your own strong feelings and beliefs, he will more likely adopt your beliefs as his own because they make sense. Teenagers do respond to logic if it is presented in the right way. Even if your teenager doesn't apply the logic now, the information will make an impression, and chances are he'll use it later if not now.

The Savings and Loan Metaphor

Help your child see the value of establishing his own standards by explaining that we all need moral and ethical standards to live by. These standards are our internal compass—they guide us in making healthy choices in our lives. They help us reach our desired destination and enable us to feel good about ourselves. They allow us to make our dreams come true.

To illustrate this, let's use what I call the savings and loan metaphor. It goes like this: Every savings and loan institution has a set of standards that it has established to define and monitor its relations with customers. These institutions have to know who you are, what your past record has been, what your credit is like, and how you plan to pay back the loan you've requested. They require references, and sometimes collateral. They never hand over the money to just anyone. They know that what they have has great value to others, which is partly why it is so important that they go through the painstaking process of getting to know who you are. They decide how much they're willing to give, when they will give it, to whom they will give, and then they carefully monitor the timing of payments and foreclose quickly in the event of nonpayment. People can't just talk their way into a loan or not follow through with their payments after receiving it. They have to prove themselves worthy. Once the savings and loan gathers the necessary information about you, it requires that you make a solid commitment to paying the institution back—a requirement that is expressed in writing, with your signature. Everything must be legal and clearly spelled out in the contract. And the institution requires that *you* give something as well: You must pay interest on the loan. After all, it has needs and goals, too.

Explain to your child that his love and his body are also special things, that they shouldn't be given away easily. It's a bit more difficult to convince a boy of this, because he doesn't usually experience the same emotional bonding that a girl does, but you will still want to teach the principle. He needs to set requirements for others to be worthy of these things.

Explain to your child that just like the savings and loan, he needs to have his own set of standards as to when it's okay for him to be sexual, how far he'll go, what he needs to know about the person first, and what kind of relationship he wants to have with that person. Once in a relationship he'll want to monitor the situation and see how it's going, and ensure that he treats his partner well and is treated well in return. It's a lot to think about, but point out that most people never consider these issues before becoming sexual, and as a result they usually find themselves in less than ideal circumstances. Your teenager will need help in determining the specifics of his standards. You will discuss these issues in greater depth as you go over the standards that are detailed later in this chapter.

Having standards is important because without them we lose a certain amount of freedom. You can help your child internalize this principle by having this topic for your family-night discussion. Ask your child these questions and help him find the best answers. Some are given here for you, but encourage your child to come up with his own answers.

Q: What's wrong with doing whatever we want, when we want?

A: There are always consequences. For example, if we ate whatever or whenever we wanted to we could ruin our teeth and health. If we stayed up all night we wouldn't get the rest we need. If we don't treat friends and family right, we won't have love and friendship.

Q: What does it mean to be truly free?

A: We're free when we make decisions based on our values rather than being forced into something; otherwise we do it for the wrong reasons.

Q: What role does responsibility play in being free?

A: When we are responsible we avoid making poor decisions that limit our freedom.

Q: Why should someone practice self-control even when he doesn't feel like it?

A: Because if we all just did whatever we wanted to do we wouldn't be responsible, functioning human beings. Gaining *pleasure* and gaining *happiness* are two different things. Self-control is what brings us happiness and peace.

Q: What separates us from the animals when it comes to sex?

A: As humans, we have the ability to reason and make choices regarding our sexuality. We have morals and values that we live by.

Q: Do we possess the power to say no even if we are really sexually aroused, or even if we have already reached a certain level sexually?

A: Yes. We always have the ability to say no. We can control our impulses and emotions—they don't have to control us.

Q: Is self-control easier for some people—why or why not?

A: Yes. Some people have better discipline. But we can learn to be more disciplined. Some people have a stronger sex drive than others, but we can learn to keep it under control. People who have high standards and make up their minds ahead of time usually find it easier to maintain self-control.

Q: Why do some people choose to be sexually involved even with all of the consequences?

A: Their resolve to wait may not be strong enough. They may not be aware of all the consequences. They may rationalize or justify their actions. They may put themselves in dangerous situations. They may drink or do drugs, which weakens their resolve.

The True or False Game

Knowing what our standards are also helps to give clarity to the role sex can play in our lives. As your child begins to understand the truth about sex and how it can affect a relationship, he will be more likely to choose to wait. Children don't need the gory details—just simple, basic information. Ask your child which statements are true and which are false. Be sure that your child is at an appropriate age level to play this game. Depending on the child, eleven and up is an acceptable age range.

FALSE STATEMENTS

• If you become intimate with a person, he or she will feel committed to you.

- Sex has to be a part of every relationship—that's just the way it is.
- You have to be sexy to get someone interested in you.
- Once you have sex, you're automatically in a relationship.
- If you can please someone sexually, that person will never leave you.
- Through sex you can get a person to love you.
- If a girl dresses sexy, it means she wants sex.
- A guy is a wimp if he doesn't "go for it."

TRUE STATEMENTS

- Sex has nothing to do with forming a commitment or gaining a marriage partner.
- Sex may keep a person interested for a while, but it's not as important as you might think. It won't necessarily keep that person interested in you.
- Sex does not have to be a part of every relationship. You do have a choice.
- Sex is not what will make a relationship great, lasting, or loving—especially if it occurs too soon.
- Sex does not affect men in the same way that it affects women. Women often bond more emotionally.
- Choosing to have sex with someone shouldn't be based on whether the other person is willing.

The Standards

Go over the following three standards with your spouse and determine which one you would like to pass on to your child. Then go over each standard carefully with your child and discuss the pros and cons. Be sure to let him know which standard you would like him to adopt. You can also just present the standard you want to teach. But if you teach only one standard, at least discuss the fact that some people live by different standards and explain why you feel strongly about the one you've selected. The point is to help your child to see clearly what his standards are. This has particular relevance to girls, who need to establish standards in a dating situation when they're confronted with a sexual advance. In deciding what you want to teach your child, don't worry about what society or your child's friends might be doing. Encourage your child to adopt solid standards regardless of these outside influences. The age at which you discuss these standards is up to you and depends largely on your child's development. I needed to have this discussion by the time I was in the fifth grade. I may not have fully understood all of the information at that time, but I needed to know what sex is, how it affects a person, and when it's acceptable to become sexual. At the very least, the concept of waiting until marriage should have been presented to me, with an explanation that many people don't wait.

Considering the idea of your child having premarital sex may be unacceptable to you. It's difficult for me to even write about other options because of the pain and devastation I've seen so many people— myself included—experience as a result of premarital sex. "Committed" relationships often end up being "casual" ones, even for adults. But I also strongly believe in the freedom to choose how we live our lives. Teenagers who are younger than eighteen should live by the rules you've determined in your home, but it is also a fact that you can't completely control their behavior. You can only do your best and trust that your child will embrace your views when he gets older and is faced with the opportunities to be sexual. Don't give up hope. Many teenagers eventually return to the counsel given them by their parents. Some teenagers even choose to follow the advice upon hearing it!

Standard #1: Abstinence until You're in a Committed Relationship

Adopting this standard means that your child agrees to refrain from sexual activity until he becomes an adult, is in love with his partner (feelings should be mutual for both partners), and marriage is the goal. Issues such as compatibility, future goals and dreams, values, and religious beliefs need to be discussed with the other person before intimacy on any level aside from kissing and hugging occurs. It's wise not to rush into making a commitment, and to allow plenty of time for both parties to get to know each other as well as possible. It's also wise to establish a date when you will discuss moving on to the next level of commitment—engagement, for example—or consider breaking up if things aren't working out.

It's important to know that there are drawbacks in choosing this standard. Clearly, this is better than endorsing only "safe sex" or not having any standards at all and therefore having completely casual relationships. But this option is complex and often dangerous. Your child could fall into the serial monogamy syndrome, whereby he goes from one committed relationship to another. By the time he's thirty years old he could have had several sexual relationships, but nothing lasting or deeply fulfilling. I embraced this standard in my late teens and early twenties, but I still felt that sex was out of context. Although my relationships became more solid and committed, over time, the intimacy just wasn't that special—and I discovered that I hadn't met my mate for life. I knew that sex was getting in the way of my creating the relationship I truly wanted. Couples who are sexually attracted to each other often make hasty decisions about commitment and compatibility in order to have a relationship. And sometimes they aren't honest about their true feelings and intentions. This option also involves physical risks. Your child will have to take responsibility in using protection from disease and unintentional pregnancy.

Pros

- You weed out some of the people who are not serious about you, or who are not ready for a real relationship.
- You gain a clear, verbal understanding of where the relationship is going.
- You feel more secure than you would if you had made no commitment or given expression of love.
- You create an opportunity to establish a foundation of love.

Cons

- Commitment does not always mean the same thing to everyone. Misunderstandings can and do occur.
- You may rush into making a commitment, possibly so that you can get close physically. Later, you may find that it was a mistake.
- Someone could end up getting hurt if the relationship doesn't work out or the other person's feelings change.
- Being in a sexual relationship outside of marriage (and as a teenager) could keep you from growing mentally, spiritually, and emotionally. Your energy could be exhausted by trying to find

ways to have sex, places in which to have sex, and in dealing with the emotional ramifications of having sex.

- The relationship, and the physical intimacy you share with each other, could become monotonous and diluted without the full commitment of marriage. It could seem less special and meaningful.

- You may become emotionally bonded with someone who is wrong for you, making it more difficult to break up if the relationship doesn't work out.

- There are always physical risks in having premarital sex: AIDS and other sexually transmitted diseases, and unintended pregnancies.

Standard #2: Abstinence until You're Engaged to Be Married

Adopting this standard means no sexual activity outside of being engaged to be married. This means that a wedding date has been set, and all of the issues mentioned in Standard #1 have been carefully considered: compatibility, future dreams and goals, values and religious beliefs, as well as how far you will go with other sexual activity prior to getting engaged.

This choice carries with it fewer physical and emotional risks than does sex without love and commitment. But it also has its drawbacks. Many women I've spoken with were devastated when their engagements were broken. They felt they had surrendered themselves to the man and the relationship. When it disintegrated, they couldn't help feeling that they had lost a part of their souls. Of course, not everyone feels this way. Many men and women are able to be sexual without experiencing emotional trauma if the relationship doesn't work out. But enough people have reported intense emotional pain as a result of their decision to be sexual to make the issue well worth our attention.

PROS

- You know the person is sincere and committed to the idea of marriage.
- Love precedes sex, which means the relationship is more solid.
- A stronger, deeper commitment has been made.
- You will feel more secure than you would if you had only made a commitment to be exclusive.

- If you wait until you're out of school to get engaged, delaying sexual involvement, you'll be able to focus on other things during your teen years.

Cons

- Engagements can be broken, which could create a lot of heartache.
- Men have been known to propose only with the intent of getting the girl to have sex.
- You could become emotionally bonded, which would make it harder to move on if the engagement is broken.
- The relationship can become stagnant. He may be less motivated to get married. Girls can become less motivated as well, but this is rare.

Standard #3: Abstinence until Marriage

Adopting this standard means that your child is committed to waiting until marriage to have sex. If you intend to encourage your child to maintain this standard, you'll also want to encourage him to avoid petting and other sexual activity in order to make this goal easier to reach.

Those who have waited until marriage say that the intimacy they share is extraordinarily powerful and fulfilling. Saving sex for that one person whom they truly love and are completely devoted to made the experience much more meaningful and profound. They looked forward to their wedding day with great anticipation. For these couples, making love wasn't a routine but, rather, an experience that consummated the love and commitment that they already shared.

Pros

- You aren't weighted down with the emotional struggles that often come with premarital sex. You can develop character, confidence, and knowledge about yourself and life when your priorities are better set.
- You will be less preoccupied with sex.
- You will be free to enjoy your teen years and better prepare for your future.

- Your reputation won't suffer. You'll be seen as a thoughtful person with high standards, and people of high character will be more attracted to you.

- You will weed out people who aren't serious, who want to use you, or who may not be ready for a real relationship.

- You will feel more secure in a relationship that's not based on sex.

- You will not have to worry about getting pregnant or contracting a disease.

- You will know that your partner cares for you completely and isn't just interested in having sex.

- You make yourself available for the right person.

- If you and your partner are virgins when you marry, you don't have to worry about comparing each other to past lovers. Parents should be careful not to discourage a teen who is not a virgin. Let him know that he can still have a healthy marriage if he re-virginates.

- You will know that your partner's intentions are sincere.

- You will experience the best kind of sex when you know that you are in love and are completely committed to that person for life.

- The relationship moves at a more natural pace rather than becoming stagnant or pressure-filled.

CONS

- You run the risk of being sexually incompatible, although there are ways of determining compatibility without having sex—through touch, chemistry, and discussions about desires, for example. Many couples who have premarital sex, however, admit that they married in spite of the fact that they didn't have the greatest sex life. So, couples knowing what each other is like sexually beforehand doesn't usually determine whether they marry anyway.

- You will probably suffer for a while, as you do when you deny yourself just about anything.

- You may lose a few people along the way, although they're the ones who won't accept your standards so this could be a blessing.

- A couple could make the mistake of rushing into mariage to become sexual. You have to take your time and make sure it's right.

I strongly believe that we should always teach the higher standard with enthusiasm and confidence. Why would we lower the moral standards we teach simply because a greater number of people seem to refuse to do the same? Even if it seems unrealistic or difficult or even improbable, you can still encourage your child to choose the higher road. It is my hope that every parent will teach abstinence until marriage. The emotional, spiritual, and physical risks can be too great otherwise.

The Flow of a Relationship

One of the things I wish I had understood before I entered the dating world was how a relationship develops. For years I was perpetually frustrated because I didn't understand that there are different stages in a relationship, that each phase must proceed at a natural pace, and that engaging in sexual activity could actually thwart the progress of the relationship. I simply didn't realize what a deep impact my response to sexual advances would be on the outcome of that relationship—and on my emotional well-being. Discuss this as you talk about the standards.

A relationship may start out as a friendship and slowly evolve into something more. Sometimes kids hang out together with a group of friends and then discover that they like each other romantically. But regardless of how two people get together, if there's a spark, and they spend time alone, eventually a sexual advance will be made. The advance can surface in a movie theater, at a party, in a house or a car—or just about anywhere. It is at that point—when your teen must respond to a sexual advance—that the course of the relationship is usually determined. That moment is so crucial that it deserves special attention as you talk to your child. Some twelve-year-olds are confronting sexual advances, so be careful not to wait until your child is older to have this discussion. But you should never assume that it's too late, either.

Draw the chart on the next page on a pad. This chart will show your child what can happen when sex, or any sexual activity, occurs too soon.

> **A couple meets . . . They date (or just hang out) . . . A sexual advance is made . . .**
>
> Explain to your child that how he responds to that advance will determine the direction of the relationship. If he chooses to have sex, or even engages in petting, it could turn into:
>
> - A one-night stand (or a one-week stand or a one-month stand).
> - A "situation." It's called a situation because it can't even be considered a real relationship. You may not be proud of the involvement or the person. You know it's not right, and you know that it's based mainly on sex.
> - A "mediocre" relationship. You may be a "couple," but perhaps the other person doesn't treat you quite right, marriage isn't the goal, and you don't experience mutual, deep feelings of love and respect for each other. It *could* turn into a solid relationship even if sex or petting occurs, but the odds are greatly reduced.

You could say, "When you say no to a sexual advance by setting your standard and the other person chooses to end the relationship, you will know his true intentions. Either he was only interested in sex or he determined that you weren't the one for him or he just wasn't ready for a committed relationship. In any of these cases, you wouldn't really want him, anyway. If he chooses to stay, a deeper bond of caring and commitment can occur if both of you are ready for commitment. You can continue to date and determine if you are compatible."

Point out that saying no to sexual advances puts the other person in the position of having to determine his true feelings for your child. He must evaluate how he really feels, and what he is willing to give to the relationship. He doesn't have to consider these issues if his partner doesn't require that of him. This can apply to both sexes. Tell your child, "Once you become intimate with another person, you can become emotionally bonded, perhaps before truly knowing the person. This doesn't allow the relationship to flow naturally. So it is when the other person makes a sexual advance that the foundation of a relationship is established, if there's going to be a relationship at all."

If two people share the same goal to wait until marriage and a sexual advance isn't made (or if they realize they aren't right for each other and they move on), they build a foundation naturally without incurring the emotional pain that often comes with premarital sex.

If your child is a boy—or an aggressive girl—understanding the flow of a relationship is still important. Tell him, "You will meet all kinds of people as you date. Some will be more open to sexual advances. Others will know what their standards are, and they will say no to sex outside of committed love or marriage. Your goal isn't to 'score' whenever you meet someone who's willing. You need to have your own set of standards. When you feel like making a sexual advance, stop and think about where you ultimately want to take the relationship."

When and How to "Set the Standard"

When it comes to giving your child an education in sexual matters, everything needs to be spelled out step-by-step. Leave no stones unturned, no questions unanswered. Your child shouldn't have to guess at when, why, or how he sets the standard in a dating or relationship situation. Self-confidence and clarity regarding what I truly believed in and what I wanted for my future were what I lacked as a preteen and as a teenager. This discussion could have made all the difference.

Explain by saying, "You set the standard when a sexual advance has been made. It's only when someone is trying to get you to go *against* your standards that you need to set the standard by telling that person clearly what your standards are. Sometimes a person might try to find out what your standards are simply by asking. At other times, that person will make a sexual advance. The fact that you know what your standards are will make it easier to respond in either situation."

As your child gets older and needs additional guidance on how to establish a solid foundation for a meaningful relationship, you could elaborate. Both sexes should be counseled to talk about their feelings for the other person and the kind of relationship they want. If they aren't sure how they feel (or their partner isn't sure), or they're not ready to be in a committed relationship, they aren't ready to be physically intimate. Once physical intimacy occurs, the relationship is never the same.

Continue the conversation by explaining additional ways your child can set the standard. Point out that we set a particular standard in various ways. For example, the way you dress sets a certain standard with those around you. How you walk, talk, and behave gives others an indication of how to treat you. You can use hypothetical examples that include kids at school. Ask your child to think of kids who elicit certain treatment by the way they look and act. Point out that they are setting the standard for others to follow based on their own set of values and beliefs.

Avoiding Going Too Far

Roxanne, nineteen, told me that although her parents taught her about how babies were made, she wanted to know more. "Now that I've had a few relationships, I know so much more," she said. "I know about the actual act of sex, but I sort of wish my parents had talked to me about what *leads up* to having sex. The whole thing sneaks up on you. You think you're in control, but you're not." This was true for me as well. I needed to be taught step-by-step exactly what to say and do if a boy tried to kiss me. Some kids seem naturally to know how to handle these situations, but many become paralyzed and unsure of what to do.

Ask your daughter what she would do or say if her date attempted to plant a serious kiss on her. You could suggest that she put her hand on his shoulder, pull away a little, and say, "Please don't take this personally, but I don't feel comfortable kissing this early in our relationship. I'd rather take it slow and just get to know you better." Or she could turn her head so that his kiss falls on her cheek. She could also give *him* a kiss on the cheek. He may frown, but he won't feel as slighted as he would if she pushed him away without any explanation or reassurance that it's not personal. Suggest giving short hugs as a way of saying good night. Some people may be hurt or slightly offended, but she needn't worry about that.

Continue the discussion by saying, "It may seem impossible to avoid going too far when it appears that everyone else is doing otherwise. But just like being honest or having integrity or being responsible, the standards you set for yourself always stay intact, regardless of what others decide to do. People may try to talk you out of your standards. They may even try to convince you that your ideas are wrong or outdated or boring. They might tell you how much they love you and how different it is between the two of you. But don't listen to them. Their motives are almost always selfish. Just stay true to yourself no matter what, and you'll be happier and healthier because of it."

Avoiding Dangerous Situations

Setting the standard is also about avoiding dangerous situations. You could say, "To be able to maintain your standards, you'll want to avoid getting into a difficult or dangerous situation." To your daughter you might say, "It's best to avoid being alone with a boy in a house, car, boat, apartment, plane [have fun with it—show a sense of humor], and so on. Know what you're going to say ahead of time when a boy makes a sexual advance. Be clear about what you will or won't do."

Before your teenager begins dating, explain that avoiding dangerous situations isn't a problem if he does the following:

- Plan dates ahead of time, and make sure the evening is filled with specific activities.
- Don't change the plans you've established.
- Don't spend too much time alone where trouble can occur.
- Spend time with other couples who share your values.
- Don't view sexual material or listen to anything of a sexual nature before going on a date. In other words, avoid getting aroused!
- Make a decision before you walk out the door as to what you will or will not do. Every choice you make throughout the evening should support that decision.
- Dress appropriately. It doesn't make sense to say no to sex verbally yet dress in a way that suggests otherwise.
- Plan dates that are in public places and include others.
- Don't go beyond light kissing and holding hands.
- Don't have casual conversations about sex or engage in sexual talk.
- Don't drink or do drugs.
- Don't send out mixed signals, such as giving someone the idea that you might be willing to fool around.

The Consequences of Making Out

Making out is probably the subject most frequently disregarded by parents. You may be so concerned with talking about "sex" that the grayer areas, such as kissing, petting, and oral sex, escape your attention. And it's difficult enough to talk about sex in a general way, let alone breaking it down to specifics. But these specifics may be even more important than talking about sexual intercourse because not all teenagers have sex, but the majority of them do make out and often go beyond just kissing. Petting usually leads very quickly to sex, so it can be dangerous. But some parents feel it's harmless. "They're kids! Let them have some fun," one father told me. But petting is anything but harmless.

Making out is really what you're teaching your child to say no to, because it's the true crux of the problem. Most adolescents can avoid having sex with little problem, provided their passions aren't awakened through heavy kissing and petting. An editorial in *USA Today* made this statement: "Parents must teach their children the need to say no, because the unwillingness or inability to say that little word makes us slaves to others and, still worse, slaves to our passions and fears. In an age of instant coffee, food and answers, there is a belief that there should also be instant gratification. Sexual promiscuity is empty and self-defeating. We cannot build families, societies, or civilizations with moral amnesia."

As you talk to your younger child about the importance of saving sex for marriage, you can also discuss the importance of not going beyond kissing when she gets older and begins dating. This will prepare her ahead of time and help to establish her standards early. You could say to your child, "I know that most kids make out. It's fun and it feels good—believe me, I know! But there are some real dangers in making out. What do you think they are? [Wait for answers.] Petting *prepares* your body for sex. When certain parts of your body are touched, you become even more aroused sexually, which usually leads to deeper levels of sexual activity. This can happen by being touched on the inside or outside of your clothing. Once you get turned on it's very difficult to think clearly. You begin to rationalize the situation. You don't care as much about your standards—you only care about satisfying your desire to feel good."

Also point out that girls can become just as emotionally attached when they make out as they do when they have intercourse. And a girl's reputation can be damaged just as severely with making out as it can with "going all the way." Of course, in some schools you become more popular as you become more sexually experienced. Either way, your daughter should know that it can be damaging to her. Diseases can be contracted as well. Even pregnancy can occur without penetration if clothes are off and genitals are close. Explain that what seems harmless to many can actually be devastating. Help your daughter to realize that if she decides *ahead of time* that she won't be sexual, she will know to stay clear of petting.

The following chart by Patricia B. Driscoll, the author of *Sexual Common Sense: Affirming Adolescent Abstinence*, illustrates the natural progression of sexual arousal. Go over this chart with your child and show him how the process works. If he is aware of when making out gets dangerous, he will be better prepared to act accordingly.

Periodically ask your child, "So, how do you feel about that?'" or, "Do you agree?" and, "What might stand in your way if you're trying to avoid these things?" Be prepared for possible rebuttals. Your child might say, "Mom, I think you're making too much of this. I know I can stop at a certain point with no problem." You can respond with something like this: "Honey, I know that you're a strong person and that you will always strive to do the right thing. I also know that when I was your age I thought that making out was fun and harmless. But now that I'm older I'm more aware of the dangers. I just want to make sure that *you're* aware of the dangers, and that you'll keep these things in mind as you date. The decisions you make now could have an enormous impact on your future." Review by asking, "So, what happens when you make out?" Make sure that you go over these answers: You get turned on, you lose a certain amount of control, you communicate less, you want to go further, you could later regret your actions and ruin your reputation. Feel free to come up with additional answers.

Here seventeen-year-old Trudy sheds some light on how times have changed: "Sometimes my friends and I say that we wish making out was like it used to be, where you'd just kiss for a long time. Now, it's expected that you go further. It would be weird not to—like, guys would think, What's the point?" These girls don't realize that *they* set the standard. They don't believe it's up to them to establish the boundaries; they don't believe they have the right, or that it would work. They adjust their standards to fit whatever the opposite sex expects, or what the times dictate. Your child needs to hear you say, "How far you go is always up to you." Every child needs to know that there can be emotional consequences even with lighter forms of affection, such as passionate kissing.

Shannon, fourteen, is already learning the hard way the results of making out. "I've only French-kissed," she told me. "I was at a friend's house. I didn't know him very well. I regretted doing it, because he

KNOW the Progression of Sexual Feeling
with Increased Physical Intimacy

Sexual Arousal

| Being Together | Hand Holding | Simple Good Night Kiss | Prolonged Kiss | Necking | Petting | Heavy Petting | Mutual Sex Play | Sexual Intercourse | End of Relationship in Its Present Form |

Beginning of danger

Male genital feeling aroused

Female genital feeling aroused

Female genital feeling aroused

No genital feeling aroused

by Patricia Driscoll, © Womanity, 1982, 1996. Used with permission.

asked my friend out after that. I found out that he does this to everyone. That hurt even though all we did was kiss."

Teenagers get conflicting messages. One teen girl said, "If you don't make out, you're a loser. If you go all the way, you're a slut." As a parent, you can sort through these messages and help your child gain clarity by saying, "Those who stand up for what they believe in regardless of what's cool or "in" gain respect in the end. They at least gain *self-respect*, which is the most important kind."

Your daughter needs to know that she has the right to say no at any time, and that she doesn't need to make out with someone in order to be liked or to be seen as cool. Seventeen-year-old Stephanie told me, "I wish my parents had taught me that it's okay to say no. One time I felt that I had gone too far with a boy, but I thought I had to keep going." In most cases, all it takes is for the child to hear the truth from a loving parent. *Someone* has to verbalize these simple, yet powerful, words.

Ann Marie, eighteen, shared this story with me: "I was with this boy . . . and we went back to his place and we kissed and made out, but I felt stuck. He's nice, but immature. He said, 'I'd really like to kiss you right now.' I said, 'Okay.' I'm so shy, so when I do get attention I really like it. We made out on his couch. Each week we went a little further. I had fun, but I felt uncomfortable. Something about it was bugging me. I knew where the whole thing was headed, and I eventually put a stop to it. We couldn't talk that well. Then I saw him flirting with other girls—I didn't want to be just one of the many girls he makes out with."

Coach your child on how to handle these situations if and when they arise. Most important, make it clear that she has the power to control her own destiny.

The Personal Pledge

When children make a formal personal pledge of abstinence they are more committed to the decision. Encourage your child to make a pledge based on the standard you choose together. The pledge is not made to *you*—it's a commitment your child makes to *himself*. Even a nine- or ten-year-old can make a pledge of abstinence until marriage, although you'll want to review this promise periodically as he gets older and begins dating. You could say, "I think it's a good idea to make a formal pledge of abstinence based on the standards you've set. It will help you feel more committed to your decision." Have your child write out the pledge and sign it in your presence. Talk about the meaning of the pledge and what is required. It could say something like the following (adjust the wording based on the chosen standard):

"I will not have sex or engage in any sexual activity outside of kissing until I am married. From this moment on, I am taking full control of my body. I will not put myself in situations that could lead to compromising my pledge."

Continuing the Conversation

It's easy for kids to forget specific points. You will want to continue the conversation at a later time. Every once in a while, ask your child:

Q: What are your standards?

A: I'm waiting until marriage, and I don't go beyond kissing.

Q: When does a person set his or her standards?

A: When a sexual advance has been made.

Q: How do you set that standard?

A: By sharing honestly and directly my goal to wait.

Q: What are the important points to consider before getting physical on any level?

A: Our feelings for each other, the future goal of the relationship, the amount of time we spend together, compatibility, how we treat each other, how long we've been together.

You may feel uncomfortable about putting your child on the hot seat like this, but these points need to be firmly established in his mind. He needs the repetition in order to eliminate any haziness or ambiguity. If these things are said in the right spirit, with love and concern, your child won't be offended.

At this point, your child will be better prepared for dating and relationship situations than are most kids his age. Someday he'll be grateful for the time and effort you invested teaching him these concepts.

❖ 8 ❖

Additional Ways to Make Abstinence the Standard

Establishing my own sexual standards has made an enormous difference in my life and radically changed the way I date. It all started when I became clear about what I wanted—and didn't want—in a relationship. I knew that I wanted to build a relationship that is based on love. I wanted to establish true emotional intimacy, whereby my partner and I share the same goals for marriage, a family, harmony, and happiness, and we openly discuss these goals with each other. I didn't want to be involved in a relationship where sex came first and then we got to know each other. I didn't want to be in a sexual relationship that dragged on for years without making clear what our true feelings for each other were or whether marriage was the goal.

Over the years, I've dated a variety of men; some have accepted my standards and some haven't. Almost all, however, have respected me for my standards, and I'm often told that it is refreshing and honorable to meet someone who has such high standards.

It's so important to learn these things early in life. In the seminars I conducted for my first book, I met countless single women in their thirties, forties, and fifties who are still trying to figure out how to build a healthy, lasting relationship. And I know that there are many men who are experiencing the same struggle. It breaks my heart to hear these women admit that they've never had a man truly love them. Many of them have only just begun to realize that they became sexual with their partners far too early, which thwarted the process of falling in love and establishing a solid foundation on which to build. Their relationships were passionate in the beginning, but eventually they fizzled and became monotonous; perhaps one day they realized that they just weren't right for each other. After years of feeling unfulfilled and frustrated, these women are finally accepting the idea that a large part of the problem stemmed from the way they approached the sexual aspect of a relationship. They are finally ready to establish standards to live by in order to avoid having these empty, futile experiences. They are learning how to say to a man who makes a sexual advance, "I really like you and I'm attracted to you, but I'm not interested in getting involved in a sexual relationship outside of marriage. I want to build a strong relationship that has a future—one that is based on love and commitment. I believe that sex is an important part of a relationship, but only in the right context."

These women are learning to have confidence in themselves, and they're seeing the value of "setting the standard" in this way, which puts the men they date in the position of having to come to terms with how they really feel about their partners, what they really want in a relationship, and what they're willing to invest. These women are now avoiding casual, sexually based relationships—and they're seeing that when they approach a relationship in this way they create the opportunity for true love to grow. The results have been astonishing. I receive letters from women all over the country who say that the men they date pursue them more consistently and express stronger interest and concern for them than they ever thought possible. Many of them are experiencing real love for the first time. Best of all, these women feel good about themselves. They're rebuilding their self-esteem, which was damaged in past relationships.

I know that as a parent you want the very best for your child. If you're like most parents, you want your child to grow up and experience the joy of being loved and of being in love. You hope that she will marry and have a family of her own. These things don't always fall into place naturally. As is evidenced by the divorce rate, we aren't properly trained in how to make a relationship work. I think much of the problem lies in how we approach a relationship in the very beginning—when we decide to bring sex into the equation. If we can learn to delay gratification, to establish love and commitment first, and spend more time getting to know the other person, I believe we will have a much better chance of being successful.

The big talk will help you to prepare your child for this aspect of her life. She will possess the power, confidence, and insight she needs to avoid dead-end relationships and to build the kind of love that she deserves. And, thanks to you, she won't have to figure this out on her own, after years of costly mistakes.

Educating your child in how to abstain from sex, however, isn't easy. There are so many details to cover in order for your child to really grasp and adopt this way of thinking. In this chapter you will find some additional suggestions on how to teach abstinence.

Dos and Don'ts in Teaching Abstinence

Go over the following list of dos and don'ts with your spouse. This will help you to determine if anything might be holding you back from teaching abstinence to your child. These can serve as your own set of guidelines as you and your child have the big talk.

Don't:

- Assume that your child already knows more than you do. She won't, particularly after you read this book.

- Assume that you can only teach your child about sex spontaneously, as opportunities present themselves—you need to have prepared, planned dialogues with her.

- Resign yourself to the fact that your child will not talk to you about the subject. She will if it is presented in the right way and with the right tone.

- Surrender to the idea that there is nothing you can do. You can have an impact on your child's life for the rest of her life.

- Subscribe to the belief that your child will have to learn on her own through life experiences. Children need guidance, but they will learn on their own as well.

- Assume that your child will learn everything she needs to know at school or through friends. She won't, and what she learns may not be correct or even helpful.

- Hand your child a book. Most kids don't read books given to them, nor do they always know how to assimilate the information and apply it to themselves. And most books don't address all of the crucial information, such as how to say no and how to build a relationship that has depth.

- Assume that you can cover the big talk in one sitting. This is a lifetime process made up of many talks.
- Wait until your child asks questions. The day may never come, or she might not ask the right questions.
- Procrastinate. It's much easier to talk to a younger child between the ages of eight and twelve about sex, and then reinforce those discussions during her teen years.

Do:

- Provide your child with a specific, step-by-step sex education.
- Take control of your child's sex education by having the big talk in its entirety with her.
- Believe that you can have a huge impact on your child's life in this area.
- Teach your child important principles regarding sex and dating before she begins dating.
- Initiate many nonthreatening, nonconfrontational conversations about sex, dating, love, and romance with your child.
- Continue to have conversations regardless of your child's response or attitude. The information will sink in even if she doesn't seem interested.
- Talk specifically about love and relationships, not just about the mechanics of sex and the anatomy.

Using Real-Life Examples

Most kids observe what their sexually active friends go through. Rosie, sixteen, said, "One girl in our school had sex with a guy. Now she's different. She used to be more bubbly and friendly. Now she's more self-conscious, tougher. The guy is like, 'No big deal.' He grabs her chest in school." Talk about your child's observations of others, but be careful not to put the other kids down. Talk about them with compassion, but help your adolescent see the differences in behavior and their consequences.

Most teenagers have at least one friend who is or was sexually active, which gives you a perfect opportunity to teach values and to reinforce the concepts you discussed when she was younger. Nineteen-year-old Gia said, "One friend of mine had sex in high school. She cared about her boyfriend a lot, and they were going steady. But since then she's had several sexual partners. Most of them she regrets, but not the first one because she said they loved each other. But she moved away, and they both acknowledged they were too young to get married. They moved on in their lives." Gia's mother can use this story to teach her daughter valuable principles.

She could start by asking Gia what she thinks about the fact that her friend had sex with any or all of these boys. The mother could say, "It's interesting that even though she felt she loved him the relationship didn't last. They both went on to have several sexual partners. Isn't that sad—to think you're in love, and to share so much of yourself, only to have it end?"

Gia and her mother could then discuss important issues that need to be considered before getting physical with someone. She could ask Gia, "What things do you think your friend should have considered first in order to protect herself?" Possible answers include: What does being in love really mean? How can I get to know this person really well before I give too much of myself? Do we agree on what commitment means—is this relationship leading to marriage? Gia needs to understand that caring about someone isn't enough. This would be a good time to reinforce her earlier decision to abstain until marriage, or at least to go over all of the options again.

Some people feel that bringing up commitment, love, and marriage prior to sexual involvement is being manipulative. Set your child straight on this. You could say, "Discussing these issues is being *wise*. We are all responsible for taking care of our own bodies. It's up to us to protect ourselves—physically, emotionally, and spiritually. People, especially girls, bond emotionally when they have sex. And girls face the risk of getting pregnant, which means they're more vulnerable when it comes to having sex. It's every person's right *and* responsibility to make sure their partner truly loves them and is committed to them before making such a serious investment in the relationship."

Your child may argue that lots of people have sex and seem fine with it. Be honest about the realities. True, some people do seem to be happy and unaffected by sexual involvement, but it's difficult to judge people simply by observing them. You can't always see their inner workings. You don't know if they go home at night and cry with heartache over the decisions they make or if they'll look back on them with regret.

If you draw on real-life examples, you can help your child see the principles you teach in action in the lives of others. Your child can actually observe others reap the consequences of having casual sex, as well as see the benefits for those who wait. Talking about the experience of others also allows you to teach principles without sounding as though you're preaching.

Boys Need to Be Educated Just as Much as Girls

For some reason a boy's sex education is practically ignored by many parents. I suppose many people feel that if girls learn how to say no to sexual advances, boys will have to follow suit. Also, many parents adopt the "boys will be boys" attitude, thinking that a boy is going to be sexually aggressive, and if the girl accepts the invitations so be it. It seems that girls are held more responsible than boys in every area of sexuality: saying no; contraceptive use; and, if they get pregnant, dealing with the decision of what to do with the child.

A study conducted by the Alan Guttmacher Institute in 1993, involving a series of focus groups made up of sexually experienced young men and women, explored the reasons unmarried males do or do not involve themselves in contraceptive practice. The study showed that in most cases men who did get involved did so because they were concerned for their own well-being, not the well-being of their partner. They were fearful of disease, of being tied down, of the financial responsibility, of angering their parents. These young men didn't mention the responsibility they would have toward their partner but, rather, the financial burden *they* would incur.

Most of the young men were more concerned about contracting STDs than about getting a girl pregnant. "Pregnancy can't kill you," said one sixteen-year-old boy. Another boy, who was nineteen, worried so much about getting a disease that he said, "Why am I going to college? I'm probably just going to find out I have AIDS in a couple of years and I've wasted all this time. I knew I was high risk. I just couldn't handle thinking about it. My mom talked me into getting tested." This boy's concerns were self-focused, and only about the physical dangers of having sex. He gave no consideration to the welfare of his partner(s).

Another nineteen-year-old boy remarked, "In one-night-stand situations, you really don't care about the girl. You just care about yourself." A sixteen-year-old said, "I wouldn't trust any girl nowadays. They go with other guys. You never know what they do, so you just use a condom all the time." As this research shows, it's obvious that boys need guidance every bit as much as girls do. Most important, boys need to learn to view the situation from the girl's point of view. Boys need to be given knowledge and skills to put sex in the proper perspective, and to learn how to delay sexual gratification. They need to learn that sex isn't just a physical experience in which they participate whenever the opportunity presents itself but, rather, that love and building a *relationship* is the goal. Even if a boy isn't interested in building a relationship now, eventually he will be and he needs to think long-term.

Boys need to know how girls feel once they become affectionate with a boy. You covered this concept when you discussed oxytocin, but reinforce it again. You could tell your son, "Girls usually take any affection very seriously. If you kiss or make out with a girl and then move on to the next girl, you could really hurt her. That one reason that it's best to save your affection for someone special."

Josh, eighteen, said, "I considered myself a 'love camel.' There was this girl I dated, and basically we just got together and kissed a lot. I wasn't in love with her, although I liked her a lot. But I didn't call her throughout the week or buy her flowers or anything romantic like that. My rationale was that like a camel, if I kissed a lot on the weekend I could store it up and then last through the week. Apparently she didn't feel the same way, because she ended the relationship." Josh's mother or father could have asked him how he thought this girl might have felt. He wasn't seeing the situation from her perspective. You have to educate your son about girls—most boys don't understand that girls are different from them in this way.

Boys also need to be instructed in how to think things through rather than acting on impulse. You could say, "Son, when you're kissing a girl and you're wanting more than anything to take it to the next level, stop and ask yourself a few crucial questions: Do I love this girl? Am I willing to make a commitment to be exclusive with her? Is she expecting more from me than I'm willing to give? Do I really want to go all the way here? Heavy make-out sessions tend to lead to sex—if not right now, then down the road. Each time you get together with that girl you're going to want to take it a little further. And if you don't love her, or aren't willing to make a commitment, you do her a disservice. You have to think about what you're doing because making out is never just a simple exercise in indulging yourself in physical pleasure. It's always more complicated."

Help your son decide how he would like others to view *him:* "He's a stud! He was with so many girls, he left a trail of broken hearts." Or: "He's a man of integrity and class! He cares about people." Remind your son that it's his choice. And he needs to know that he won't be seen as a wimp if he has high standards. Those who would view him this way aren't people of high character, so their opinion shouldn't matter.

Mark, seventeen, and his sixteen-year-old girlfriend, Diana, broke up recently. The breakup was precipitated by Diana's telling her mother that they almost had sex. Diana's mother insisted they stop seeing each other. Mark said, "We've been good friends for a long time. We really love each other. But we were both raised with the idea that you should wait until marriage. It all started with me tickling her chest around her bra, then I'd slowly go underneath her bra. All the while I would be thinking, This is wrong, but it was fun and even addictive. I'd get this rush. But afterward we always felt guilty and agreed to stop. Then it became hard for me to be around her. I really don't know why. It's like I couldn't be myself, or like I had this chip on my shoulder. I don't understand it all. But then she got weird and wondered what was wrong. I guess it finally destroyed our friendship."

Mark is learning the consequences of making out through experience. He is aware of having negative feelings, but he doesn't understand them or know what to do with them. He needs guidance in sorting through these emotions. Sometimes experience is the only way teenagers can truly learn the lesson. But if you explain to your son what could and probably will happen if he participates in making out, he'll be able to quickly identify what's happening to him at a particular moment rather than being confused by the experience.

Give your child concrete ways to break free of dangerous situations. Seventeen-year-old Kurt said, "My girlfriend and I have decided to wait until we're married, but it's hard. Sometimes I have to just jump up and say, 'Let's go get a milkshake!' She's really great about it. I told her to just push me away. Or we have a saying when things get too heated. We say, 'Time to take a cold shower!' That's our cue to back off." You can suggest these ideas to your child.

If you've waited until your child is a teenager and she's already being confronted with these types of situations, you might meet with some resistance. But don't avoid having this discussion. Although some teenagers refuse to be open, most will listen and even welcome suggestions. Patsy, the mother of seventeen-year-old Mitchell, said, "When my son Mitchell started having trouble refraining from sex, I asked him how far he and his girlfriend had gone. He was very open. They had gone too far, but not all the way. I told him that when two people spend as much time alone as they do, it makes it harder to say no. I suggested that they spend time together in groups. He agreed." Teenagers know when you're right, and quite often they share your values. Patsy was smart. She didn't overreact or make Mitchell feel like a bad guy. She simply stated a fact and suggested a solution. She needs to continue the discussion and to talk about how sexual activity affects a person (particularly girls) emotionally, and how it can destroy a relationship and derail our spiritual progress. She can also point out that being physically intimate with the one person we fall in love with and marry is infinitely more special and meaningful when we save it for that time.

Teach What Is Expected

In addition to helping your child to establish her own value system, determine and discuss the rules and guidelines you expect her to follow in order to protect herself. You may think it's ridiculous and a complete waste of time to tell your child not to do these things, but what you're really doing is telling her what is expected of her and what you believe is the best way for her to behave if she wants to be a happy, healthy, well-adjusted human being. That's your job as a parent!

You could say something like this: "The guidelines we expect you to follow are: always keep your clothes on; no French kissing until you're in a serious relationship with someone and you've both made a verbal commitment to be exclusive and have expressed your feelings for each other; and no petting or oral sex. The choice is always yours of course, but these are the guidelines that will protect you from potential dangers."

The Browns, who are the parents of two sons, said, "We tell our kids that if they're touching below the waist—or a girl's breasts—that's too far. Kissing is okay, but we explain the dangers. They know right from wrong. We remind them that their consciences will make it clear."

As you convey to your child what is expected, also be careful not to add to your child's struggle. James, twenty-two, shared this with me: "My family used to sit around the dinner table and talk about sex on a regular basis. Dirty jokes and innuendos were just part of life for us. In fact, it was *admirable* to come up with a dirty joke! I think this gave me a very sexual view of the world, and it made it more difficult to refrain from sex when I was younger. I started having sex at sixteen."

It's important to know where your child stands on these issues. Many teenagers don't experience intense sexual feelings. These teens are more capable of keeping their impulses in check. It is doable. Wallace, sixteen, said, "I've never even kissed a girl. No big deal, I can wait. My friends can wait, too. Adults think teens can't wait to get rid of their virginity. But that's not true."

Sometimes parents assume that their teenager is unable to delay sexual gratification and therefore avoid discussing their expectations. This can have a negative effect on your child, particularly if she feels that you don't really understand her or know her true values. Selma, the mother of an eighteen-year-old daughter, told me, "My daughter was visiting from college and her boyfriend spent the night. We live in a big house, so I didn't know where he slept, but I assumed they slept together. So I approached her one day and said, 'Don't you think you need contraception?' She was offended. She said, 'Mom! I'm not having sex. He's been sleeping on the floor.' I couldn't believe that, so I said, 'Don't you think that's a little unrealistic? I mean, don't you think eventually you won't be able to maintain that attitude?' She surprised me when she said, 'Mom, I don't *want* to sleep with him. If I wanted to, I would. But I'm not ready for that.' Sometimes my kids blow my mind with their strength and wisdom. I certainly wasn't like that when I was their age!"

As is the case with many parents, Selma didn't really believe that abstaining is possible. Selma's daughter intuitively knows how to control her sexual feelings. But Selma needed to know in advance what her daughter's standards were rather than coming to her own conclusions, and she needed to be clear about her own expectations for her daughter. And even though her daughter acknowledged that she wasn't ready, Selma needed to find out when her daughter felt she would be ready. Her daughter needs more guidance in the matter. Giving the boyfriend a room to sleep in would have been appropriate as well.

If you have the big talk consistently throughout your child's life—

even throughout her college years—you'll always know where she stands on these issues, and she'll know your stance.

What Teenagers Think

Most teens I talk with don't believe it's okay to be sexually permissive. They want their sexual experiences to be special. But they have unclear answers as to how that goal is achieved. They're missing important pieces to the puzzle. Fifteen-year-old Paul said, "Having sex is supposed to come from the heart. You should love each other and know the person for a long time." Nicholas, sixteen, said, "I'd have to be in a real long relationship before I'd have sex. I've seen my friends lose their girlfriends a couple of weeks after having sex. You can't be the same after that—sex ruins it." These kids are on the right track and their ideas are very noble, but they need more information. Again, telling your child to wait until she's "in love" or is in a relationship for "a long time" isn't clear enough. If your adolescent is going to have premarital sex in spite of being encouraged to choose a higher standard—waiting until marriage, for example—she needs to know the issues that should be discussed with her partner (love, commitment, marriage, goals, beliefs, compatibility). She also needs to know what condition the relationship should be in order for it to have a chance of being successful. She needs to ask herself, Do we treat each other well? Is ours a mature relationship based on trust, respect, and love? It's doubtful that any teenager has the skills and the emotional maturity required to build this kind of relationship, but anyone who chooses to be sexually active needs to consider these points.

Unfortunately, even though teenagers don't want to be promiscuous, they often think that waiting until marriage is unrealistic. Reilly, sixteen, said, "I'd like to wait, but I don't see how that would be possible. I probably won't get married for a long time." Reilly may not marry for a while, but she needs to know that she *can* wait until she marries. Perhaps all she needs is someone to inspire her to believe in her own ability to achieve this goal. And she needs to see the value of waiting until marriage. When I was a teenager, it never occurred to me that sex could be so much more rewarding with someone who truly loved me and was committed to sharing my life. I thought that sex was sex and nothing more.

The fact that most teenagers have sex by the time they graduate from high school makes it clear that for many teens abstaining isn't always easy or even desirable. Kent, seventeen, told me, "I really love sex! It's fun. I'm not ready to settle down with one girl, so I fool around with the girls who want sex as much as I do." Kent has made up his mind that he just wants to have a good time, and he claims that there are plenty of girls who want the same thing. It would be easy to give up on any chance of him changing his behavior anytime soon. But as we talked further, and I explained that a girl becomes emotionally attached when she has sex and is therefore more vulnerable to getting hurt, he seemed genuinely affected. I could see that the wheels were turning in his mind. He even expressed remorse about a girl he had seen recently who wanted more from the relationship than he was willing to give. Kent may not change his ways right now, but I like to think that an impact was made.

It may be hard to believe, but kids want their parents to play a more active role in their emotional, spiritual, mental, and sexual education. In an article published by *Focus on the Family* (January 1997) entitled "Hey Mom and Dad," the author, Dayle Shockley, wrote about one of her experiences as a teacher. A distraught parent told Shockley that he didn't know what to do with his rebellious son. Shockley related the story to her high school students and asked for their opinions. This led her to take a survey of two school districts, with more than three hundred teenagers. She said it was like "opening a floodgate." Here's a sample of what these teenagers said:

- Don't allow your child to bring company into the house unless you know them personally. (sixteen-year-old African-American female)
- Don't let your small kids watch a lot of TV. If you do, they'll adopt the bad attitudes seen on TV and end up not respecting you. (seventeen-year-old Asian-American female)
- When you're trying to talk to your children about private subjects like sex, just sensitively say it. If you beat around the bush, it makes you both nervous. (fifteen-year-old Hispanic male)
- Look for things that are good about your children instead of constantly finding ways to put them down. (thirteen-year-old ethnic Hawaiian male)
- Be consistent in what you say; follow through with your decision. (fifteen-year-old white female)

- Don't curse or smoke unless you want your children to do the same. (sixteen-year-old Hispanic female)

- When you let your children go out, give them a curfew. Let them know you love them and want them to be safe. (sixteen-year-old Hispanic female)

- Play with your kids. Have fun and laugh. (fifteen-year-old white female)

- Fathers, tell your daughter you love her often. If you don't, she'll go out looking for love in boys or friends, but she'll never find the kind of love she wants. (fifteen-year-old Hispanic female)

- Accept the fact that adults are not always right. If you're wrong, admit it. (fifteen-year-old Asian-American female)

- Teach your children that a true friend will understand that when you say no, you mean no. (fifteen-year-old white female)

- Don't hold the past against your child. What happened, happened; it cannot be changed. (eighteen-year-old white male)

- If your daughter tells you she's not having sex, believe her. (seventeen-year-old white female)

- Guide your children toward good marriages by giving them a good example to follow. (fifteen-year-old Hispanic female)

- Sit with your children and just talk. Ask them questions like How was school? Did you make any new friends? (sixteen-year-old Hispanic male)

- Don't jump to conclusions. (fifteen-year-old white female)

- Turn the TV off and talk to your children. You can't carry on a good conversation if you're constantly worried about your show. (sixteen-year-old white female who says her mom knows *TV Guide* backward and forward but has trouble remembering her family's birthdays)

- When your children are very small, let them have only wholesome friends. If you allow your children to have bad friends, they will soon be bad, too. (sixteen-year-old Hispanic male)

- Get involved in school activities. Acting concerned isn't enough; you need to show your concern by getting involved. (fifteen-year-old white female)

- If your child tells you something wrong is going on, believe her. Don't ignore your child. (sixteen-year-old white male)

- Be there for your teens, even when they try to push you away. The harder they resist, the more they need you. (fourteen-year-old white female)

- Know how to take control. Don't be a pushover. (sixteen-year-old Hispanic female)

- Teach your kids manners, like how a lady sits and how a gentleman opens the door for a lady. (sixteen-year-old white female)

- Teach your children right and wrong, and that each action brings either a bad consequence or a reward. When they do right, reward them, and when they do wrong, punish them. (eighteen-year-old Hispanic male)

Warning Signs That Your Child Needs Information Fast

The ultimate goal of having the big talk, beginning the discussions when your child is young and reinforcing the ideas throughout her teen years, is that your child will internalize the principles outlined in this book at an early age and consistently live in accordance with them. But things don't always work out perfectly. And chances are you're just beginning to have the big talk with an older child who is already experiencing some problems. Remember, it's never too late to start having these discussions. Begin the process now if you haven't done so already, particularly if you see the following warning signs.

These warning signs are not etched in stone, but they are common among sexually active teens who find themselves in sexually based relationships or situations. If you notice these behaviors in your child consistently, you need to have a heart-to-heart as soon as possible. And start having the big talk now, beginning with establishing some standards.

WARNING SIGNS:

- Immodest dressing
- Wearing heavy makeup
- Letters or conversations full of strong sexual innuendo
- Speaking to the opposite sex for hours on the phone, particularly if she always wants to talk privately
- Spending an inordinate amount of time with the same person of the opposite sex

- Sex books or magazines in his room. (This is more often a problem with boys than with girls.)
- An obvious fascination with the opposite sex, and with sexual things in general. This isn't always a serious problem, but be vigilant.
- A rebellious and defiant attitude
- Depression or increased moodiness beyond normal changes due to puberty

At fourteen, I exhibited all of these behaviors. I empathize with my father, who was completely powerless and must have felt overwhelmed by me at the time. I wish we had had the kind of relationship that allowed us to talk about my behavior and get to the heart of the problem—to determine why I acted the way I did. But my father responded to my actions with anger and disgust, which further alienated me. It wasn't until I became an adult that I fully understood why I acted out as I did. Talk to your child from the heart—express your love, concern, and hopes for her. Know that she isn't trying to make your life miserable or to ruin her own life. She's only doing what she thinks she has to do in order to get the attention and love she so desperately wants. Lovingly teach her that there is a better way.

Your teenager may need counseling for serious behavior problems. You'll need to evaluate the cause of the symptoms and determine the best course to take. But begin having the big talk in any case. Also in the way of observing warning signs that your child may need stronger guidance, make a point of scrutinizing your child's character as objectively as possible. Is your son honest? Does he have compassion for others? Does your daughter have integrity? Does she possess the courage to do what is right? If you know your adolescent's strengths and weaknesses, you will know which areas need work. Building a better self image is an important first step.

If your child is exhibiting these warning signs, chances are she needs to gain clarity as to what her talents are, what her goals are, and what she wants her life to be like. We know that kids don't respond well to preaching, blatant demands, or boring lectures. But we all respond to information that helps us get what we want.

What do teenagers want? Teens want to be popular among their peers, to be seen as unique and important, to have fun, to get good grades, to gain more freedom and autonomy, and to achieve success in all their endeavors. When you attempt to teach your child valuable principles relating to sex, love, and relationships, come from the perspective of what she wants to achieve and how; by putting sex in the right context, she will be better able to reach those goals. Also, as you strive to fulfill some of her needs (to feel important, loved, appreciated), she'll feel less inclined to use sex as a way to find fulfillment.

After sharing the insights outlined in this chapter, if you haven't done so already, encourage your child to make a commitment to abstinence. Consider the three standards presented in chapter 7 and ask your child to make a formal pledge.

❖ 9 ❖

It's Never Too Late to *Re-Virginate!*

Hopefully you won't need this chapter. It's my hope, too, that every parent will begin having the big talk when their child is young, and that every child will grasp and internalize the information and save sex for marriage. But life isn't always so neat and perfect. It could be that your child has already been sexual and now you're wondering what you should do. This chapter could be the life preserver that aids you in helping your child to get back on track.

It's rare for a teenager who is sexually active to feel completely at peace with his decision. Although both sexes often experience remorse, guilt, shame, and heartache when they become sexually involved, girls seem to experience more regret. But rather than recommit to a higher standard, so often these teenagers go on to make the same mistake again and again. They may become promiscuous because, as they put it, "What's the point? I've already done it, so it doesn't matter anymore." On a deeper level, the belief is "I'm now damaged, unlovable, used goods, too experienced to be innocent, less than adequate as a person, unworthy of someone really special." What a sad, devastating set of beliefs to adopt! Your own child may be internalizing these same beliefs. It took me years to work through these kinds of feelings. Unfortunately, I didn't have an informed, supportive adult to explain to me that I held the keys to my future, that I was not a bad person, that I was still capable and worthy of real love, and that I could start over. You can help him realize these truths. He won't have to go through years of pain and self-doubt. He can re-virginate and begin to feel better about himself.

When one woman heard me talk about re-virginating on a radio program in New York, she immediately called her teenage son and said, "You know, son, it's never too late to start over. Although you've been sexually active in the past, you can *re-virginate* and put love first in the future." She said that the concept of re-virginating captured his attention when nothing else had in the past. He wanted to know more. This initiated an open discussion between this mother and her son.

Some teenagers are dealing with very stressful and overwhelming feelings. These feelings may be deeply harbored and therefore not easily detected. These teens are longing to know that there's a way out of the prison they seem to be locked into—that dilemma of not wanting to get caught up in sexually based relationships yet not being able to avoid them due to feelings beyond their understanding. The sad reality is that many parents have no idea that their teenagers are sexually active. These teenagers are so afraid of how their parents will react that they do all they can to keep them from knowing the truth. As a result, these teens are all alone, struggling with the challenges that come with premarital sex in addition to the many other challenges of being a teenager. Talk to your teenager often, and stay in tune with what he may be going through. Always be ready to provide the counsel and support he needs.

What It Means to Re-Virginate

If your teenager is or has been sexually active, you can help him establish new standards by teaching him how to re-virginate. You can be the rescuer and the safe haven that your child is seeking, in spite of the fact that he may not even be consciously aware of his search. In my own case, I knew that I was unhappy, but I didn't correlate my feelings of emptiness with my sexual activity. There were other reasons for my feelings, of course, but the fact that I didn't have strong moral standards made me feel powerless and largely contributed to my low self-esteem.

Teach this concept if your teenager is or has been sexually active. He can re-virginate even if he hasn't gone all the way. Teens re-virginate when they have gone against the standards they've set for themselves and they want to change. If you haven't helped your child determine his sexual standards, you'll want to have the discussions outlined in chapter 7, along with the discussions in this chapter. To re-virginate means to make a decision to reestablish those standards, or to establish them for the first time if your child has never considered these issues or his standards haven't been sufficiently well defined. Some people call this secondary virginity.

As you talk to your adolescent and determine that he has been sexual and would like to start over, be understanding and offer hope. Tell him something like this: "I can see that you regret your decision. I'm sorry that you have to deal with these feelings—I know how hard it is. Of course I'm disappointed. But it's important to begin focusing on the solution rather than dwelling on the mistake. Do you know you can start over? You can recommit to a way of life that's more in line with your values. You can re-virginate! This means that you make a decision to live by a new standard." You can then go over the different standards and how a person sets the standard. Be sure to make it clear that he can still commit to waiting until marriage and talk about how much more special sex will be within that context.

Explain that re-virginating means your child makes a pledge to abstain (or recommits to his prior pledge) and recommits to doing whatever it takes to be true to that pledge. Doing this will help restore peaceful feelings, his self-esteem will grow, and he'll soon be back on his way to achieving his goals. It's always more inspiring, uplifting, and encouraging to focus on the positive—on how much better he will feel and on what he can achieve and create in his life once he establishes and maintains high moral standards rather than focusing on what he has lost and the mistakes he has made. I'll never forget the feeling I had when I decided to re-virginate (hopefully your child won't take so long!). With just a small shift in my thinking and attitude, I felt an incredible source of power and confidence. I felt that I could achieve anything and, best of all, I knew that stagnating, unfulfilling relationships were a thing of the past and had no place in my future. I knew that re-virginating wouldn't guarantee that I would meet the man of my dreams, but I also knew that I would feel good about myself and how I lived my life.

When you talk to your teenager in this way, you create open communication and trust. Your teenager won't feel that you're coming down on him. He'll feel your love and support. Many parents make the mistake of saying things like "How could you do this?" or "What were you thinking?" or "I thought you knew better!" But these reactions only close the door to communication and perpetuate the problem. Kids are then left to figure out solutions on their own, which usually doesn't happen. Your child needs to be *led* back to maintaining high standards by a wise and forgiving parent. Go over the consequences of having sex and the benefits of abstaining, as discussed in chapter 7 in order to help your child internalize his decision to re-virginate. He has to want this for himself as a result of understanding all the facts.

How to Convince Your Child to Re-Virginate

The concept of re-virginating is a powerful one, and it carries with it many rewards if it is applied. It can literally change your child's life, because where there seemed to be no hope, there is now absolute hope! In my experience, girls tend to be more open to the concept of re-virginating because of the emotional pain they experience when they have casual sex. Begin by reassuring your child that just because she made a decision that she knew wasn't right doesn't mean her life is over, that her innocence is completely destroyed, or that she's a bad person. She made a mistake. We all make mistakes. Let her know that the best thing to do is to move on and focus on how she can avoid this in the future. Tell her that someone will still love, respect, and want to marry her. Explain that as time passes her pain will heal and she will again be the carefree and happy person she used to be. But stress that time must pass, and that she needs to be completely recommitted to her new standards. That's why re-virginating is so important—it's the only way for good feelings to return. When you live in accordance with your values, you feel a sense of renewed hope for the future. You have more confidence. Be sure to make the connection between your daughter's happiness and her resolution to maintain her sexual standards. Your teenager needs to understand that compromising her standards is what brings about feelings of despair.

Unfortunately, boys are encouraged to see having sex as a reflection of their manliness. For them it's sometimes seen as an advantage to score. But not all boys feel good about their choice to have sex without love, especially if they have strong religious beliefs that oppose premarital sex. These boys will be more open to re-virginating. Still, if you explain to your son that he could seriously hurt a girl and go over the benefits of delaying sexual gratification, he will probably respond positively.

The Plant Metaphor

In order to create a mental picture of what it means to re-virginate, share this plant metaphor with your adolescent. When a plant has been neglected it shows signs of that neglect: wilted leaves, dry, cracked dirt. But with a certain amount of care and attention—a rededication by its owner—it can be brought back to life. Before long it can be a thriving, brilliant plant again. Those who see the plant cannot detect that there was ever a problem because they see it as it is today. Of course, if the plant is neglected for too long, it becomes very difficult to recover.

Point out that this is similar to your child's situation. If she gets back to what she knows is right, she can redeem herself and become a thriving, happy person again. Help her to see the damage that premarital sex creates in her life: heartache, wanting to isolate herself from family, a melancholy spirit, poor grades, fear of what others think of her, depleted energy and passion in her life, and so on. She may not be experiencing all of these things, but point out the things that you notice. She may not even be aware of what is happening to her. But chances are her inner voice is telling her that something isn't right. If she neglects that inner voice that exhorts her to change, she can cause more serious damage. That's why it's so important to re-virginate now. Obviously you can't force your child to re-virginate—you can only guide and support her in her decision to do so. Your part is to help her to realize that it's possible and that it's her only hope of becoming fully revived and vibrant once again.

Timing Is Everything

It seems that the best time for change to take place is when the individual is open, meek, and humble—which is usually during times of pain. As a parent, you need to have eagle eyes, and be particularly watchful for when your teenager seems to be experiencing the heartache that comes from unfulfilling relationships. At these times you can approach him with love, concern, and answers. This unconditional love is the bridge that will eventually lead you into your child's mind and heart. It takes time to have an impact, but it will come.

Guilt Is an Inner Guide

Jennifer, sixteen, said, "I always felt so guilty, but I didn't want to say no. At a certain point, the guilt was so strong that I cried and cried. My boyfriend felt bad, too. The whole thing has been horrible for me. I couldn't get it out of my mind, yet I felt like I couldn't tell anyone. People could see the change. I didn't want to go anywhere. I took long naps. Basically, I just isolated myself. I only wanted to be with my boyfriend. I had to pretend. I was living a lie, and it was killing me." Jennifer decided to re-virginate when she realized that being in a sexual relationship was causing her more pain than pleasure. Not all teenagers are able to gain this kind of clarity on their own; they need their parents to help them see that their unhappiness is self-inflicted.

Many parents say, "I don't want to give my kids the burden of guilt when it comes to sex." The fact is, you don't have to give guilt—it's already built-in when kids know they're doing the wrong thing. Guilt can be a healthy emotion. It helps us know when we are off track.

Seventeen-year-old Antoinette had only one sexual experience, but *guilt* got her back on track. "My goal is to be able to say yes when that special guy asks me to marry him, without feeling unworthy or ashamed," she said. "I don't want to go through all that pain anymore."

Explain this concept to your child by saying, "Usually, if you *feel* guilty you *are* guilty! Those nagging feelings of guilt, remorse, or shame are signs that you've made a poor decision. When you realign your actions to fit your values, guilt usually dissolves like cotton candy." Stress that your child shouldn't alter his values to *accommodate* guilt; in other words, he shouldn't lower his standards to avoid feeling guilt. He should elevate his actions so that he can honestly feel good about himself and avoid feelings of guilt altogether. Use examples of how fear, worry, or anxiety prevents him from making poor choices. He avoids going too close to a ledge, for example, because he doesn't want to fall and hurt himself. He doesn't touch fire because he doesn't want to get burned. Instruct your child to listen to his inner voice, which will tell him when a situation doesn't feel morally right. Once he has made the decision to re-virginate, for instance, you can then help him learn ways to say no to the sexual advances he might incur in the future.

Steps to Take

A good time to approach your child with answers is when a relationship has ended, or soon after a sexual experience. Ideally, you won't have to wait for these events to occur, but if these opportunities do occur, use them to teach valuable principles. They typically enhance receptivity. Perhaps your child had a sexual encounter with someone and it turned out to be a one-night stand. Or maybe he realized that the other person didn't care as much as he did.

If you discover that your child is or has been sexually active and the timing is right, here are the steps to take to turn things around:

1. Let him know that he is loved. Put your arms around him and say, "I know that you're going through some tough times right

now. We're going to get through them together." This will encourage him to be more open with you and more receptive to advice.

2. Help him see the correlation between his actions (having sex, getting involved with someone who's not good for him) and his feelings of remorse. Ask questions such as: Do you want to start over and prevent this from happening again? What can you do differently next time? What do you feel led to this happening in the first place? What are some obstacles that might stand in your way of living by a new standard? Ask all of these questions in a loving tone, and avoid sounding accusatory or critical. If he's receptive, go over the information in chapters 5 (to discuss sacredness), 7 (to discuss various standards), this chapter (to re-virginate), 10 (to discuss ways to abstain), and 11 (to discuss ways to control sexual impulses).

3. Discuss the other person who's involved. Find out how your child feels about this person: what kind of relationship they had; how the other person treated your child. Determine if amends are in order. If your child hurt another person's reputation, or put pressure on that person to have sex, he needs to humbly apologize. Insist on this. Your child needs to promise to call the other person or approach her privately and say something like "I just want you to know that I'm really sorry for hurting you. I should have handled the situation differently—I'm sorry."

4. Discuss where the relationship stands now. Re-virginating means ending a sexual relationship if it's still going on. But don't say, "Well, there's no way you can see *her* again!" Instead, help your teenager to come to this conclusion himself. When you ask him questions about the other person's true intentions (as well as his own intentions) and his new standards, he should eventually realize that he has to let go. Suggest that he screen his calls, and that after he has been honest with her he avoid her at school and in other activities. Give him encouragement by explaining that the longer he is separated from this person without hearing her voice or seeing her, the easier it will get. If he leaves himself open to talking to her, letting go becomes more difficult.

Your teenager may want to remain in the relationship but just stop having sex. If this is the case, discuss whether this is even feasible. Help him prepare to talk to his partner about this decision. It's best if younger teens avoid serious relationships altogether. But if your child is older than seventeen and wants to be in a committed relationship, you should discuss this information. Emphasize that he needs to tell the other person about his decision to start over. Ask, "Do you know what you're going to say? How do you think she'll react?" Tell him that you believe if he is honest and lets his friend know that he's doing this for his own well-being and for the good of the relationship, she will be more understanding. Advise him to let her know that it isn't personal and that he still cares about her. But stress that he must be firm. This person should know that he has made up his mind. He should tell her how unhappy he feels about having a sexual relationship. If the other person really cares, she will be sympathetic. But let your child know that he has to be willing to let the girl go and walk away from the relationship if she isn't willing to see him nonsexually. Ask him if he's confident about doing this. Breaking off the relationship is almost always the best course. It's extremely difficult to be nonsexual when you've been sexual in the past. I must admit, I've tried this in the past, and it *never* worked. I think that the only time it really could work is if the couple immediately gets engaged and marries in the near future. Of course, if both parties are highly committed to abstaining and they do everything humanly possible to avoid dangerous situations, it can work. But it's very difficult. It's wise to suggest that he date other people to avoid being too focused on one person.

5. Fill up your child's time with more family time, one-on-one activities with you, and so on. Additional ideas for keeping your child busy will be covered in chapter 11. It's a simple yet effective way to keep his mind and energies on productive activities.

If Your Child Resists

You may have a sexually active teenager who does not seem to be experiencing emotional pain with his decision. He may feel happy that he finally experienced this wonderful aspect of life and have no desire to re-virginate. You may have to approach this situation in a different way. Some parents choose to forbid the adolescent from seeing the other person; some simply insist that he stop sexual activity altogether. Many parents accept and ignore the reality, giving up all hope that there's anything they can do. Typically, these approaches aren't effective. I agree that if your teenager is set on being sexually active you probably won't have much luck trying to talk him out of it right now. But you can present your views, and the practical reasons that make it a mistake.

You could say, "We have talked about why premarital sex isn't a wise or healthy choice, especially during the teen years. We're extremely disappointed that you've chosen to go against our wishes. But we can't force you. This is your choice. We do, however, reserve the right to tell you, whenever possible, the damage this choice is causing you." Point out any negative changes that you've noticed. Have his grades slipped? Is he less able to concentrate on his goals when he's wrapped up in a serious relationship? Is he more moody than before? Is he less interested in being with the family? Let your child know that it hurts you to see these changes because you want the best for him. Ask him to think about these things and let him know that if he changes his mind you'll help him to start over.

❖ **III** ❖

Handling Sexual Pressures

❖ 10 ❖

How to Say No

Just as we wouldn't send a child out of the house without warm clothing and shoes on a cold winter's day, we shouldn't be willing to send her out into the world without equipping her with ways to deal with sexual advances. You'll want to know if your child has been confronted with sexual pressures in the past, and you'll want to coach her in how to deal with them in the future. The "just say no" approach doesn't always work. Children need to know about the dangers of drugs, alcohol, and date rape when it comes to the ability to say no. Role-playing exercises and advice on how to tell if a person is only interested in sex will also give your child more confidence in dealing with sexual advances.

Dealing with Sexual Pressure

At this point your child knows that sex is sacred and that it will be much more meaningful and rewarding within a committed, loving relationship. She knows that sex is more than a physical experience, that it has a powerful effect on our emotions. She has made her pledge to abstain, and she knows how and when to set the standard in dating situations. But she needs additional coaching in exactly how to deal with sexual advances.

Many teenagers don't know how to say no to sexual pressure. It seems so simple, doesn't it? When we are just two years old, one of the first words out of our mouths is no! Most little children are naturally confident when it comes to knowing what they will or will not do. But something happens when we hit puberty. Suddenly every insecurity boils to the surface and we feel our tongues are tied, particularly when we're with someone we really like or someone who's older or physically attractive (or attracted) to us. We say and do things and then later ask ourselves in exasperation, "What was I *thinking?*" The truth is, we weren't thinking at all. No one taught us how to think. No one showed us how to project into the future or to pre-

131

pare for potential situations. No one coached us and instilled in us the confidence and self-assurance that we need in this sexually focused world. You have discussed with your child *why* it's important not to have sex; now it's time to discuss *how* she should go about doing that.

When a girl—and even a boy—realizes that she has the *right* to say no—that it's *okay* to say no—and she is well prepared with exactly what she will say when the moment arrives, she develops a deep sense of self-worth and confidence. She is free to be herself, to enjoy life, date, and eventually build a healthy relationship with someone special. People will come and go in her life as she dates a variety of people, but she won't get stuck along the way in dead-end situations. She won't allow that to happen because of the standards she's established. She will learn that the opposite sex won't necessarily lose interest just because she won't participate in sexual activity. In fact, she will see that by rejecting sexual advances she will gain respect and admiration. She will realize her own sense of power, not to manipulate others but to direct her life for *good*. She will not be a victim as is the case with so many adolescents who are sexually active.

You may be saying, "But my kid isn't even interested in these things!" Teenagers don't always exude sexual energy or interest, particularly around their parents. In the life of a teenager, things can change from one day to the next. It's always best to prepare your child in advance for a sexual experience than to wait until she's faced with the real thing. I was only twelve when I was confronted with my first sexual advance. I was baby-sitting, and the husband came home before his wife did. Luckily, I didn't succumb to his advances, but I do remember feeling unsure of what to say. I think every child should be forewarned that these situations can happen and they should know what to do and say. Your child will encounter a sexual advance sooner or later. As one father said, "Don't assume that everyone has had sex, but do assume everyone will be faced with the decision at some point in their lives!"

Younger teens (thirteen through fifteen) who have sex are often coerced into the decision by someone older. According to studies done by the Alan Guttmacher Institute, the youngest teenagers who have had sex have done so because they were forced to, not necessarily because of sheer physical force but because these teens felt that they had to say yes to sex. They didn't know how to say no to the pressure placed on them.

I've spoken with teens who encountered sexual advances while baby-sitting (sometimes by the person who hired them, at other times by a boy or a girl who showed up to visit them), during summer camp, at a sleepover, while cousins were visiting, when their parents were out of town, or even while the parents were home in another part of the house. Oftentimes parents never find out about these experiences.

Young girls in particular need to be prepared with ways to respond to sexual advances. Boys need to learn that it's wrong to manipulate and coerce someone into participating in sexual activity. The research done by the Guttmacher Institute also notes: "While traditional sex education has been successful in achieving the limited goal of increasing knowledge, students do not appear to change their sexual behavior . . . unless the program provides specific information on *how to resist sexual pressures.*"

"My teenager has such a strong personality that I really don't worry about her" is a common statement made by parents. But even the strongest personalities can become timid and unsure of what to do, especially in the presence of someone they really like and want to impress. This was true for me. My dad often said, "I'm more concerned about the *guys* Laurie meets—she can take care of herself!" We laughed at this comment, but it simply wasn't the case.

Has Your Child Confronted Sexual Pressure Before?

Every parent has the right and the responsibility to know what their teenager is going through in his or her life. Building trust and establishing open communication will enable you to know what's really going on in your child's mind and life. But sometimes teens find themselves in painful situations where they simply don't feel comfortable talking with their parents. They may be afraid of how you might respond. Do what you can to get her to open up with you. You can't force her to divulge information to you, but at least try. Spend more one-on-one time with your child. Show her that you care, and that you can be trusted with whatever information she shares with you. Make every attempt to tap into exactly what she's dealing with, and try to do this without coming across as a controlling, prying parent.

You know when your child is troubled. You may notice that she's quieter and more introverted than usual. It's important that you know how far your adolescent has gone sexually. "That's too private!" said one mother. "My teenager shouldn't have to divulge that information to me!" Why not? What if your daughter was date raped? What if she thinks she's pregnant? What if your son is receiving tremendous pressure to have sex with a girl? Your teenager may be dealing with heavy-duty issues, and she may not be open with you unless you ask. How else will you be able to intervene and help your child? Until she's eighteen, she's in your care. She isn't developmentally mature enough to always know how to handle situations. She needs your guidance, yet she's probably not going to offer information without some probing. If you're in the habit of asking her how she's doing and what's going on in her life, she won't see this gentle questioning as being too invasive. Even if your teenager does think you're being invasive, if you can intervene before serious problems occur, it's worth it.

Find time to be alone with your child and ask her:

1. Has anyone ever tried to pressure you into having sex or performing any type of sexual activity?
2. Have you ever made out? (Be specific: Kissing? Touching? Where? Oral sex? Intercourse?)
3. How did you handle the situation?
4. How did you feel? (Did she regret it, or was she glad she did it?)
5. What could you have done differently?
6. Help her reestablish high standards if necessary—re-virginate, make a personal pledge.

Drugs and Alcohol

Most of the teenagers I spoke with admitted that the reason they went too far sexually was that they were drunk or on drugs. Have this discussion when your child is between eight and twelve years old. Talk about the dangers of drugs and alcohol in order to encourage appropriate behavior when she's older. Point out to your child that when kids drink or do drugs they aren't always able to make healthy decisions. Help her understand that peer pressure to drink, do drugs, skip school, and so on can lead to sexual pressure. Even if she has clear standards, being high causes a person to compromise. You can't think clearly; your judgment is clouded and you may lose self-control. Emphasize your hope that she will stay away from drinking and drugs so that it will be easier for her to be true to her decision to abstain. Share additional reasons to avoid the use of alcohol and drugs: physical health and safety, spiritual reasons, to avoid problems with the law.

DATE RAPE

Rape is forcing sex upon another person without his or her consent. According to the U.S. Department of Justice, a rape occurs every seven minutes in the United States. Eighty percent of rapes are committed by a person who knows the victim. Half of the rapes occur on dates. The sad and frightening reality today is that date rape is more common than ever before.

Tyne, eighteen, says that in her small town in Virginia she and several other girls she knows have been date raped. "I was a junior in high school when I was date raped," she told me. "My friend was dating this boy from school, and they wanted to skip school and go to her house. The boys brought alcohol. We were just sitting around. Then my friend went off to a bedroom with her boyfriend. I was stuck in a room with one of the boys. I thought I would just kiss him, but he kept going lower and lower with his hands. I yelled, 'Get off me!' My friend later said that she heard me but she thought we were just messing around. When it was over, he got up like nothing happened. I didn't want to be weird about it. I felt stupid. His attitude was 'no big deal.' We couldn't look at each other after that. He did tell one friend. And I actually think he felt guilty, even though he never admitted that. Boys don't seem to have as much feeling. I just try to forget about it."

Seventeen-year-old Renee was raped by her boyfriend while they were horseback riding in the country. "I always thought making out was so fun," she said. "But I always stopped it at a certain point. I never had any intentions of going all the way. I always intended to wait until marriage. But my boyfriend trapped me in the middle of nowhere. We stopped riding the horses and found a little spot in a field where we started kissing. He just wouldn't listen to me when I kept screaming no."

You can't be with your child all the time. That's why you want to have these discussions with her when she's young enough to be prepared well in advance. Boys need to understand the seriousness of these actions. Girls also have a certain responsibility in the matter. They need to know that making out isn't just a fun pastime—it has serious consequences. Point out to your child that being alone in an isolated place with someone who has made serious sexual advances in the past, especially when she absolutely doesn't want to go all the way, isn't wise. According to Ann Landers, "the notion that a woman has the right to change her mind after two hours of passionate stimulation may be LEGALLY SOUND, but it flies in the face of the most basic facts of procreational and biological human drives." The real issue is learning what can be done to prevent date rape from happening. Just as we coach kids in how to say no to sexual advances, we need to teach them how to do everything in their power to avoid date rape. Explain to your child what date rape is, why it's wrong, and how to avoid it.

Here is what your child needs to know about how to avoid date rape. These points should be discussed with both sexes:

- Never go out with someone of questionable character. If you get an uneasy feeling about someone, trust that feeling and stay away from him. Always follow that inner voice.

- Do not dress in a way that would invite sexual advances. Sometimes sexual advances are made no matter how you dress, but it's important to dress modestly to avoid encouraging sexual attention. Boys need to know that there is no excuse for pressuring a girl to have sex. It is always wrong.

- Alcohol and drugs are usually present in date-rape situations. Our defenses are down when we're high. It's best to avoid drinking and using drugs altogether.

- Never go beyond kissing. Usually a person can stop kissing with little trouble, but when you get into petting the feelings become more intense. The last thing you want to do is lead someone on when you have no intentions of following through. This is dangerous.

- "No" means no under all circumstances. You are morally responsible when you pressure someone to go further than they want to go. Even if you think that person "wants it," you are responsible for your own actions.

Your daughter needs to know that no matter where she is or what time it is, if she is in danger she is to call you immediately and you will come and get her. If you can't be reached she should have a backup person to call, or she can always call the police if necessary. Her personal safety is the most important thing, and she should do whatever it takes to protect herself.

Warning Signs That a Person Is Not Being Sincere

Unfortunately, there are boys and sometimes girls who will say whatever it takes to have sex with your teenager. Just before your adolescent begins dating, after you've had all the other talks about sex, say, "When you set the standard you put the other person in the position where he has to determine how he really feels about you. He has to consider whether he wants to make a commitment to be exclusive. He has to think about whether he loves you or he just wants a casual fling. If the other person isn't interested in having a real relationship that's based on true caring, he'll move on. He'll realize that this is what's required to be intimate with you on any level, whether it's a matter of holding hands, kissing, or sharing deep feelings. You have to be willing to lose that person if he can't accept your standards." Ask your child how she thinks she might know whether someone is interested in only one thing. Share the following warning signs:

- He only wants to be alone with you in private places.
- He's very touchy right away (puts his hands on your waist, touches your hair a lot, etc.).
- He makes very aggressive physical advances right away, within the first couple of dates.
- He asks very personal questions relating to sex very early in the relationship.
- He tries to change your views about sex, attempting to convince you that you're wrong.
- He's constantly staring at your breasts or other private areas.
- He doesn't seem interested in getting to know *you*.
- He strongly encourages you to drink or take drugs.

If your child suspects that her date is only interested in sex, then the wisest thing for her to do is to stop seeing him. He may change his ways down the road, but the risk is too high. Remind her that she doesn't want to give anyone an excuse to take advantage of her. Remind her of her pledge. Tell her to take her time and be very observant as she begins dating someone new. Your daughter shouldn't be fearful about dating, or get the impression that sexual issues are the primary concern, but in today's world it isn't possible to be too careful.

Your teenager also needs to be aware of the fact that most people will be persistent. Her partner may disappear for a while, but his interest may intensify, partly because of the challenge. He may be back only to try to talk her out of her standards.

Stella's daughter did the right thing by saying no, but the boy came back a second time hoping to change her mind. "My daughter's boyfriend dumped her because she wouldn't have sex with him," Stella told me. "He pressured her and she just wouldn't give in. After they had broken up for a while he called again. She thought he wanted to get back together, under different circumstances. But he just tried to push her into having sex again. He just didn't get the message." This can happen to both boys and girls. Remind your child of her goals, and warn her to be cautious.

Girls Are Also Sexually Aggressive

We typically think of boys as the ones who are sexually aggressive. But today this just isn't the case. In fact, many boys claim that girls are more aggressive than ever. Nina has experienced this firsthand: "I don't worry about sexual advances that my daughter might receive because *she's* the sexual one. She's the one who would most likely make the advance. Right now she's so tall, and big. So boys aren't interested right now. But she's beautiful, and I know she'll blossom into a gorgeous young woman in time. If she had the chance to make out, I'm sure she'd do it." Another parent said, "Boys aren't nearly as sexual as the girls! Girls seem to be the instigators—they chase the boys these days. Boys just talk about it, whereas the girls go for it!"

Belinda, sixteen, said, "At school all the girls care about are sex and relationships. It's like no big deal—you're in a relationship and sex is just part of it. A couple of weeks later, you get a new boyfriend." If you suspect that your daughter might be the aggressor, help her to establish her sexual standards. Help her determine her relationship goals, and point out the benefits of waiting. Attach meaning to sex—teach your child that it's sacred, that it is neither insignificant nor common. Teach her that delaying sexual gratification can help her reach her goals and maintain a positive self-image. Make a point of introducing role-playing ways for her to respond to advances. Regardless of how aggressive she is, she will still be confronted with them at some point.

Saying No Without Hurting the Other Person's Feelings

Much of the big talk has to do with teaching kids to consider the other person's feelings in dating situations. We'll discuss the situation for girls first. Say to your daughter, "When a boy makes a sexual advance, you already know what to do. But here are some tips on how to treat him." Remind her that this advice applies to *nice* guys.

Boys who have only one thing in mind and don't seem to care about her feelings or standards should be dropped immediately. Then share these points in your own words:

1. *Put yourself in his shoes.* Always be considerate as to how a boy might be feeling. The boy you're with has feelings for you. He has a strong desire to express those feelings and get close to you. Remember, he's only reacting to the way he feels, and he usually feels that making an advance is the right and natural thing to do.

   Sometimes girls tease boys by acting as though they want to make out, then when the boy tries they act offended. Be honest with the person. Explain your feelings, and then when he respects your wishes be appreciative.

2. *Appreciate his attraction to you.* If a boy really likes you, and you've been dating for a while, let him know that you appreciate the fact that he's attracted to you. If you're attracted to him too, tell him so. But then set your standard.

3. *Let him know it's not personal.* A boy sometimes takes rejection personally, which can seriously affect his pride. Assure him that it's only because of your need to do what's right for you, and not because there's anything unappealing about him.

4. *Be firm.* In addition to being considerate and understanding, you must also be firm about your convictions. He needs to know that you mean what you say, which will only deepen his respect for you. This firmness should be obvious to him from the very beginning, and he must not see you questioning your own resolve.

Continue your discussion with your daughter by explaining that all she can do is set her standard and see how the other person responds. Boys love challenges, and when a girl sets sexual boundaries, boys will sometimes try everything they possibly can to break through them. It's their nature. Let your daughter know that if she's prepared for this in advance, she'll do just fine.

Advise her to be careful to not criticize a boy by calling him an animal or a jerk. It's natural for boys to be the aggressors. After all, that's how we're able to get married and create families! But it's up to her to set her standard and channel that sexual energy into either a friendship (if she isn't interested in the boy romantically) or a committed relationship (if she is interested in him romantically and she's emotionally ready for a serious relationship). Impress upon your daughter that giving in when a boy puts pressure on her is a big mistake—one that she'll probably regret. Remind her that she alone determines her standards and lives by them.

As I mentioned earlier, this topic is rarely discussed with boys. It seems they grow up thinking they should "go for it" whenever the opportunity arises. The pressure is on the girls to fend for themselves, whereas boys are usually given free rein to do what they want. Talk to your son by saying, "Some guys don't think about how a girl might feel. Sometimes they make sexual advances without much regard for what she might be thinking or feeling. Here are some ideas to keep in mind as you date." Share the following concepts with your son:

1. *Never pressure a girl to do something she doesn't want to do.* When a girl says no you need to respect that, even if you think you may be able to change her mind. She has a right to say no regardless of the way she dresses, walks, talks, and so on. A girl never "owes" you sex, regardless of what you do for her.

2. *Girls are not sexual objects created for your pleasure—they have feelings.* Girls are not there simply to be sexual partners. You build a relationship with a girl for lots of reasons: companionship, love, to have fun, to learn from each other, to eventually get married and have a family, and so on. The focus shouldn't be on sex.

3. *Listen to your date/girlfriend—care about her feelings and what she has to say.* Some boys don't seem to care about girls' feelings or what's important to them. But this isn't the way to relate to girls. They're just as intelligent as boys, and they deserve to be heard. When a girl attempts to share her feelings and thoughts with you, give her your full attention—if you do, her feelings for you will deepen.

4. *Don't take her rejection personally—she may just not want to be intimate at this point.* (This concept should be discussed with an older teen who is involved in a serious relationship.) Just because a girl doesn't want to kiss you or be intimate with you doesn't mean she isn't interested in you at all. She has her reasons, and she'll probably share them with you if you ask. Some boys get angry and then treat girls poorly when they turn them down, but you can have more integrity and confidence in yourself. Appreciate a girl who has standards that she lives by. This shows that she has character. You need to live by your own standards as well, particularly if you want to be worthy of a girl who has character.

5. *If she makes the sexual advance, appreciate her attraction to you, but be firm in saying no.* You don't have to be sexual with a girl just because she makes an advance or you know she's open to your advances. You aren't less of a man just because you aren't willing to be sexual. Be polite, and just say no thanks. Let her know that you appreciate the fact that she likes you but that you just aren't interested in her in that way, or that you aren't ready for that level of closeness. Most girls will appreciate your honesty.

Coaching Your Child in How to Say No

Brandy, seventeen, has had sex with seven different partners. Yet she has never been in love; nor have any of her partners been in love with her. With each experience, Brandy said it "just happened." One was a one-night stand while she was on a trip to Hawaii with a friend. Her friend's mother was supposed to be chaperoning, but she was barhopping while the girls spent time with some local boys. Two of the encounters were with friends. One of the boys came over for a swim while her parents were out of town for the day. She thought other kids were coming, too, but it ended up being just the two of them. One of the boys was known as "the stud" of the school, and she just wanted to be able to say that she "did it" with him. Her parents were upstairs the entire time. Brandy's current boyfriend is ten years older than she is. She says she's not in love, but she likes the attention. Perhaps she isn't getting enough attention at home.

Brandy has never been adequately prepared to deal with sexual advances. The real issue is that she doesn't know why she should avoid sex at this point in her life. Her sexual standards were never established, and she lacked the emotional and moral courage to say no. Role-play with your child in order to help her come up with specific responses to sexual advances.

Role-Playing

You need to adjust the wording for this exercise depending on whether you're talking to your son or your daughter. Have fun with this project. You can play the role of the guy who makes a sexual advance. Your daughter has to respond in the best way she knows how. Then go over some of these potential responses. Ask your daughter how she would handle the situation if she a) really liked the boy, b) was extremely attracted to him, or c) thought he might lose interest if she didn't do something physical. Dad can do the same with his daughter. Or Mom and Dad can role-play with each other and give the kids an entertaining view of potential dating situations. Go through several hypothetical situations based on the following possible lines teens might hear. Some of these responses are more appropriate for older teens who are considering a more serious relationship.

Line: "We won't do anything; I just want to hold you and kiss you."

Response: "I would love to get close to you, but I just don't want to put us in a dangerous situation."

Line: "Let's just watch a movie at my house. My parents are going out tonight."

Response: "I'd rather not be alone at your place. I just don't feel comfortable with that." (If he persists, you can suggest getting together another time.)

Line: "You're being so immature!"

Response: "I think it's immature to jump into having sex or making out too soon. I'm waiting until I get married to be sexual."

Line: "Why can't we just see what happens, play it by ear, and let it progress naturally? This isn't a business, you know."

Response: "I agree, we should let the relationship progress naturally. We can take as long as we have to. I'm in no rush. But for me sex isn't casual."

Line: "But I love you."

Response: "If you really love me, then you'll respect my feelings when it comes to this."

Line: "But sex is a natural part of a relationship."

Response: I agree that it's a natural part of a *committed* relationship, but we're not fully committed to each other at this point. Let's just have fun and hang out—I'm not ready to get sexual."

Line: "But I *am* committed to you!"

Response: "We know we're boyfriend-girlfriend, but we don't know that we're going to be together forever. Besides, we're too young to be considering all that. If you can't be in a relationship with me without having sex, then we'll just have to be friends."

Line: "But even marriage isn't a guarantee."

Response: "True, but it is the highest level of commitment two people can make. It's the only commitment that's honored legally and the only one that would make me feel secure enough to give myself sexually."

Line: "I'm a very sexual guy, there's no way I can't be physical."

Response: "I understand how difficult it must be for you—it is for me, too. (Remember to be understanding even if he isn't.) But I can't go against my feelings and compromise on my standards. I'd rather miss out on the temporary satisfaction I'd get by having sex now than miss out on the possibility of building a solid, lasting relationship." (If he persists, you'll need to be confident enough to suggest that maybe you aren't the right girl for him.)

Line: "I'm just so attracted to you, I can't help myself. You drive me crazy."

Response: "I'm attracted to you too, but we're going to have to exert some self-discipline because it will only destroy our relationship. We shouldn't just react to our physical drives. We have the ability to control our bodies and not let them control us."

Line: "But this is the '90s—everyone's doing it!"

Response: "I know everyone is *not* doing it, but even if they were, it doesn't matter to me. It just doesn't feel right to me, and I won't compromise my values. We're not just everyone else. We're special together."

Line: "If you really loved me you would do it."

Response: "Do what? Ruin our relationship? I feel that if you really loved me, you wouldn't pressure me to do something that I don't want to do." (You need to convey the message that you care about *yourself*, which he should respect.)

Line: "If you're not going to do it, then I'll get it somewhere else!"

Response: "Good luck. Don't let the door hit you on the way out!"

Line: "Your views are just too old-fashioned and outdated."

Response: "I'm sorry you feel that way. They feel right to me. I'm sure there are plenty of girls out there who will go along with your way, but I'm not one of them. I would hope you would see abstinence as a way for our love to grow."

Line: "But you've already done it before, so what's the difference?"

Response: "I have a different set of values today, and I've got to be true to them. I believe a person can start over anytime, and that's what I've chosen to do. Besides, I'd hoped that you might want to be part of a new, more evolved relationship."

Line: "There's no way I could marry someone without knowing what she's like sexually."

Response: "I can see how you would feel that way. I realize it's scary, but if two people truly love each other and communicate their emotions, I know they can create a beautiful sex life when the time is right." (Again, you must be willing to say that you may not be the right girl for him instead of trying to persuade him to see things your way.)

Line: "How do I know you're not frigid, that you're a sexual person?"

Response: "I think you can easily see that I'm a very affectionate, warm person. If I had any hang-ups, or lack of desire, I would tell you. Besides, our chemistry speaks for itself."

Line: "How will we know if we're compatible sexually?"

Response: "There are ways of finding out compatibility—by talking about sex openly and honestly, and by the way we hug and kiss. If we truly love each other and are physically attracted to each other, chances are we'll be compatible. We've got to have faith that we can work things out no matter what."

Line: "It's unnatural to suppress your sexual urges."

Response: "No one has ever died from not having sex. Even though we may strongly desire to have sex, we don't necessarily *need* to have sex in order to survive."

Line: "I really need sex—you get me all worked up and it's painful to stop what we're doing."

Response: "Needing sex and wanting sex are two different things. We don't need to have sex. We can control our desires and delay sex. Lots of people do this. I think we should stop making out so much, because I understand that it's uncomfortable for you to stop at a certain point. Let's just focus on building our relationship in other ways. If you don't want to do this, maybe we should just be friends."

Line: "Don't you find me attractive?"

Response: "Of course I do! But I don't want to move too fast. Sex can ruin a good thing, and I don't want that to happen."

Line: "Are you gay, or what?"

Response: "No, I'm not gay. And I love kissing you, but I don't feel that we're ready to be so intimate. I plan to wait until I'm married before having sex. I just think it's better that way."

Line: "C'mon, it won't hurt our relationship—it will only make it stronger."

Response: "I don't agree. Not only would our relationship change but I wouldn't feel good about myself. We're too young to be having sex. I'm just not ready for that kind of a relationship."

The "What If" Game

Continue to role-play a variety of situations with your teenager. For example, lots of teenagers watch videos together—sometimes when parents aren't home. Ask your adolescent son or daughter, What If . . .

- A boy suggests that you lie on the floor or the couch together? (I would suggest that we sit on the couch and just talk. I would tell him that I'm not comfortable being so close. If he persists, I would say I have to leave.)
- A girl started rubbing your back underneath your shirt? (I would ask her to stop.)
- A boy pinched your butt? (I would ask him to not do that again.)
- A girl started talking to you about her sexual fantasies? (I would act uninterested and change the subject. Or I would tell her that I'm not interested in talking about those things.)

- A boy invites you over to his house when he knows his parents won't be home? (I'd say that I'm not comfortable being alone with him in his house, and that I would rather see a movie or some other activity.)
- A boy kept making sexual jokes or innuendos? (I wouldn't laugh. If he persisted, I would ask him not to talk like that around me.)
- Your boyfriend breaks up with you because you won't go beyond kissing? (I'd let him go, and I'd feel good about being true to my standards.)

Listen closely to what your child says. Try to tune in to what she may be feeling or going through. Remind her that when she responds to these scenarios she can do so in a polite way without offending the other person, but that sometimes offense will be taken—in which case it's an acceptable trade-off for maintaining her values.

Learning how to say no to sexual advances and developing the confidence required to say no will be a big step in your child's development. But even with all of this coaching, hormones and sexual impulses are strong. We'll discuss ways of dealing with these feelings in the next chapter.

❖ 11 ❖

Controlling Sexual Impulses

There's no surefire way to eliminate or reduce the sexual impulses your child will eventually experience. But what you can do is teach your child that these feelings are healthy and normal, and, most important, show him how to control them. Rather than being over-powered or obsessed with these newfound feelings, your child can be prepared in advance for what to expect and he'll learn not to allow these feelings to compromise his standards.

Sexual Feelings Are Normal and Positive

One of the first things you can teach your child is that sexual feelings are a good thing and a natural part of life. When I think back on my own teen years, I remember feeling overwhelmed at times with sexual feelings. There was the neighbor boy, who seemed too cute for words. And rock stars who took my breath away. Sometimes these feelings were so strong, I felt I couldn't contain them. I didn't understand them at all; nor was I able to balance what I was feeling with what my values were. Actually, the bigger problem was that I didn't know what my values were. I didn't realize that just because you *feel* something, it doesn't mean you have to *act* on those feelings. Some kids seem to possess a natural wisdom or ability to know what is right or appro-priate behavior. Perhaps some kids are better able to observe and learn from the examples of others. But most adolescents need to be shown and taught what to do with sexual feelings. These feelings need to be understood, explained, and demystified for preteens and teenagers. They start kicking in at puberty, which is a good time to have these discussions. When you're a child you think that whatever you're go-ing through at the moment will last forever. It can be very helpful, even soothing, to know that it's temporary and than an entirely new world is right around the corner.

Impulses Need to Be Controlled

Kids don't hear enough about the importance of self-control. We live in a world that is constantly implying that immediate gratification is the way to go. But what kids need to understand is that with immediate gratification there are consequences. The only way to avoid incurring those consequences is to exercise control. Yes, it's difficult, uncomfortable, and even agonizing at times. But it isn't impossible or unrealistic. Your child must first see the value of avoiding situations that lead him down a dangerous path in the first place.

The Potato Chip Game

The potato chip game illustrates this point. This game is appropriate for teenagers and most preteens, depending on their level of development. Bring a bag of potato chips (your child's favorite brand) to one of your family-night discussions. Instruct your child to take only two chips, then pass the bag back to you. Close up the bag and set it beside you, in clear view. Be sure not to allow him to take the bag or have another chip.

Begin the discussion: Find out what your child thinks making out means, and what his thoughts on the subject are. How far does he feel it's okay for an unmarried couple to go? Does sexual activity affect girls differently than boys? Is it okay for a boy to try to go as far as a girl will let him get away with going? How does making out change a relationship and affect us on an emotional level?

You have discussed making-out issues in previous talks, but these ideas should be covered many times and in various ways in order for your child to really get it.

Pretty soon it will become obvious that he wants another chip. He may find it difficult to focus on the discussion. You'll see his eyes wandering back to the bag of chips sitting next to you. He might ask for more. The answer must be *no*. Keep the discussion going. At the end of the discussion, make your point using the chips. You might want to ask him how making out and eating potato chips are similar before sharing your views. Then you could say, "Making out is just like eating potato chips. When you have just one chip, you want more. You *crave* more. Sometimes you think you're going to die if you don't get more. And you can hardly concentrate on anything else. You can't focus on building a beautiful relationship with the person; you don't spend many hours talking and finding out what's important to that person or if she's even right for you. You can't concentrate on school or studies. You just become obsessed with making out, and then going further. And the intimacy becomes less special and meaningful when it becomes a routine part of a relationship that isn't based on love and commitment."

Point out that he had a difficult time staying focused on the discussion because all he could think about was the chips. Tell him that if he ate the entire bag of chips he would feel stuffed and might even regret eating the whole bag. He probably feels lousy now because he can't indulge himself at all, because you won't let him have any more chips. Ask, "Don't you almost wish you hadn't eaten that first chip? At least then you wouldn't have whet your appetite. The thought of having another chip wouldn't be plaguing your mind."

Draw parallels between the potato chip exercise and making out. Point out that once you get started it's extremely difficult to stop. The intimacy feels good while you're doing it, but that feeling soon wears off. And because we're humans and not potato chips we have emotions—and so does the person with whom you are making out.

Share the following quote from the book *Finding the Love of Your Life,* by Dr. Neil Clark Warren: "Each level of sexual experience is so immediately rewarding that it's nearly impossible to be satisfied by previous levels." Your teenager needs to understand the senselessness of adopting a set of morals that says casual sex isn't for him but it's okay to participate in everything but intercourse. Your child needs to see clearly that if he's going to be true to his pledge, it would be wise to abstain from other sexual activity as well. He should be sold on the fact that lines need to be drawn *before* he finds himself in a compromising situation. He should know that sexual impulses can be as strong as the desire to have a potato chip (stronger, actually) but they can be overcome.

The Horse-and-Bridle Metaphor

In their best-selling book *Teaching Your Children Values,* Linda and Richard Eyre use what they call the horse-and-bridle metaphor to help adolescents understand and control their sexual desires. Here is their suggested dialogue:

Q: What is the purpose of a bridle for a horse?

A: To control the horse, to make it do what we wish it to.

Q: Is there any other more *complete* way to control a horse?

A: Tie it up, hobble it, shoot it.

Q: What's undesirable about these other ways?

A: They take the pleasure and purpose out of owning a horse in the first place.

Q: Why worry about controlling the horse?

A: It can run away with you; it can hurt you.

Q: Now, here's a tough question. What is similar about the horse and about our sexual desires and drives?

A: Both are very strong; both can be much stronger than we are.

Q: Why do we need to control our sexual appetites?

A: They can run away with us and hurt us or other people.

Q: Are these desires evil or bad, then?

A: No, just as the horse isn't bad; they are wonderful and beautiful.

Q: So how could we completely control them?

A: Take vows of celibacy; try to deny them or overcome them.

Q: Why not do that?

A: Because sexual desire is good and right and natural, even though it can be dangerous.

Q: So what to do?

A: Bridle it.

Q: How?

A: By deciding in advance that we will put limits on ourselves, that we'll be true and faithful in marriage and save the deepest forms of physical affection for the commitment of marriage.

The Fallen Sparrow Metaphor

This metaphor further illustrates that it is better to refrain from certain behaviors altogether than to compromise and be tempted to go on to deeper levels.

A lark was perched on a high branch of a tree safe from harm. He saw a traveler walking through the forest carrying a mysterious little black box. The lark flew down and perched on the traveler's shoulder. "What do you have in the little black box?" he asked.

"Worms," the traveler replied.

"Are they for sale?"

"Yes, and very cheaply, too. The price is only one feather for a worm."

The lark thought for a moment. "I must have a million feathers," he said. "Surely I'll never miss one of them. Here is an opportunity to get a good dinner for no work at all." So he told the man he would buy one. He searched carefully under his wing for a tiny feather. He winced a bit as he pulled it out, but the size and quality of the worm made him quickly forget the pain. High up in the tree again, he began to sing as beautifully as before.

The next day he saw the same man and once again he exchanged a feather for a worm. What a wonderful, effortless way to get dinner!

Each day thereafter the lark surrendered a feather, and each loss seemed to hurt less and less. In the beginning he had many feathers, but as the days passed he found it more difficult to fly. Finally, after the loss of one of his primary feathers, he could no longer reach the top of the tree, let alone fly up into the sky. In fact, he could do no more than flutter a few feet into the air, and was forced to seek his food with the quarrelsome, bickering sparrows.

The man with the worms came no more, for there were no feathers to pay for the meals. The lark no longer sang because he was so ashamed of his fallen state.

Ask your child what he learned from this story. Then add, "Sometimes we think that just this once it won't make a difference. But 'just this once' usually turns into many more times until our conscience is severed and we forget how painful it is to go against our standards. It's better to refrain completely than to get started on a path that can lead to despair."

Ways to Manage Sexual Impulses

Suggesting ways for your child to spend his time will help him a lot. As a teenager, I was full of angst and frustration. My time wasn't being used wisely. I was bored, with very few productive activities to occupy my overactive imagination. I needed to understand that my feelings were very real, powerful, and normal. I also needed to know what to do with my feelings. It wasn't clear to me that I needed to rein them in in order to avoid pain and heartache. It can help a teenager to know that someday he'll be a sexually active person, but in the meantime there are others ways of channeling this energy.

Sometimes the best you can do (apart from having the big talk in its entirety) is to fill up your child's life with as many interesting and stimulating activities as possible, thereby reducing the opportunity for obsessive behavior. Homework, extracurricular activities, sports, lots of family time, and so on can make a huge difference.

Sexual impulses are not more powerful than teenagers. If your child is adequately prepared to know what to expect when puberty hits, is given suggestions on how to avoid dangerous situations, and has a full, busy life, he can deal with his sexual urges. It may not be easy, but he doesn't have to succumb.

Also, be sensitive to your teenager. Acknowledge and accept his sexual feelings, and help him to compartmentalize them. Bill's mother had the right idea: "My mother could tell when I was restless. But instead of yelling at me or criticizing, she just redirected me. She'd say, 'Hey, Billy, let's do this. . . .' She kept me actively involved and diverted my attention away from unhealthy situations."

We want our children to avoid being sexually active, yet we give them few if any outlets to help them cope with their newfound feelings. We give them far too many hours alone with nothing but the television, the telephone, the neighbor boy or girl, and their own active minds busily searching for something that interests them. Think of the amount of time and effort it takes for a teenager to have a sexual relationship with the opposite sex: the telephone conversations, dates, finding a place to be intimate, and so on. A life brimming over with family, friends, learning (at school, home, everywhere), sports, talent-developing, work, church, temple, love, and service is too full for him to get weighted down with the kind of emotional energy and time commitment this kind of relationship requires! Filling your child's time isn't always a surefire way to eliminate sexual activity, but it can make an enormous difference.

Fran clearly recognized this fact. She is the mother of three children, two of whom are already grown. Her youngest daughter, sixteen, was faced with a summer alone now that her older siblings had moved out of the house. Fran insisted that she get a summer job. The older siblings wanted to know why their little sister couldn't just have fun and enjoy her summer. Fran's wisdom became apparent to them very quickly. She said, "Because for years she had you guys to interact with and to keep an eye on her. Now she has no one, which means she'll be sitting around bored, and with no supervision. That's when trouble happens." Fran trusts her daughter, but she also understands human nature and recognizes that precautions need to be taken regardless of how excellent her daughter's track record has been.

Ruling Our Emotions

Stacey, the mother of four, said, "Sexual feelings can be seen as a built-in challenge. Either we learn how to control them at a young age or we spend the rest of our lives in subjugation to them. It's difficult for everyone, but we don't have to be enslaved by any emotion or desire we might have." This is a good topic for the entire family to discuss during family night. Ask your child the following questions:

"Do you believe that your emotions rule you, or that you rule your emotions?"

"Does each of us possess the ability to do what we know is right, in spite of strong feelings to do otherwise?"

"How do we practice self-control?"

Talk about areas in which your child has already learned self-mastery. Some examples might be learning how to play an instrument, attending school every day and completing each grade level, playing on athletic teams that required him to attend practice every day after school. When you draw your child's attention to the fact that he *already* possesses the ability to be disciplined and self-controlled, he'll realize that this principle or ability can apply to every area of his life. He will have more confidence when he's confronted with situations that require self-control.

Parents—Eliminate Opportunity!

When a murder case goes to trial, a prosecutor has three things to prove: 1) means (which is usually the murder weapon); 2) motive (why the murder was committed); and 3) opportunity (when it happened, and if the person on trial could have committed the crime).

If we apply the same methodology to teenagers and sexual activity, we could say that teens have 1) the means (their bodies); 2) motive (sexual impulses, curiosity, wanting to get the other person interested); and 3) opportunity (sleepovers, nights out with friends, parties, out-of-town trips).

It's a parent's job to *eliminate the opportunity,* whenever possible. This isn't easy, however. One mother said, "You can't lock your child up!" Another mother remarked, "I'm a working mom. There's no way I can keep track of what my kid is doing every second." But this isn't what's required. Adjustments in your lifestyle may need to be made for the welfare of your child, but you don't have to be with him every minute of the day.

Amber, the mother of an eleven-year-old daughter, has the right idea. "When my daughter asked if she could go to her friend's slumber party, I called the friend's mother to find out more," she said. As it turned out, the slumber party was coed. I told my daughter she couldn't go. Of course, she had a fit. But I sat her down and said, 'I know everyone is going to this slumber party. But I promise you that one day some of those kids might regret it, but you won't. In these situations you aren't always safe. It's unfortunate that you can't go. I feel terrible that you have to miss out on it. But it's my job to protect you.' My daughter understood what I was saying, and she respected it. At first she moaned and groaned, but she listened and she got it."

This mother is eliminating opportunity. It would have been easy for her to rationalize "They'll be chaperoned" or "These kids are only eleven, it's a harmless situation." But she followed her better judgment and stuck to her guns even at the risk of having her daughter angry with her.

Colleen has a seven-year-old daughter. "My daughter wanted to see a certain movie," she told me. "I said, 'Look, sweetie, that isn't a movie I really want you to see. I work very hard to teach you good things, and that movie teaches bad things. I'm sorry that I have to say no.' "

Colleen isn't being a mean, overprotective mom. She's teaching her child important values. She explained why she wouldn't let her daughter see the movie, and her explanation went beyond the standard "because I said so!" retort. "I know that my daughter feels secure because I have strict rules for her. She doesn't always like it, of course. But in the end she responds really well, because she knows she can count on me to have her best interests in mind."

This mother is eliminating the opportunity for her daughter to listen to and watch something that counters what she teaches at home. Of course, kids are being exposed daily to negative, unwholesome behavior and ideas. But it is possible to limit them.

Parties are often where sexual activity occurs. Fifteen-year-old Kaloni is still a virgin, but she has already been confronted with sexual advances. She's an attractive girl who is sought after by many boys. Every time she encountered sexual pressure from boys she was at a party. At one of these parties there was no adult supervision, but at the other the parents were upstairs. "This boy tried to get me into the bedroom. I just said that I don't believe in that kind of thing," she told me. Luckily Kaloni had a response. It is possible not to allow your child to go to these parties. She may not be happy about your decision, but at least she'll be protected.

The busier your child is, the more harmonious your home life is, the more family time you establish, and the more there are established rules to follow, the less likely it is that your child will be obsessed or overwhelmed with sexual feelings. Obviously some kids are naturally more sexual than others, but you can work with whatever sexual inclination your child has. I find that kids who spend an inordinate amount of time in the shower, in their rooms alone with the door shut, and who seem mysterious and antisocial have the most trouble with the issue of sexual impulses. You have to keep his life *moving*.

Prayer as an Aid to Coping with Impulses

Countless teens—and single adults, too, for that matter—have told me that they simply don't believe they alone have the power to cope with their sexual desires, in spite of the fact that they want to delay having sex. Many of these people have turned to prayer as a source of power and strength, with tremendous success. This has worked in my own life as well. You don't have to be religious to suggest that your child use prayer as a way to maintain his standards. As human beings we possess only so much power on our own. With something as important as this, praying daily for added strength makes a lot of sense. If you're comfortable with the idea of prayer, tell your child that he doesn't have to rely on his own abilities—he can gain power through prayer.

Talking About Masturbation

There is some debate about whether masturbation is a normal, healthy practice. Some people think it's unhealthy or even immoral. Most therapists believe it's a harmless practice, that it can help a teenager relieve some of the tension he feels, and that it can help him learn more about his body and how to gain pleasure.

Your child is probably going to think about masturbating, and it's highly likely that he'll actually do it at some point—usually beginning at around age twelve or thirteen. Aside from whatever your religious beliefs may be, there are some very important *practical* reasons that it's best to encourage your child not to masturbate. Present your child with the ideas in this chapter even if you aren't morally or religiously opposed to masturbation in order to give him a more complete view of the subject. Kids generally hear only two sides of the issue: either that masturbation is a serious sin or that it's a normal, healthy practice that should be done in private. I've found that there are additional aspects of the subject that should be addressed.

When and How to Discuss Masturbation

This subject could be discussed when your child is about twelve or thirteen years old. If possible, you want to prepare your preadolescent child for these feelings *before* they kick in. You could express the awkwardness of the topic by saying, "I want to talk to you about something that's fairly uncomfortable but needs to be talked about—masturbation." As he rolls his eyes and groans, you could say, "Yeah, I know. But it's important that we discuss it." Be sure to find a time when you have privacy, and when you feel your child would be receptive to discussing something so personal. There's really no easy way or perfect time to bring it up, but don't let that dissuade you from talking about it.

You could say, "Masturbation means self-stimulation. It's something that practically every teenager deals with at some point in their lives. When you go through puberty, hormones surge through your body. These hormones create strong sexual feelings. These feelings can be very intense. Some people choose to masturbate to relieve those feelings. It seems like the natural thing to do, and you're not a bad person to feel this way. But we believe that no matter how strong a desire may be, we always have the ability to transcend those feelings if we choose to. You don't have to masturbate or have sex with someone simply because you have the desire. When we become masters of our bodies, we become masters of our souls. We want to share with you the realities of masturbating. Obviously we can't make you *not* masturbate—it's your choice. But we want you to have the facts."

The Dangers of Masturbating

The following points evolved through many conversations with teenagers and single adults who have experienced these feelings with consistent masturbation. Convey the following points about masturbation to your child.

- Masturbation can actually *intensify* one's sexual appetite. Although it can sometimes temporarily satisfy sexual feelings, many people claim that it rarely leads to lasting, real satisfaction. Passions are often flared up even more, creating just as much angst as before.

- Masturbation can bring about feelings of emptiness, remorse, shame, and guilt. This is especially true if your child has been raised with strong religious beliefs that oppose masturbation. But even without religious teaching, many kids say they feel empty and remorseful after engaging in masturbation. More girls expressed these feelings than did boys. Many girls said that what they really wanted was an emotional connection, not a sexual release.

- Masturbation may desensitize some people sexually, making it more difficult for them to achieve orgasm with a mate. Many women and men have told me that with consistent masturbation they became somewhat desensitized. This desensitization can also alter a person's natural energy flow, preventing him from exuding a natural, sexual, and sensual energy. This can frustrate the courtship process and prevent a relationship from taking its natural course. Some experts believe, however, that for women masturbation can be an aid to achieving orgasm because they learn how their bodies work. But this is a discussion you could have with your engaged child in order to help her achieve a positive sex life with her mate. It isn't something that a teenager needs to know, particularly if you're encouraging her to abstain from sexual activity.

- Masturbation can lead to obsessive behavior, sometimes with pornography at the center. This conjures up sexual images that can play on your child's mind and deter him from focusing on what is most important, such as getting an education and so on. If you masturbate once, you usually want to do it again. This can lead to an ongoing pattern that doesn't always feel good emotionally or spiritually. You end up wanting to take the sexual experience to the next level: with another person. You can remind your child of the potato chip exercise, and let him know that if he has made a pledge to abstain until marriage yet he masturbates he's creating an uncomfortable situation for himself. He then has to fight these overwhelming sexual feelings, which need to remain somewhat dormant until the time is right. While some boys said that masturbation helped them abstain from sex temporarily, most of them admitted that masturbating led them to having sex sooner rather than later.

You may feel that I'm painting an overly negative picture of masturbation. But based on my research these truths about masturbation need to be presented to teens—if for no other reason than to prepare them in advance for what *could* happen. And if you offer this information to your child he may just choose to occupy his time with more worthwhile, productive activities that are in sync with his goals.

This is a good time to discuss the issue of pornography with your child. You might want to explain what pornography is and then point out why it isn't healthy to view this material. At some point your child will probably come across some kind of pornographic material. You'll want him to know your views on the subject.

Delaying Gratification

Part of why it's best to encourage your child not to masturbate is that masturbation isn't an isolated experience. It's usually only one step that eventually progresses to further sexual activity. Fourteen-year-old Daniel invited his friend James, fifteen, over to look at his father's *Playboy* magazines, which were hidden in the closet. Daniel's father didn't see this as a problem. "So what? They're curious. We all go through that phase," he said. The problem with this perspective is that it fails to see the bigger picture. Remember, the goal is to help your child establish high standards that will enable him to put sex in the right context: on the back burner until marriage, or at least until he's in love and committed. Delaying gratification is what we're striving for here. That goal is almost impossible if a child is spending his afternoons staring at naked bodies and masturbating!

The boys spent hours poring over those magazines. The pictures created mental images in their minds that eventually led to their first sexual experience. We often create what we visualize. Looking at pictures is often the first step in the process of making thought a reality. Daniel admitted that simply looking at the pictures wasn't enough at a certain point. Masturbating while thinking about the pictures eventually wasn't enough. Ultimately, he needed the real thing. The "real thing" was a real girl who had no idea that she was just a pawn in the process—a body that had all the right "parts" necessary for this boy to act out his fantasy. The experience had nothing to do with love—it had to do with a physical need. The young girl, however, didn't realize that. She thought they had something special.

Be Careful Not to Give Your Child a Complex

We have all heard the tale that masturbation can make you go blind. In response, one little boy asked his dad, "Well, can I just do it until I have to wear glasses?" Another myth is that masturbation causes acne. One father, when discussing this subject with his son, said, "Masturbation doesn't *cause* acne, but it can make it more tolerable!" You may not want to use these lines on your child, but you do want to be prepared with the facts on masturbation. Actually, kids will appreciate having a little humor interspersed in these talks.

As you present the potential problems of masturbation, you also want to be careful that you don't send the message that doing so makes your child a bad person or a sexual deviant. This was Shelly's concern. She has a thirteen-year-old son. She hasn't begun having the big talk yet, but she feels the urgency. "I have no idea what I'm going to say, except that it's okay to masturbate as long as he does it in private," she remarked. I asked her why she felt this way. She said, "Well, if it's true that guys think about sex every few seconds, then it seems pretty silly to think that they won't masturbate on a pretty regular basis!" I said, "Are there other reasons why you feel it's okay?" She said, "I just think that a kid could get real mixed up if you tell him it's wrong, or that he's bad to do that. I don't want my son to have any hang-ups."

There's a big difference between educating your child about the practical, real aspects of masturbation and giving him a serious complex. I'm not suggesting that you instill fear or self-doubt in your child. You don't want to imply that the child is bad, dirty, or evil if he masturbates. The message is an educational, practical one that offers kids information about masturbation. Explaining that masturbation can create obsessiveness, or that it can be unfulfilling, is very different from saying that it's a disgusting, dirty practice. Simply preface your discussion with the fact that practically everyone feels compelled to do this at some point in their lives, and that it doesn't make him a bad person. It's normal!

At this point your child will have a solid understanding of how important it is to delay sexual gratification, and he'll know how to maintain his standards. Another aspect of helping your child make healthy choices is guiding him in establishing his priorities throughout life.

❖ 12 ❖

Establishing Priorities

It's easy for teenagers to get sidetracked and lose touch with what they should spend their time focusing on, such as attending school, spending time with family, and planning and preparing for the future. If you have the discussions in this chapter when your child is younger (between the ages of eight and twelve), her teen years will flow much smoother. She'll already be clear about what her priorities should be. You can help your child establish her priorities by making sure that she understands the importance of thinking through decisions she makes today if she is to have a positive, successful future. In this chapter we will discuss how to help your child focus on building positive memories, how to adopt a bird's-eye view by creating a time line of her life, and how she can control her thoughts to bring about more positive results. Each of these discussions will aid your child in putting her priorities in order.

Building Positive Memories

When I was a teenager and "doing my thing," I never thought, I'm building memories right here in this moment. It never occurred to me that I would be plagued with these remembrances that would eventually be out of sync with my values. With every choice I made, I was creating what is now my history. And although it isn't recorded on paper, it is recorded in my mind. I will never forget most of my past. I will forever experience flashbacks from my childhood and teen years. I enjoy reflecting on the good memories. But I have many memories that aren't as positive, and they have created pain in my life. Forgiving oneself and letting go of the past aren't easy for anyone. That's why it's important to teach your child how to create memories that she'll be proud of. Fortunately, all of our experiences, whether they are good or bad, can make us better, stronger human beings. If we learn from our mistakes we can take a negative experience and turn it into a positive one. But certain painful experiences are unnecessary

161

and the cost is too high. Still, we can avoid these experiences if we're taught to plan ahead and think things through.

Imagine if your own parent had said to you, "Remember that what you do in this moment will be a fact forever. You cannot completely erase it in your mind, and you will reflect on this decision in the future. What kinds of memories do you want to create?"

Gentry, seventeen, says she "kind of has a boyfriend." She lost her virginity at fifteen, when she spent the summer with her family in Florida. "I was with some friends at this boy's house. I was really drunk," she said, giggling. "I felt really bad, though. I just did it to be a rebel, not because I wanted to. I was mad because of my parents' strict rules. I liked this boy, but not that much. I think I was just a piece to him," she continued with no emotion. "So, this boy sort of became my boyfriend. I mean, we saw each other a couple of times, but he told all of his friends that we had sex. I was at a softball game, and I overheard his friends teasing him about me. They didn't know I was there. I felt humiliated. It was like a joke to everybody."

Gentry is finding it difficult to get over these painful experiences. She feels insecure, wears heavy makeup, revealing tops, and tight jeans to make herself more attractive. She spends little time with her family. She says she can't get the painful memories from her past out of her mind.

Think of the memories *you* have accumulated over the years. Some of the teenagers I spoke with are building memories of having sex at parties, and in cars, with people they barely know. Many are building memories of being used, lied to, and abused by one or several people over the course of their youth. Some have only memories that are based on what others tell them happened because they were too drunk or high to remember. But the memories are there and, like a slide projector, scenes from their lives flash on the screens of their minds to haunt them forever. These scenes affect how they feel about themselves and influence their decisions.

Even seemingly innocent memories of light petting can make an indelible mark on a teenager's psyche. I'm not referring only to the guilt your child might naturally feel but to the fact that our memories cannot be erased. They affect us on an emotional and sometimes a subconscious level.

Many of the women I've spoken with said they were haunted by memories of past lovers. One woman, who is married today, said, "It took my husband and me a long time to develop a satisfying sex life because I just couldn't stop these flashbacks from popping up in my mind during our lovemaking. I felt like I was constantly comparing these past lovers to my husband."

When to Start

Introduce the memory-building concept early in your child's life. When you celebrate a holiday or birthday or whenever you are having a particularly great time, say, "Isn't this fun? We're building such happy memories in our lives! It's so much better to build happy, positive memories than to build bad ones!" You can have your child help you organize the family pictures into an album, watch home movies of fun times, and so on. When tragedy occurs, or anything that creates sadness or tension in your lives, you can say, "This is a sad memory that we will have, but that's part of life. There are some things that we cannot control. It seems that we need the good and the bad so that we will really appreciate the good."

When your child consciously makes a poor choice that has obviously caused her pain, you can help her to see that she has created an unhappy memory for herself. When she is contemplating a certain decision you can say, "Would that choice help you feel better about yourself? Will that decision create a good memory?"

The idea is to help your child to get used to thinking through her decisions ahead of time and to make the concept of memory-building a well-established principle in your home. Be sure to point out that negative or painful memories can also be seen as "learning memories."

Thoughts Are Powerful

I love cheese, but my thighs don't. I know from many years of experience that if the thought of cheese pops into my mind, and I choose to dwell on that thought for a while, chances are I'm on my way to a market or a restaurant where I can get what my mind has been focused on. Once I've allowed myself to fantasize about a big chunk of cheddar, I'm a goner. Thoughts have a life of their own. Highly successful people often say that one of the ways they achieved success was through visualization, a technique that brings about dramatic results. This is a powerful concept, but it is rarely understood by children and teenagers. If you teach your child that thoughts are powerful, you will help her to recognize the correlation between fantasizing about something and making it a reality.

Children often don't realize that what they choose to dwell on in the private recesses of their minds will have more influence on them than anything else. For this reason, it's important to know what your child spends most of her time thinking about or talking about with her friends. You don't need to spy on your child; simply pay attention and keep the lines of communication open.

Zane, the father of fifteen-year-old Maria, said, "I inadvertently came across a letter my daughter received from a friend. In it her friend wrote about someone else who was 'doing it.'" Then he added defensively, "That doesn't mean my daughter is 'doing it.'" Still, I think he should be concerned. I find that if kids are making sex a big part of their daily conversation, and caring enough about the subject to write about it, it's only a matter of time before they, too, begin doing it. It's a natural progression. What we think about, talk about, and make a priority in our life eventually becomes a reality. It's naive of parents to think otherwise. Of course, there may not be much you can do to direct your child's thoughts, but if you can gain insight into what holds her attention you'll know which aspects of the big talk you need to focus on. Zane could have asked his daughter what she thought about her friend and the other person mentioned in the letter. Not only would he have gained insights about his daughter, but this would help Maria learn to think for herself and determine her own views of the situation. The following exercises will aid you in teaching your child about the power of thoughts.

The Walls of Your Mind

Steven Cramer, the author of *Conquering Your Goliath,* says, "I will allow no picture to hang on the walls of my imagination that I would not hang on the walls of my home. And I will not allow myself to imagine something mentally that I would not do physically."

This is an excellent point to make to a younger child. You could say, "Let's pretend that our minds have walls just like those in our home. And our thoughts are like pictures that we hang on those walls. What kind of pictures would you want to have hanging on your walls? They should be the kind of pictures that you would be proud to have on our walls at home." With your child, brainstorm the positive images she should keep in mind—family, friends, goals, fun times. This is an exercise that your child will never forget. Be sure to acknowledge, however, that it isn't humanly possible to always have positive, pure thoughts. We all have sexual thoughts at times, and that's normal. (Be sure that your child is at the appropriate age—just prior to puberty.) The point of this exercise is to encourage your child to strive to focus on productive things rather than dwelling on thoughts that might get her sidetracked. She should simply understand the power of her thoughts.

The Lemon Test

Give your child the lemon test to further elaborate on the idea that thoughts are powerful. Ask her to close her eyes and keep them closed until you say to open them. Then say, "Imagine you are holding a lemon in your hand. Feel the lemon—the skin, the bumpy ends. Imagine how yellow it is. Make it a vivid picture in your mind. Now cut the lemon in half. Take one of the halves and bring it to your nose. Keep your eyes closed. Breathe in the fragrance of the lemon. You can almost taste it in your mouth. Now lick the surface of the lemon with your tongue and then take a big bite out of it. You're sinking your teeth right into the lemon and filling your mouth with its juices." Pause. Then say, "Okay, open your eyes."

No doubt your child's mouth watered during this exercise. Tell her, "You see how powerful our thoughts are? It's amazing, but even when we *think* about something we can make it real. This can work in positive or negative ways. If you think negative thoughts, you could eventually create that reality. If, however, you think about the things that should be important to you right now then those things become your reality. Isn't it amazing how much control you have over your life?"

Paint a Bigger-Picture Perspective

Find a time when you can be alone with your child and talk about "the big picture" of her life. You can begin by saying something like this: "Everything evolves over time. When you were a baby, you crawled until you could walk. You nursed until you could eat solid food. You lost your baby teeth only to have them replaced with permanent teeth. You finished each grade in elementary school. One day you'll graduate. And one day you'll marry and share physical and emotional intimacy with your partner. Everything has its time and place. The key is to be patient for all things to happen at the *right* time. And to know that I will be there for you no matter what."

Draw a Time Line for Your Child

Get a writing pad and two pens. Draw a time line (see below) and discuss the various stages of life with your child. As you discuss the stages together, write down the priorities that your child should focus on at each stage. Some priorities have been added in the sample time line, but fill in the blanks with additional priorities that you and your child feel are important. Put them in order of importance. Point out to your child that this will help her to plan ahead and look to the future. You can have this discussion as your child approaches puberty.

SAMPLE TIME LINE

Teens	Twenties	Thirties	Forties	Fifties
Spiritual growth	Spiritual growth	Spiritual growth	Spiritual growth	Spiritual growth
Dating	Marriage, family	Family	Family	Family
Get good grades	College	Career	Career	Career
Friends	Dating	Financial security		Retirement planning

Show your child that during her teen years she will go through puberty and experience many of the frustrating aspects that go with that period in her development: acne, physical and emotional changes, perhaps lack of dates, peer pressure to be whatever is in, trying to figure out who she is, learning about the opposite sex. Point out that there are good things about that period of life, too: less responsibility than you have when you're an adult, fun with friends, dating a variety of people, attending proms, learning to drive. Be sure to mention that the teen years will pass by quickly, and that she should enjoy this time and not be too focused on becoming an adult.

Time passes, and then you move into your twenties. You are then a full-fledged adult: no more acne, less awkwardness. You get better at things: how to interact with people, how to behave on dates, you get to know yourself better, and you become more self-confident. You enter the workforce and build a career, or you continue with your education. Eventually you'll find a mate and begin a family. Some people never do, of course, but this is rare. You continue through your thirties, forties, fifties, and beyond with your family, friends, career, and whatever goals you've set for yourself. Be sure to make the point that your child will go through many changes throughout each of these phases of her life. She won't be the same person one year from now.

Get comments, feedback, and/or questions from your child. Talk about some of the changes that might occur. Say, "It's interesting that decisions we make back here in our teens can seriously affect our lives when we reach our forties. The goal is to continue growing and improving with each stage in life, and to make choices that will perpetuate that growth, as well as create positive memories."

We do everything we can to suppress certain behaviors in our children. We say, "Don't grow up so fast! Be a kid—have fun. You'll be an adult soon enough." But these little pep talks don't address the real issues. They don't *teach* children anything or help them demystify the things that consume their thoughts.

Preteens and teenagers need perspective, balance. They need to be assured that they aren't crazy, deviant, bizarre, or lacking in any way. They need to know that this, too, shall pass, that feelings are intensified during their youth, particularly during puberty. As you review your child's time line with her, you could say, "During the teen phase you sometimes have these overwhelming sexual feelings to deal with because they're just being awakened for the first time. They're new to you, and they're intense. But, as with everything else, they will subside somewhat with time. You'll be better equipped to deal with these feelings as you develop into an adult mentally, physically, and emotionally."

Kids live for the moment. They don't usually think about what might happen several years from now. They're concerned with having fun, being cool, hanging out with friends, and fitting in. If your son is awkward and shy, he may think he'll always be that way. If your daughter is gangly and unpopular, she may think this will be her plight forever. Teenagers' decisions tend to be based on emotion and the immediate gratification of needs and desires that they are experiencing at the moment. Adolescents don't always think about how those decisions may affect them long-term. That's where you come in. You can help your child project into the future when necessary so that she can see that her life will change even as she begins to understand that the choices she makes now will affect her future. Ask your child questions such as, "How do you want to feel about yourself ten years from now? How do you want your future partner to view you?"

The Staying on Track Metaphor

This metaphor applies to many situations, particularly when it comes to being true to oneself. As you help your child see the bigger picture of her life, also let her know that none of us glide through life without learning lessons. We all make mistakes. Make it clear that you will be there to help her as she goes through each stage of her life. This metaphor can help you make the point. It goes like this:

Trains always have a destination. They know where they're going, and they know how to get there. But they can get to their final destination only by staying on the track that leads them there.

Sometimes trains get derailed—they get off the track. They're stuck. They don't have the freedom to continue on their journey, and they must sit there and wait for help. Something must be done to fix the problem. Usually someone has to be brought in from the outside to come and help the trains get back on the track.

Getting off the track is very costly. The conductor loses valuable time, and the railroad loses a considerable amount of money. It takes a lot of time and energy to start again. The physical safety of those who ride the trains may also be in jeopardy.

Ask your child how this metaphor relates to her. You could say, "You are on a certain track in life. You want to finish school, go to college, get married, have a family, and be happy, healthy, and successful. As your parent I help you figure out the course to take, the schedule, and where the stops are along the way. But you will be faced with choices. Depending on the choices you make, you could get derailed."

Ask her how she thinks this could happen. Answers should include: by taking drugs, getting involved with a bad crowd, being lazy and irresponsible, not setting goals, having casual relationships. Point out that sometimes we cause a derailment ourselves, and that other times we allow others to derail us. But either way *we* are responsible for our decisions, including the decision to get back on track.

Talk about the fact that many people feel it's okay to get off the track for a little while. They get involved in situations they know aren't helping them reach their destination, but they rationalize and justify their actions. They say, "I'll start over tomorrow" or, "I just want to have a little fun for a while." But a little while often turns into years. Their lives are off schedule. Sometimes addictions are formed, unwanted pregnancies occur, diseases are contracted—all kinds of things happen that they don't plan on. Their dreams are sometimes shattered or seriously delayed.

If your child is on the right track now, commend her for that and express your pride in her. Let her know that you want to help her stay on that track so that she can reach her own destinations in life. If she ever feels that life is getting too overwhelming she should know that she can always come to you and say, "Mom, Dad, I'm having a hard time staying on track," and you will do whatever you can to help.

You can use this metaphor throughout your child's life to consistently reinforce that all choices have consequences, and that if her priorities are set she will have a much easier time making the right choices. When your child is on the edge of making a poor choice, you can say, "Honey, I'm afraid that if you make that choice you'll be derailed. It would be a shame if you were prevented from being all that you can be."

You can also use this metaphor to find out where your child is at the moment. "Honey, are you off track?" Or if you know she's off track, you can say, "You seem to be off track. Are you ready to talk about how to get back on track?" Set yourself up from the beginning as the person who comes in when a derailment occurs.

Prepare Your Child for Her Own Family

Eventually your child is probably going to want her own family. You can help her think ahead about what she wants her future family life to be like. She will stand out as unusual in this regard, but with your encouragement she could even set a new standard among her peers.

Delaying gratification is easier for kids when they have a goal. If you can help your child project into the future, and visualize that one day she will meet someone, fall in love, and have a family, she'll find it easier to delay sexual gratification.

We usually think of our teenage years as a time to have fun and to be carefree. But it's also a time to prepare for our future family. Having several sexual relationships that have no goal and aren't based on love is a very poor training ground for managing a successful, loving family. Maintaining fidelity becomes more difficult, comparing partners sexually often happens, and overall selfishness on the part of both partners is common because they are so used to being in less committed relationships. You can help your child avoid some of these problems by encouraging her to look to the future, when she'll be a wife and a mother.

The goal of the discussions and exercises outlined in this chapter is to help your child realize that she has tremendous power over her choices, thoughts, and actions and that the decisions she makes will affect her future life. By being focused on the things that are important for her at this time in her life, she can one day look back and be proud of the memories she has created. If she can clearly grasp what her priorities need to be right now, she will be able to enjoy her teen years all the more.

❖ 13 ❖

Contraception, STDs, and Pregnancy

Y ou will have to decide for yourself how specific you would like to get in discussing contraception and sexually transmitted diseases (STDs) with your child based on your own moral and religious values. If you're like many of the parents I've spoken with, you would like your child to abstain from sex for as long as possible—ideally until he's married. But if he chooses to be sexual now, you hope he uses contraception. You may be unsure of how to approach the situation. One the one hand, you want to provide your child with the information he may need, but at the same time you don't want to encourage him to be sexual or give him the impression that you approve of his being sexually active. The most important message to convey is that sex is serious. It has all kinds of emotional *and* physical implications. If your child is going to be sexual, he should know about contraception, STDs, and pregnancy. It's difficult to always know if your child is sexually active, but it is possible if you communicate often with your child. I will offer information about these topics, and then you can decide what you want to pass on to your child.

Has the "Safe Sex" Message Worked?

The statistics regarding the "safe sex" message are alarming, and indicate that it isn't sufficiently effective. According to *Testing Positive,* a study conducted by the Alan Guttmacher Institute, more than one in five Americans are believed to be infected with a viral STD other than AIDS. Two-thirds of those who contract STDs are younger than twenty-five, and one-fourth are teenagers. Many of these young people suffer long-term health problems as a result of their infection. One million teenage girls become pregnant each year. Thirty-six percent of women in their early twenties will get pregnant within one year. Eighteen percent of teenage girls will get pregnant during their first year of using oral contraceptives. *Pediatrics* magazine reported that at least $3 billion has been spent on safe-sex programs, but there is no evidence that these programs have reduced sexually transmitted diseases or the teenage pregnancy rate. Now we say "safer" sex, but even though many teenagers know that contraception isn't always safe they often don't change their behavior. It's obvious that we need to try another approach. Perhaps this is why the Clinton administration is now spending more than $250 million on abstinence-only sex-education curriculums for schools across the country.

It isn't that I'm opposed to talking to adolescents about contraception, particularly if they're sexually active. But discussing *only* contraceptives and leaving out the rest, as though it were inevitable that your child is going to have sex and protecting herself from pregnancy and disease is the primary concern your teen should have, is dangerous. Not every teenager is going to have sex—and most teenagers will, and do, choose to abstain if they understand the consequences of not waiting as well as the benefits of waiting. I learned about contraception by going to Planned Parenthood when I was fourteen. But what I didn't learn until many years later was that there were many emotional and relational aspects of sex that I needed protection from.

By discussing only contraception, we are basically saying that we don't trust the child's ability to abstain. We show doubt in his moral character. If a boy is with a girl who says no to his sexual advances, we would advise him to respect her feelings. In that case, he would have to abstain. Why would it be possible for him to abstain then but not otherwise? We have to believe in a teenager's ability to exercise self-control. Equally important is that parents maintain their own integrity and not compromise their true feelings and desires for their child simply because it appears to be a hopeless cause. It's always better to take the high road: to impart the highest standards, to have faith in your child's ability to live true to them, and to stand firm regardless of what others seem to be doing. I've spoken to many parents with grown children who never discussed contraception with their children, and with positive results. They taught only the principles they truly believed in—abstinence, sacredness, the importance of caring for one's body, and not hurting others, for example. Many of these children trusted in their parents' wisdom and complied out of respect for their parents, and because they saw the value of what they were being taught.

Probably the most dangerous part of the safe-sex message is that it conveys to kids the idea that when it comes to their sexuality being "responsible" only means using contraception. Why not teach that being *abstinent,* and considering the *emotional* costs of having sex, and being *in love* and *committed* to their partner is what being responsible really means?

If we only talk about contraception, we can actually encourage teenagers to be sexual. According to a Harris poll commissioned by Planned Parenthood, kids who receive contraceptive-based education are 53 percent more likely to become sexually active than are kids who do not.

Promiscuity skyrocketed once the pill came out on the market. One of the inventors of the pill, Dr. Robert Kistner, of Harvard Medical School, said in 1977, "About ten years ago I declared that the pill would not lead to promiscuity. Well, I was wrong." Once we bought into the idea that we could have sex without fear of disease or pregnancy, it appeared that nothing should hold us back. It seems that teenagers are embracing the same message. Many teenagers now believe that if two people are willing to participate in sex, and they have discussed and agreed to use contraception, everything will be okay and no one will get hurt. Clearly, it isn't that simple.

The Truth About Contraception

The truth about contraception is that it simply doesn't always work, or work well. Although contraception *can* help to protect your adolescent from disease and pregnancy, teenagers don't usually use contraceptives properly, or every time they have sex. Even if they do, contraceptives aren't 100 percent safe, and they can't protect a person from being hurt emotionally.

Pamela discovered that her daughter Megan was having sex, in spite of the fact that Pamela had had the big talk with her. Pamela took Megan out to dinner, expressed her disappointment, and then asked her daughter if she was happy with her decision or if she wanted to make a change. Megan said she wasn't sure. Pamela ended the conversation this way: "Well, you know how I feel. I'm truly disappointed. But I'll always love you. Please remember that if and when you decide to start over, I'll help you make the transition."

Even with detailed knowledge about condoms and other forms of contraception, many teenagers don't use contraceptives at all. Either they are embarrassed to buy them or they don't want to plan ahead. This is one of the major issues to consider. Most teenagers don't even want to acknowledge that they're sexually active. According to Doug Goldsmith, "Most teenagers end up having *spontaneous* sex, because they tell themselves, 'If I plan to have sex, I'm bad. If I don't plan it, and it just happens, it wasn't my fault.'" The education teenagers are receiving about contraceptive use doesn't seem to have an effect on their ability to make conscious decisions about having sex. We need to help teenagers establish clear sexual standards as to when they will be sexual and then, if necessary, discuss the use of contraceptives with them.

Most experts agree that it can do little harm to simply discuss the facts about contraception. In fact, it can even help in convincing your child to abstain. Mary Kay Lehto says, "When parents talk to me about their fears of discussing contraception with their teenagers, I say, 'Didn't you raise your child to be an independent thinker?' If you helped him form moral values, then talking to him about contraception isn't going to change those values. Instead, you're letting him know that you trust him with information. Plus, you might not know if your child chooses to be sexual."

For your own information, you should know about the various forms of contraception. There are additional contraceptives besides the ones I mention here (the rhythm method, withdrawal, IUDs), but either they aren't effective enough to be discussed or they aren't recommended for teenagers.

Condoms and Spermicide

Condoms can reduce the chances of contracting a disease, but they aren't foolproof. They could be defective, or not used properly. They can slip or tear. Many teenagers, in the heat of the moment, decide not to use a condom because it's a hassle or they don't always have one available. They also complain that condoms reduce the level of pleasure they experience.

The Pill

The pill is considered by many to be the safest form of birth control. The drawbacks are remembering to take it regularly and properly (many girls don't allow enough time to pass after starting the pill for it to take effect); weight gain; and other potential side effects (headaches, nausea, depression, spotting). Some girls think that if they skip a day or two they're still protected. And many fail to continue taking the pill once their initial prescription runs out. The pill also doesn't protect a person from STDs.

Diaphragm or Cervical Cap and Spermicide

The diaphragm and the cervical cap are very similar. A doctor must measure and fit a diaphragm or cervical cap to the girl. Then it must be checked yearly to make sure the fit is still right, since there are many factors that affect the size needed, such as a change in weight. Diaphragms and cervical caps work only if they fit properly and are not damaged in any way. There's always the chance that a tear or a hole will develop. Then there's the issue of making sure it's inserted properly and that it stays in place. You have to put a small amount of spermicidal jelly or cream into the diaphragm or cap prior to having intercourse, urinate, and wash your hands before inserting it. Then you have to leave it in for several hours after intercourse, remove it, wash it, and store it in a place where it won't be exposed to heat. Among the problems many girls have is that their diaphragms don't fit, they don't use them properly, they run out of jelly, and they don't plan ahead in order to have the diaphragm with them when they need it.

Contraceptive Sponge

The sponge is inserted and left in place for several hours after intercourse. Many women claim that the sponge irritates them and is difficult to remove because it expands. The problems that apply to other contraceptives also apply to the sponge: it can be confusing and difficult to use; it's difficult to anticipate when you're going to be sexual, so it isn't easy to plan ahead; and it's embarrassing for a teenager to admit that she uses one, unless she's in a serious relationship with a boy and they've discussed contraception.

Norplant

Norplant is several little tubes that are implanted in an area under the skin of the upper arm. This procedure is performed under local anesthetic and begins working within twenty-four hours. It can prevent pregnancy for up to five years, and it can be removed anytime. It is very effective, but it is expensive (several hundred dollars), and there are side effects—including headaches, weight gain, spotting or bleeding, and the fact that Norplant offers no protection from STDs.

As you can see, there is an awful lot to consider when it comes to using contraceptives. As I've mentioned before, it isn't enough to just say "be careful." If your child is sexually active, after going over the three standards and the consequences and benefits of having sex or abstaining, you can decide whether you want to discuss these methods of contraception with your child or whether you want to take your child to a doctor who can provide the information she needs. If you're opposed to discussing the issue of contraception in detail because of religious beliefs, or because you only want to teach abstinence without sending a mixed message, it's still important to share your views on the subject.

There is a difference between *discussing* realities and issues that exist and *promoting* them. If you withhold the truth from your child about what is going on in the world and avoid these issues altogether, your child could develop beliefs that are contrary to those you consider to be healthy and good. And if you discuss the inconvenience and complexity of using contraception, your child may become even more convinced that it's wise to delay sexual activity.

Find the right moment and say, "You hear a lot about contraception and sexually transmitted diseases—whether on television or at school. We want you to know how we as a family feel about those subjects. (You might want to explain what contraception is—some kids don't know.) You know from previous talks we've had that having premarital sex is a big risk physically, which is why everyone stresses having safe sex these days. We don't go into detail about contraception and STDs because we hope that you'll follow our counsel and wait until marriage. Then you won't have to worry about these dangers. You've made your pledge, and we trust that you're being true to yourself. If for some reason you feel that you're going to fall short of that, we hope you'll come to us and talk about it first."

There are no guarantees that your teen will do as you suggest, but if you create open communication and present her with the information she needs to establish high standards and avoid having casual sex, you'll have done your part.

Patty insisted that her sixteen-year-old daughter, Julia, go on the pill when she discovered that Julia was having sex. But Julia ended up getting pregnant, anyway, because she secretly stopped taking the pills. There are no guarantees that a teenager will use contraceptives consistently or properly.

As you talk to your child about contraception (regardless of how much detail you provide), also talk about love, dating nonsexually, and how to say no to sexual advances. Remind your child that the physical part of sex is only one aspect, and that there are many other sides to consider. Also, be sure to explain that contraception is not always effective, and that abstinence is the only safe method of avoiding pregnancy and disease. Even though she is probably learning about these things at school, she needs to hear *you* say these words.

The Dangers of Sexually Transmitted Diseases

Most sex-education classes held in schools cover fairly detailed information about sexually transmitted diseases. You may not feel comfortable discussing this issue with your child, or even feel that it's necessary, but by doing so you just might convince her to abstain until marriage. Better yet, she might convince herself. It isn't that you want to scare your child into abstaining, but you do want her to know the truth about what could happen. In any case, you should be aware of them yourself.

More than 13 million Americans contract a sexually transmitted disease each year. Almost two-thirds of these cases occur in people under twenty-five. Many people don't even know they have a disease, because the symptoms aren't always detected and they often continue to spread the disease to others without realizing it. At least 1 million women suffer from pelvic inflammatory disease (PID) yearly as a result of having a sexually transmitted disease. Many women are diagnosed with lifelong infertility, which plagues one in five couples.

The only way to be completely safe from contracting a disease is to not have sex at all until you're either married or you're with someone who has never had sex with anyone else and you're free from disease yourself.

Some of the more common STDs are:

AIDS

There is currently no cure for AIDS, a disease that weakens the immune system. People often think that AIDS is primarily spread by homosexuals and drug users, but AIDS cases are rapidly growing among teenagers, women, and minorities. Those who are HIV-positive experience symptoms such as fever, fatigue, weight loss, or lesions. These symptoms sometimes don't surface for several years after an individual has been diagnosed as HIV-positive.

Gonorrhea

This disease is not easily detected. If left untreated, it can lead to all kinds of health problems. One of the more serious is pelvic inflammatory disease, which can scar a woman's fallopian tubes and make it difficult or impossible for her to get pregnant in the future. If gonorrhea is detected early enough, it can be cured with antibiotics.

Chlamydia

Chlamydia is very common, so much so that it's become an epidemic. Girls fifteen to nineteen appear to have the highest infection rate. Most women never experience symptoms until it's too late—that is, until they discover that they're infertile. But if it is detected early enough, chlamydia can be cured with antibiotics.

Genital Warts

Genital warts, also known as human papillomavirus (HPV), is a very contagious and serious disease. The warts are usually so small that you can't see them, and symptoms are often undetectable. Cervical cancer is thought to be associated with HPV. Cervical cancer rates among sexually active young girls who have multiple partners are skyrocketing. This disease can be treated through laser surgery, burning, freezing, or medication, but quite often the warts return and are again undetected.

Genital Herpes

Herpes simplex II is recurrent sores in the genital area. It can be spread through direct contact, and not only through sexual intercourse. Condoms can't protect a person from this virus because the sores aren't always directly on the penis or inside the vagina. There is no cure for genital herpes, which means the sores reappear periodically and sufferers experience burning, itching, pain, and sometimes fever.

Syphilis

This disease, if left untreated, can be devastating. It can cause damage to the brain, heart, and blood vessels. If syphilis is detected early enough, it can be treated and cured with antibiotics.

There are other health problems that can be spread through sexual contact, including vaginitis, crabs, and cystitis, but these are not really STDs.

What to Do If Your Daughter Is Pregnant

You may find yourself flooded with emotions if your daughter tells you that she's pregnant. Your first inclination may be to get angry or show strong disappointment. But the most important thing you can do is express your love for her and let her know that you're there for her regardless of how you feel about her being pregnant. Don't blurt out right away what you think she should do.

If you react with hurtful comments, such as "What in the world is wrong with you?" or "As if you didn't know right from wrong!" or "Well, now you've really messed up your life!", a huge wall will come between you and your child. Your teenager will be on the defensive, she'll feel misunderstood, and you'll get nowhere. Your adolescent didn't do this to *you*—she created problems for *herself* by making poor choices. You can help her see that, but not by belittling her. Perhaps you didn't give her the tools she needed to make better choices. Acknowledge your own mistakes. Show your hurt and disappointment, but acknowledge that this was her choice and now she has to decide on the solution.

Next, talk about the boy: How do they feel about each other? Where does the relationship stand now? Does he know that she's pregnant, and how did he react? Do his parents know? If the boy is serious about your daughter, whether or not they are open to the idea of marriage, you will want to have a meeting with both of them together, along with his parents, so that decisions can be made. If his parents don't know, suggest that your daughter encourage him to tell his parents as soon as possible because you will be calling them. But first talk privately about the options that are available to your daughter.

Vicky Burgess says, "Parents need to explore all of the alternatives with their child. Most high schools have parenting classes, and teenagers can arrange meetings with girls who have kept their babies to find out what to expect should they decide to keep the child. Teenagers need to *see* the struggle. Teenagers don't really think that it could happen to them, but if they see others going through the process of raising a child, it becomes more real to them."

Is Abortion an Option? You have probably considered your feelings on abortion prior to this moment, possibly more from a political or a religious standpoint than as the result of a personal experience. You probably have very strong feelings about the issue. Either you support the freedom of every woman to be able to choose what to do with her body or you believe that the spirit and the fetus of the child she is carrying have the right to come into the world, regardless of the circumstances. You may believe that to terminate this new life simply because it isn't convenient or didn't come to be in the ideal way is selfish. Or you may not be opposed to abortion.

It isn't my intent to impress upon you my personal beliefs about this issue, as much as I would like to encourage you, in the event you're ever confronted with this dilemma, to present the various sides of the issue to your adolescent. If you and your adolescent are completely opposed to abortion for religious reasons, you may not even want to consider it as an option. This is up to you. But quite often teenagers don't have the same beliefs, and they feel they should be presented with all of the choices.

It's difficult to be calm and present your teenager with all sides and options, particularly when you feel adamant about a particular choice. It's difficult to think these things through at all when you're emotionally distraught with the knowledge that your child is faced with this kind of problem. But it's important that you be loving, honest, and open so that your teenager, with your assistance, can make the wisest choice based on your sound and honest guidance.

It's true that some of the most talented, gifted human beings came into this world out of wedlock and even endured much hardship, yet they made tremendous contributions to society in spite of the disadvantages of their birth. As you discuss this option with your teenager, share your own moral or religious beliefs on the issue. If you do discuss abortion, your teenager should have a complete understanding of the choice. Abortion isn't just a simple operation that makes the problem go away. There are often serious emotional and sometimes physical repercussions—if not right after the abortion, then years later. The girl often wishes she could go back in time and reverse her decision. According to a nationwide survey by the *Los Angeles Times,* "For a woman who has an abortion, the experience can be traumatic, leading often to feelings of guilt and sometimes even regret about her decision not to bear the child. Her partner typically is nagged even more by guilt and regret."

Dr. Irving Klitsner says, "Many teenage girls who have abortions do so because the parents insist on it, not because they chose to do so. Some girls have abortions because their boyfriends insist. But I feel the girl should choose. When the decision is not their own, guilt and depression often lead to repeat pregnancies. Parents need to go over the options available. Fathers need to share their thoughts also. But the final decision about how to deal with the pregnancy should be made by the pregnant teen."

The Adoption Choice: In my opinion adoption is the best choice if the girl is unable to care for her child. There are many couples who are trying to adopt and are capable of providing financially and emotionally for a child. Help your daughter see the situation from the child's perspective. It is the well-being of the baby that matters most. The child deserves the best opportunities in life—two loving parents, if possible, and a stable home environment.

Raising the Child Alone: As a teenager, your daughter is probably too young to be able to take adequate care of a child. But many teenage girls have chosen to keep their babies, and although they found it challenging they raised these children as best they could, often with the help of the grandparents. But these lives are frequently filled with difficult trials. The question is, Does your daughter want to keep the child even after considering each option carefully, and in your best judgment does it seem feasible that she will rise to the occasion and be a responsible parent? She needs to know what the future holds for her. She would have to get a job, find someone to care for the child while she works, stay up late, and get very little sleep while caring for her infant. There would be very little time for friends or dating. Her education may be thwarted, her reputation will suffer, boys may not be interested in a serious relationship with a young girl who has a child. There would be a considerable loss of freedom, financial responsibility, and so on.

Getting Married and Raising the Child: This is an option that rarely happens for teenagers. Sometimes the boy even denies that the baby is his, is unwilling to get married, or may never want to see the girl again. Sometimes it's the reverse—the boy wants to get married and the girl doesn't. But teens do get married, and it is something that should be discussed if your daughter and the boy are serious about each other. Sometimes they come to you saying, "We're in love, and we're getting married." If this is the case, you could say, "Okay, but let's talk about this to make sure you've thought things through." Then explain the realities: loss of freedom, financial and emotional burdens, potential marital problems when couples marry too young, the fact that people change as they mature, the shift in their dreams and goals. Suggest that your daughter take one month to think things over before deciding for certain. Tell her that marriage is forever, and that thinking about it for one month won't hurt. After all, it's a huge decision that will affect them both forever. If after this time she's still adamant about getting married, she deserves your support. You can then focus on teaching her how to build a strong marriage.

What to Do If Your Son's Girlfriend Is Pregnant

Show love and support for your son from the very beginning. Let him know that although you're not pleased with what has happened, you're there to help him. Ultimately, it's up to the girl to decide what to do with the baby. But your son needs to consider the options as well. He needs to consider how he truly feels about the girl and if he wants to marry her and raise the baby. Ask him what the girl wants to do and if they've talked about the options.

Some points should be made clear: He needs to be willing to provide financially if the girl decides to keep the baby. He should be encouraged to do whatever it takes to be responsible, and to see himself as responsible financially. If the girl chooses to keep the baby but they don't marry, he should still be a committed father by spending time with the child and fulfilling other fatherly duties for the child's sake. If your son wants to marry the girl, help him prepare to talk to her. Suggest that he go to her and express his feelings for her and his desire to marry her, raise the child, and build a life together. If she refuses, he can still promise to provide for the child financially and emotionally. Since most teenage marriages aren't successful, you may want to suggest that he encourage her to put the baby up for adoption, for the baby's benefit. If he's adamantly opposed to abortion, he should tell the girl.

The most important point to discuss with your son is that he needs to think about the situation from the girl's perspective as well as from the point of view of the baby's welfare. The girl is obviously in a very vulnerable position, and she needs your son's reassurance. Even if he doesn't want to marry her, he was intimate with this girl and he needs to be caring toward her. As you talk with him, be sure to say, "You know, son, even if you don't love this girl, you did have sex with her. You are responsible. Imagine how she feels right now. She's probably embarrassed and scared to death. You can go on with your life, but she has to deal with her reputation, and nine months of physical changes or the difficulty of an abortion if she chooses to have one. She may have thought that having sex with you would make you love her more, or that you did love her in the first place. She needs your kindness right now. Call her and let her know that you won't abandon her or act like it's not your problem, too."

Plan a time to meet together with the girl's parents to discuss all of the options mentioned above. This could be a difficult meeting, especially if the other parents aren't as rational or as solution-oriented as you are. But it has to happen. The young couple needs adult guidance and mediation. Call the girl's parents and say, "We obviously have a situation here, and we think it would be wise for all of us to meet and talk about what to do next. Would you and your husband (or wife) and daughter be willing to come to our home this evening and talk about this?" Be sure to make it clear what the tone of the evening should be. Say, "We don't want to have an angry confrontation or blaming session—we just want to find a solution that's best for everyone. We've already talked to our son about the options available." You may want to suggest that both families see a counselor in order to help you come up with the best solution. It can be helpful to have a mediator, particularly one who has had years of experience in dealing with these situations.

Get to the Heart of the Matter

Adam was aware that his fourteen-year-old daughter, Clara, was having sex. He insisted that she go on the pill. There was no discussion about the fact that she was having sex, no questions asked about her behavior. His daughter was deeply offended, not so much by the idea of using contraception but by the level of disdain her father seemed to have toward her. "I wasn't a human being with feelings or fears," she said. "To him I was nothing more than an irresponsible kid who was out of control. I was embarrassed and even disgusted with myself."

Clara needed further interaction with her father about these serious issues. She needed mediation in thinking through the decisions she was making. No one ever tried to find out *why* she was sexually active. Adam could have said, "Clara, the fact that you're sexually active disappoints me, but I think it's important that we talk about some important issues here. There are the physical concerns, of course, which include making sure that you use protection. But I'm curious to know why you decided to become sexually active with this person. Do you feel you're in love with him?"

Adam and Clara need to talk about the relationship Clara has with her partner, where the relationship is going, if these issues have been discussed, and how Clara truly feels about being sexual. The fact that Clara told me she felt "disgusted with herself" shows that she has remorse. Her parent needs to uncover those feelings and let her know that there is a way out, rather than just becoming resigned to the idea of her being sexual. Clara may not want to be on the pill; she may be longing for guidance in how to stop having sex and build a more healthy relationship with someone in the future. Working through these obstacles together in a loving, open way will strengthen Clara's relationship with her father. She will be more willing to go to him with future problems and concerns rather than keeping them a secret, as most teenagers do.

The first thing that needs to be done is to get to the heart of the matter. *Why* is your child sexually active? Does she think she will lose the boy if she says no? Was it just a matter of sexual impulses? Was it a mistake in her mind? Once you find the answers to these questions, you can determine what area you need to work on in your teenager's emotional and spiritual development.

One mother thought the way out of an awkward conversation was to invite someone else to talk with her son. "Dwight's father and I divorced when Dwight was born. When Dwight was eleven I set him up with a 'Big Brother' so that he would have a male influence in his life. Dwight is shy but very talented. I worry about him because he doesn't talk to me as much as he used to. He's wearing his pants real low, and listening to heavy rock music. I suggested he talk to his big brother about sex. His big brother told him to always use a condom. I just went along with that advice because I didn't know what else to tell him."

This mother needs to take control of her son's sex education. She can research the subject at the library, talk to professionals in the field, attend the sex-ed class at Dwight's school, and read books like this one. Dwight needs to know a lot more than to just use a condom. If his mother has the big talk with him, he may not need a condom because he might choose not to have sex until he's engaged or married. In fact, when I spoke one-on-one with Dwight he told me that he's still a virgin and he has no intention of being sexually active at this point in his life. He asked me questions about dating and girls— these are the things he needs to learn about now. Dwight's mother could suggest to the big brother that he tell Dwight to talk to her about his sexuality. She could also communicate her values to the big brother so that he will be able to back her up if her son asks questions about sexual issues.

By encouraging your teenager to abstain through the talks, hypo- thetical examples, metaphors, and role-playing that make up *The Big Talk,* you will teach him that sex and making out are not to be taken lightly. He will learn how and why to say no, and how to think things through rather than pursuing immediate gratification. If you have the big talk in its entirety, and go over the information many times, you may not have to discuss sexually transmitted diseases and contracep- tion in great detail.

The primary goal of the big talk is to help your child determine his sexual standards *before* he begins dating, and to teach him how to incorporate these standards into his life. Teaching your child how to say no to casual sex, how to set high moral standards for himself, and how to build a relationship based on love and commitment will help him avoid having to deal with the issues outlined in this chapter. In- stead of focusing primarily on the physical aspects of sexuality, spend more time reinforcing ways to *prevent* problems such as pregnancy and disease.

❖ IV ❖

Establishing a Healthy Relationship

✦ 14 ✦

Setting Dating Guidelines

Most people don't consider making discussions about dating, love, and how to attract the opposite sex part of the big talk. After all, the big talk is about sex—the birds and the bees, puberty issues, and so on. But I don't think we can separate the two. Sexual advances occur when two people date each other, so it makes sense for us to learn how to date and interact with the opposite sex as we learn about sex itself. Part of the goal is to help your child learn how to build a loving, lasting, healthy relationship by putting sex in the proper context. For this reason, discussions about love, dating, and relationships go hand in hand with discussions about sex.

Dating can be a time of great learning and fun for your adolescent—or it can be traumatic and frustrating. What took most of us many years (or decades!) to figure out can be presented to your child even before she begins dating. She will still have to learn a lot through experience, but at least she'll have a foundation and a basic understanding of the purpose of dating, how to behave on dates and what to expect, and how to treat the opposite sex. First, you will want to establish some rules for dating in your home so that your child will know exactly what's expected of her.

Establishing Rules

Having rules, particularly regarding dating, gives teenagers a feeling of being loved and of being secure. This also creates more respect from their friends. The Parsons shared their experience on this issue. "We have two daughters who have gone out with seniors to the senior prom. They wanted to stay out past their curfew because their friends were allowed to stay out until one or two in the morning, but we wouldn't allow it. There just isn't any reason to be out so late—

that's usually when the problems start. In both cases, it worked out great. In fact, one boy said he was relieved that he had to bring our daughter home early because he had to take an ACT test the next day."

Come to an understanding with your spouse about the rules you feel strongly about before you talk to your child. Susan, the mother of two teenagers, said, "My husband and I may not always agree on everything, but we present a united front to our children. We do this so that they can't play us against each other and so there is unity in our decisions and rules." Have a family-council meeting and include your child in the decision-making process. Explain that you want to establish dating guidelines that will protect her as well as make the experience more enjoyable for her.

The following guidelines can help ensure that your child feels safe and loved—and they'll give you more peace of mind! You may want to come up with additional ones.

- Know where she's going, and whether she's going someplace else later. There should be no surprises.
- Know with whom she is going and if others will be joining them later.
- Don't allow her to date someone who's much older than she is.
- Discuss the types of activities that are unacceptable for dates: drinking, drugs, isolated locations, unsupervised parties.
- No exclusive dating until she's older than seventeen.
- Know when she'll be home. Specify the time, and don't let her extend that time except in special cases.
- Obtain a phone number where she can be reached. If there is no phone, she should call you if anything happens.
- Always meet her dates and friends.

One large family issued an edict whereby every family member had to be home by 10 P.M. every weeknight. Only the teenagers ever stayed out that late, however. The only exceptions ever allowed were very special cases. After one week, the parents realized this was the best thing they had ever done. One of their daughters said, "Mom, my life is so peaceful now!" Until then, this family had lost order and peace in their home. People were coming and going, and it was almost impossible to get the entire family together for dinner and other activities that were important. Mom and Dad felt that they couldn't sleep comfortably because they had to wait for one or another of the kids to get home at night. Enforcing this rule brought harmony and peace back into their lives, and even the kids, however reluctant at first, noticed the difference.

Why It's Important to Establish Rules

It's important to set down clear rules for dating so that your teenager knows exactly what is expected of her, as well as to protect her from getting into trouble. Practically every corporation and organization has a set of rules and policies that its employees and members must follow to ensure harmony and safety within the organization. The same concept can apply to our home life. Teens usually feel restricted and annoyed with rules rather than seeing the benefits. Explain to your child why it's important to have rules. The rollerblading metaphor will help you to get this point across.

THE ROLLERBLADING METAPHOR

The best way to instill an idea is through metaphors that your child can relate to. Lots of kids Rollerblade today. Share this metaphor with your child in your own words:

One day I saw a girl Rollerblading. She didn't like wearing the knee pads and wrist guards. It was a hassle for her to put them on. She seemed to feel confined, less free. But I realized that the guards were there to protect this girl, not to limit her enjoyment. She was viewing the guards as a negative, a restriction, something that held her back. But the truth is, they gave her the freedom to enjoy herself even more. They allowed her to Rollerblade more confidently, with less worry or fear that she might hurt herself.

As I watched her, it dawned on me that we all feel this way to a certain degree about things that confine us. Most of us don't like rules. We sometimes think they limit us. But just like the guards, they are there to protect us and give us even more freedom to truly enjoy ourselves without fear or worry.

The Age Question

Many teenagers want to begin dating at an age when they aren't emotionally mature enough to handle the issues that arise with dating, such as dealing with sexual advances. You'll want to establish a specific time when it's okay for your child to start dating. This will depend largely on her emotional development, but sixteen is usually a safe age to begin dating in groups.

NO DATING UNTIL 16!

According to research done by Brent C. Miller of Utah State University and Terrence D. Olsen of Brigham Young University, among 2,400 teens the findings were: "The younger a girl begins to date, the more likely she is to have sex before graduating from high school. It is also true of girls and boys who go steady in the ninth grade. Of girls who begin dating at twelve, 91 percent had sex before graduation—compared to 56 percent who had dated at fourteen, 40 percent who dated at fifteen, and 20 percent who dated at sixteen. Of boys with a ninth-grade steady, 70 percent said that they'd had sex compared to 60 percent of girls. Of boys who dated occasionally as freshmen, 52 percent had sex compared to 35 percent of girls." These findings show that early dating increases the chances of sexual activity for teens. It's hard enough for most teens to say no to sex when they're older, let alone when they begin spending lots of time alone with the opposite sex too soon.

Teenagers shouldn't be preoccupied and overwhelmed with heavy-duty relationship issues that even adults find taxing. Their teen years should be full of family, friends, school, and wholesome activities—all of which will help to prepare them for their own future families. Fourteen- and fifteen-year-olds aren't emotionally ready for serious involvement with the opposite sex. Some teens appear to be mature enough—they may seem more grounded than their peers. Fifteen-year-old Alicia, for example, seemed way beyond her age emotionally. She seemed to know what a healthy relationship is all about. She said, "My boyfriend respects how I feel about things. We talk about everything. We both know that we aren't ready to have sex." Sounds good so far. But although Alicia and her boyfriend Darrin, sixteen, are still virgins, they do everything but have sex. They spend most of their time together, and have done so for the past six months. I asked Alicia what she plans to do when they go off to college, particularly if they attend different colleges. "Well, I don't know," she said. "It will be hard because we really love each other." I asked her if they plan to get married someday. "We joke about it, but we really don't know. We don't really talk about that in a serious way. But we did decide that if we were to break up we would stay friends." Chances are Alicia and Darrin won't get married. Yet there's a growing physical and emotional intimacy between them that prevents them from focusing on other areas of their lives. They have created a marriagelike situation for themselves at the tender ages of fifteen and sixteen that may end up in a divorcelike situation down the road; even if they do part as friends it won't be easy. And even though they aren't having intercourse right now, they're certainly moving in that direction.

If teens don't begin dating until sixteen, and then don't date one-on-one until seventeen, they will be more likely to delay sexual activity. It helps to prepare them in advance for this kind of dating. Remind your child when she's younger by saying, "When you're sixteen, you can go out on dates like your older brother." Make it part of your family culture.

Byron hadn't thought through the age question ahead of time, therefore he wasn't prepared when his daughter Jennifer, fourteen, asked him about dating: "As we were driving one day, Jennifer asked me when she could date one-on-one. I thought about it for a few blocks and then said, 'Well, I'm assuming you want to date guys who can drive?' She looked at me as if to say *duh*. 'So, at what age can you legally drive?' She thought for a moment, then looked at me with complete horror, '*Sixteen!* I have to wait until I'm sixteen to date one-on-one?'" Byron said, "Well, depending on your level of maturity and your grades, maybe even at fifteen and a half!"

This father's lack of preparation created problems. His daughter knew that he wasn't clear and resolved. She knew she had an edge, and that there was room for negotiation. Some rules can be negotiable, but others are established to protect your teenager and shouldn't be compromised. The fact that his daughter had to ask him at all means that rules regarding dating had not been taught all along in their home. Byron wavered on his decision based on the reaction he received from his daughter. Sometimes in an attempt to remain on friendly terms with kids, parents—particularly divorced parents—cave in to appease the child. But this does more damage than good. Byron hadn't really thought through why he even said sixteen, other than the fact that sixteen is the legal driving age. A lot of thought needs to be given to these issues long before kids ask the questions.

DON'T LET YOUR TEENAGER DATE SOMEONE WHO'S TOO MUCH OLDER

Many young girls are attracted to older men, and I was no exception. Older guys seem wiser, more experienced. Young girls sometimes go to great lengths to measure up—to be mature enough to maintain the man's interest. I'm talking about more than a five-year difference. Girls mature faster than boys do, and dating someone a year or two older is common, but some girls are drawn to much older men.

One eighteen-year-old girl I spoke with told me that she's seeing a thirty-five-year-old man who lives near the college she attends. She stops by his place at least three times a week. Their meetings include sex, of course, and they rarely go out. Yet this girl considers him to be her boyfriend. She still lives at home, yet her mother has no idea that she's involved with this man. In fact, the mother still believes her daughter has had only one sexual experience—a couple of years ago with a boy from her high school. You can solve this problem if you insist on meeting the boys your daughter dates. She might still date someone older behind your back, but if you keep close tabs she'll have a much harder time pulling it off. If you know that your daughter is attracted to older men, talk to her about the dangers and help her establish sexual standards and future goals.

Courting/Dating

Dating in groups is often safer than dating one-on-one, and it's a good idea for teens who are just beginning to date. But once teenagers get a little older they need to learn how to date one-on-one. Whether your adolescent goes out on a single or double date, courting is a great way to learn how to build a relationship with the opposite sex. Today, *dating* can mean meeting someone at a movie theater and going dutch. But *courting* brings back good, old-fashioned behaviors, such as the boy picking up the girl at her home and meeting both parents.

Teens need to get excited about the date as they prepare for the evening. Boys need to learn how to ask a girl out, make plans, pick her up, open the door for her, and so on. Girls need to learn how to create interesting conversation and appreciate their partner's chivalry. Hopefully you are teaching your son to be chivalrous—it should never go out of style.

I once read an article that featured the story of a father who dispensed with dating and issued a new (or old) way of relating called "courting." His daughter agreed to the terms, which consisted of having a boy who asks her out talk to her dad first. The boy has to get permission to go out with her, and he has to know what's required of him if he wants to spend time with this girl. Furthermore, her parents expect him to be spiritually and financially prepared to marry her if they fall in love; otherwise he shouldn't be starting a relationship. This is a good way to approach the situation when your adolescent is a little older and is ready to date more seriously.

One of the benefits of courting is the fact that much of the burden is taken off the child's shoulders. Girls don't experience as much pressure, and they don't have to worry about how to deal with sexual advances or agonize over whether a boy is truly interested. Also, this gives the parents a chance to get to know the boy who's showing interest in their daughter. And the boy will be spending time with the entire family, not just alone with your child.

In the book *She Calls Me Daddy*, by Robert D. Wolgemuth, the author shares a personal story about his sixteen-year-old daughter and a boy she wanted to date. Here's the story:

In the fall of 1990, Julie, our second daughter, turned sixteen. Coming home from work one evening, an unfamiliar two-door European sedan parked in front of our house caught my eye. "Nice," I remember whispering out loud. "Very nice."

Steven was a senior. I had suspected that he was interested in Julie because of his recent visits to our church. Julie was only a week short of her sixteenth birthday, and Steven knew the rules: 1) no (single) dating until Julie had turned sixteen, and 2) boys must be interviewed by me.

I walked through the kitchen and into the family room, where my wife, Bobbie, Julie, and Steven were making small talk.

Steven quickly stood to his feet.

"Good evening, Mr. Wolgemuth," he said, squeezing a thin, nervous smile.

"Hi, Steven, how are you?" I replied, firmly shaking his hand.

"Fine."

Following a few seconds of silence, I spoke again.

"How about if we go into the next room for a few minutes?"

His visit to our house was to get this meeting out of the way. He knew it was part of the deal, and he was ready.

He followed me into my study, where I invited him to sit in the chair across from my desk.

"I couldn't help but notice the car out front when I drove in. Is it yours?"

"Yes, sir," Steven replied. "My dad is helping with the payments, but I cover the insurance and gas. We bought it last summer, and I spend a lot of time fixing it up. The engine was in pretty good shape, but the body needed some work."

This was more information than I was looking for, but I let him run. He was taking the bait. After a few minutes of detail about what he had done to the car, I leaned back in my chair.

"It sounds like this is a pretty special car," I said.

He nodded as I continued, "Now, can I ask you a question?"

"Okay, go ahead," he replied.

"What if I had come to your house last night, and asked you if I could borrow your car for the evening? What would you have said?"

Steven took no time to respond. "I'd have said 'No way.'"

"Why?" I replied, acting as though his answer fascinated me.

"Well, because I don't know you. I don't know how you drive. I don't know how you'd treat my car. I'm not sure I can trust you. That car's important to me."

"That's interesting, Steven," I finally said. "If I were you, I'd do the same thing."

He smiled and, for the first time, looked a little relaxed. "You would?"

"Absolutely," I reassured him.

"And do you know why? Because tonight you've come to my house and asked if you can borrow our daughter for the evening. And before I let you do that, I want to find out who you are."

A shocked but dawning look of understanding crossed his face. I had his undivided attention.

As we talked, I reminded him that, as an eighteen-year-old, he was far more experienced than Julie, and that I expected him to treat her like he treated his four-wheeled import. No, actually, better.

He understood.

When we finished our conversation, we both stood up. I shook his hand.

"You know, Mr. Wolgemuth, if I ever have a sixteen-year-old daughter of my own someday, I'll do what you did today."

Don't Be Fooled by Your Child's Rebellion

When I hit my teens the last thing I wanted was my parents quizzing me about where I was going, whom I was going with, and so on. But

I hadn't been raised with that kind of treatment up to that point, so I wasn't seasoned. As I got older, I was ready to take my freedom and independence to a new level. But the truth is, even though I appeared to be uncontrollable, I desperately wanted to have guidelines. I wanted to know that my parents worried about me and stayed up all night waiting for my return. I wanted them to not allow me to do things that could be dangerous to my safety. And I wanted all of this to be in the spirit of love and tenderness, not that of a dictatorial parent. Your teenager will accept and adjust to your rules if you remain steadfast. But give her large doses of love. Eventually she'll even appreciate you for setting rules.

Here's what the Thompsons did: "We gathered as a family and my husband and I said, 'Here are the rules: no dating until sixteen, no sex before marriage, curfew is midnight on Fridays and eleven-thirty on Saturdays, boys are not allowed upstairs.' We just spelled it all out for our children, and we feel very fortunate that they have accepted our guidelines." Part of the reason I think the Thompsons have been so successful is that they prepared their kids early. They had these discussions when their children were in grade school. Their kids therefore accepted these rules as part of life, and they didn't rebel as they grew older.

Of course, there will be times when you'll want to be flexible. One sixteen-year-old girl said she really appreciated it when her parents allowed her to stay out beyond her curfew for special occasions. You don't want to be Gestapo-like in enforcing rules; there are times when rules can be bent.

Preparing Your Child for Dating

Once you've set clear rules for dating, prepare your child for the dating process. These talks will help her to understand the purpose of dating as well as how to behave on and in between dates. And these are the discussions your child will probably enjoy the most.

The Purpose of Dating

Dating isn't just a time to have fun and hang out. Share the following list with your child as you discuss the purpose of dating, and ask her for additional ideas. Through dating, teenagers learn how to:

1. Be around and relate to the opposite sex.
2. Build friendships and special bonds with another person.
3. Treat others with respect and kindness.
4. Have meaningful conversations.
5. Determine what they want in a future mate.
6. Figure out who they are—what they think about various issues, what they like and don't like.
7. Be unselfish and do what others like to do.
8. Be responsible and plan ahead.

EXCLUSIVITY

For teenagers, the purpose of dating is not to get seriously involved with just one person or to find a mate; that will be down the road. Talk to your child about the dangers of dating exclusively during her high school years. You can have this discussion before your child begins dating, maybe even as early as eleven or twelve years old. Kids sometimes start thinking about dating this early, and many of them develop crushes. During family night you could say, "We prefer that you not date the same person more than once or twice during high school because it's not a good idea to get too serious about one person while you're so young." Help her to see your logic by giving her a bigger perspective. Say, "Someday you'll get married and have a family, but that won't be for several years. What are you going to do with the boyfriend you have now when you go to college? And what about your pledge? It just doesn't make sense to get wrapped up in a serious relationship with one person when you and your life are going to change so much."

Casual dating in high school is fun, but it shouldn't be your child's main focus. I feel strongly about this, partly because of my own experiences but also because of conversations I've had with teenagers. I've spoken to many teens between the ages of fourteen and seventeen who are seriously involved with one person. Almost without exception, they are sexually involved in one way or the other. How could it be otherwise? They spend hours on the telephone together, they spend several nights per week and almost every weekend together. They hang out together at school during the day. They go through all of the phases of an adult relationship: they sometimes argue and fight; they break up then get back together; they struggle with jealousies and insecurities. When they aren't together, they obsess over each other and the relationship. This is too much for a teenager to deal with.

Teenagers sometimes worry that they won't find a suitable person to marry. Priscilla, the mother of sixteen-year-old Shoshana, shared this experience with me: "My daughter tells me all the time, 'Mom, I'm never going to meet the right person. The ones I like never like me!' I worry about her, but I feel like there's nothing I can do." Priscilla can ease her daughter's fears by explaining that finding an appropriate mate is not always easy. Sometimes it takes a lot longer than we anticipate, and unfortunately sometimes people aren't who we think they are. Meeting the right person and falling in love is not something that is guaranteed to a person simply because they arrive at a particular age, but eventually most people do meet someone they want to marry.

You don't want to paint a bleak picture, whereby your child gets the impression that finding someone is like searching for a guppy in the ocean, but you do want to be honest about the reality that it may take many years before she finds someone with whom she would consider sharing her life. Explain to your child that it's scary to think that she may not find the right person. And when the day comes when she thinks she's found that person, she may have doubts and fears. But if she takes her time, doesn't date exclusively too early or rush into making a commitment, she will usually make the right choice.

Be sure to explain that once your child is in a committed relationship she shouldn't shop around for something better. And the focus isn't just on finding what she wants in a mate—she still needs to work at being the best she can be as well. Ask your child, "How can you make sure that a person is right for you and that you are making a good choice?" Some of the answers might be: date a variety of people; don't get too serious too soon; get to know them really well through long conversations about various subjects; date them for at least one year.

How to Tell If Someone Is Interested

If a girl really likes a boy, she may go crazy trying to figure out whether he feels the same way about her. You could say, "Sometimes it's really hard to tell if a boy likes you. It's easy to get impatient because sometimes it takes boys a long time to call no matter how interested they are. But if they truly are interested, eventually they do call. If a boy continues to pursue you, he's interested."

Boys often experience similar feelings. You could say, "Girls usually give off signals. If she lights up around you, if she takes your calls and usually says yes when you ask her out, then she probably likes you. You'll want to go slow so as to not scare her away. Give her time to develop feelings for you. And if you still can't figure it out, and you're dying to know, you can always ask, 'So, how do you feel about me?' Girls usually like it when you're confident enough to be direct."

Talk to your son (or daughter) about how to deal with rejection. Explain that just as he isn't going to be attracted to every girl he meets, some girls won't be attracted to him. Rejection is part of life, and he shouldn't allow it to get him down too much. He'll meet plenty of girls who will find him appealing.

Fun Dating Ideas

As a family, come up with fun dating ideas for your teenager who's approaching sixteen. Be sensitive, however, to a teen who may not be ready even at sixteen to begin dating. Some teens never get asked out in high school, or they're rejected when they do the asking. Preface the discussion with something like this: "Let's come up with some fun ideas for when you do date, even if it isn't in the near future." Make notes as family members offer ideas. Type up the list for future reference. Here are some suggestions for some fun ideas:

- Dinner at a fun restaurant
- Carnival
- Day at the beach (take a Frisbee or other games to play)
- Picnic
- Take-out food and a video (it's best to have parental supervision)
- Movies
- Cook together
- Have a party (preferably at your home, with you present)
- Play games (Trivial Pursuit, Monopoly, etc.)
- Theater
- Bike ride
- Rollerblading
- Any sporting activity

Share Your Own Dating Memories

Remember when you were in love with the cutest boy in the whole school—and then you discovered that he was in love with the cutest girl in the school and it wasn't you? Remember the geek who followed you everywhere? What about your first date? Or were you the guy who couldn't get a date? Early dating experiences are difficult even under the best of circumstances.

Share a few "date disasters" from your past with your teenager. The evening will be a riot! Your child will love to hear about your nightmare dates, and she'll learn from them, too. She'll remember these stories and be sure not to make the same mistakes.

Dating is all about relating, and we learn to relate from the time we're very young. Now is the time to teach your child how to relate to others with confidence and enthusiasm. Think of the criticisms you've had about dates in your present or past: he didn't look me in the eyes; she talked about herself the entire time; he looked disheveled; she's constantly late. Share these examples with your teenager.

Talk to Your Teen Before (and After) Dates

Take the time to ensure that your adolescent is living in accordance with the values you teach her. This means taking the extra fifteen minutes before the date to chat about what they have planned for the evening and so on. After the date, you can talk about what happened on the date and how she feels about the person. Ask, Did you have a good time? What did you do? What do you think of him? Do you plan to see him again? Don't grill your child with these questions, but do ask one or two of them after each date. Be nonchalant in expressing your curiosity. If you notice that your older teenager is seeing the same person often, say, "It seems like you two are getting pretty serious. How's it going?" Show your child that you're interested and that you care about her dating life. Ask her if she and her date are struggling with anything, and watch for signs of depression or worry. Try to see situations from your child's perspective.

Dating Etiquette for Boys and Girls

Your adolescent is entering into a whole new world when she begins to date. She has never done this before, and she's going to need some advice on how to behave. I've separated some of the advice for boys and girls because the roles and sexes are so different. Some of this advice will overlap, of course, and the differences aren't etched in stone, but there are some specific differences in how boys and girls relate to each other.

Boys need advice on dating just as much as girls do. We can't expect boys to know what to do on a date if we've never given them any suggestions. Trey, sixteen, said, "My mom yelled at me because I didn't walk my date to the door when I took her home. I felt really dumb, but I didn't know what to do." Travis, sixteen, is working on getting a girlfriend. "I know how to start things, like starting a conversation, but to take it to the next level is a mystery to me," he said. The talks in this chapter will help you answer these types of questions.

Role-Playing

Role-playing various dating scenarios is a great way to teach appropriate behavior. Your teenager will be able to observe hypothetical scenarios and actually practice various ways of handling different situations. The process can also be a lot of fun. You can role-play how to ask someone out, how to get dates, how to turn someone down, how to behave on a date, and discuss what to do in between dates.

How to Ask Someone Out

You could play the role of the girl, or you could play your son's role. Pretend you're calling the girl on the phone: "Would you like to go out to dinner Friday night? Great. How's seven-thirty? Okay, what's your address?" Then go over the other details of preparing for the date: decide where they will go (or he could have a couple of things in mind and ask her what she'd prefer to do), pick her up on time, open her door, have a clean car with plenty of gas, go to the ATM machine *before* he picks her up, and then just have fun!

Suggest to your son that before he asks a girl out he might want to get some indication that she's interested or receptive. Positive signs are that she seems interested in talking to him, exudes warmth, and she smiles at him a lot. Let him know that it might be wise not to ask her out on the spot unless the vibes seem right. Instead, he could try to find out what classes she takes, where she works, whom she knows— some connection, so that he'll know where to find her. Suggest that he wait a few days or so, and when he runs into her again, and the time is right, he could say, "So, maybe we could go out sometime." Stress the importance of his saying it with confidence and looking her directly in the eyes. He can then watch for her reaction. If she says "Sure!" he should get her number and tell her that he'll call. Suggest that he wait a few days before calling to set up the date. If it feels right, he could ask her out right then, but sometimes it's good to wait a couple of days. You probably have your own suggestions on how to ask a girl out—share them with your son.

Today, girls have the option of asking boys out, but based on my own dating experiences, as well as conversations I've had with teenagers and single adults, it seems to work better if the boy does the pursuing. This doesn't mean that girls can't open the door by smiling and being friendly, but I would teach her to wait for the boy to ask her out on a date. You can explain that the dating process often flows smoother this way because of the differences between boys and girls, not because they aren't equal in value and aren't both capable of pursuing. If you feel strongly about telling your daughter that she can ask boys out, tell her to be cognizant of how effective this approach is for her. If she isn't successful, she can then wait for boys to ask her out. Tell her, "If you're interested in a boy, just be friendly. If he's interested, he'll eventually ask you out. If he doesn't, someone else will come along."

How to Get Asked Out

Begin each of these talks with a question to find out what your teenager thinks. Ask, "How do you think a girl gets asked out?" Girls need to be taught to be approachable, not stuck-up or intimidating, and to be as attractive as possible. You could say, "Boys are sensitive. They have their pride to consider! Imagine how scary it would be to ask a girl out and be rejected. Go easy on boys. Be friendly. Make them feel comfortable. If you're not interested in a boy romantically, you can still be nice without giving him the indication that you want to go out."

How to Turn Someone Down

Ask your teenager what she would do if someone she wasn't interested in asked her out. See if she has given this much thought. Unfortunately, many people lie and say they're seeing someone else or they have plans for that evening, which usually backfires and ends up hurting the other person.

You could say, "I've found that it's always best to be honest and upfront. The last thing you want to do is string the person along or make up excuses. Just nip it in the bud by saying 'Thanks, but I'd rather just be friends.' Or, 'I don't really think we're right for each other, but I appreciate the offer!'"

THE "WHAT IF" GAME

If you give your adolescent a series of hypothetical situations, she will be better able to handle these scenarios as they come up in real life. Discuss these hypothetical situations and come up with additional ones:

What if . . . your best friend likes a particular boy and he asks you out?

What if . . . you like a boy but he doesn't know you exist?

What if . . . a boy says he likes you but he won't talk to you at school?

What if . . . you like a boy but he has a bad reputation?

What if . . . you aren't sure how a person feels about you but you want to know?

HOW TO BEHAVE ON A DATE

Boys usually have more to actually do while on a date than do girls (planning the date, picking her up, making sure she has a good time). Girls need only show up, have fun, and be interesting conversationalists. Tell your daughter that she doesn't have to try too hard to impress the boy—she should give him plenty of space to impress her. Tell her that she shouldn't worry too much about doing everything right—she only needs to be herself and have a good time. Her date will take care of everything else.

Thad, seventeen, said, "My biggest fear is that I won't know how to show the girl a good time and impress her." Boys can learn that most girls appreciate it when they have a plan or ask for suggestions. And girls almost always have a great time when the boy gets them talking and shows interest in what they have to say. You could offer this advice: "When you're on a date you can talk about common interests—music, school, sports, family, plans for the summer, what you did during spring break or on holidays. Find out about her and what she likes to do. Remember to be a good listener. Get to know the person you're with and let her know the real you. And don't worry too much about doing everything right."

THE IMPORTANCE OF BEING A GOOD CONVERSATIONALIST

Some teens are painfully shy. One fifteen-year-old boy said, "I wish I was more confident around girls, but I don't know what to say." Make this a family-night topic. Ask, "What do you think it takes to be an interesting conversationalist? Being one will help you develop more friendships, get more dates, and be more confident."

Explain that a good conversationalist has a little bit of knowledge about many subjects. Encourage your child to read a lot. Suggest that she ask questions about the other person in order to learn about his interests. Advise her to listen intently to what the other person is saying. This will give her other interesting topics to discuss.

You and your spouse could role-play various situations pertaining to initiating conversation as your child watches and learns. For example, pretend you're at a party and you've just met for the first time. One person must initiate the conversation. Offer your teenager suggestions on how to talk to people and what to say: "Hi! I'm John. What's your name?" Or, "What classes are you taking?"

Include the following points in your role-playing:

- Speak up—don't talk too loudly or too softly.
- Look people in the eye.
- Answer questions clearly and distinctly.
- Handle phone calls appropriately.
- Keep it light!
- Have fun—be fun!
- Be yourself—let your personality shine through!
- Be flexible—you don't always have to be right.
- Talk, but not too much!
- Be interested in the other person.
- Don't be critical of others or gossip. Be positive.

HOW TO TREAT THE OPPOSITE SEX

Both genders need to learn to treat each other with respect, kindness, consideration, and honor. Girls needs to realize that boys sometimes put a lot of thought and effort into a date. Appreciation and a good attitude will go a long way.

Boys needs to be taught to treat girls with respect and tenderness. Instruct your son to ask a girl how she feels, or what she thinks about various things. Tell him that he shouldn't leave her hanging when they're in a group situation, and he shouldn't tease too much.

What to Do Between Dates

Girls often pine for boys between dates. They can become obsessed and may even call the boy, which usually doesn't go over very well. Say, "One thing I learned the hard way is not to obsess in between dates! Keep yourself busy, and don't worry about whether he'll call. As hard as this is, it's the best way. If you get impatient and call him, you could scare him away or give him the impression you're too interested in him. Just be patient and he'll probably call you. If he doesn't, someone else will come along."

Boys don't realize that girls often wait by the phone for days or weeks after a date, waiting for their call. Some boys promise to call but never do, which creates a lot of frustration for girls. Tell your son that he isn't obligated to call a girl if he isn't interested but that if he promised to call he should do so. It's better for him to be upfront with a girl and tell her that he just wants to be friends than to lead her into thinking that he might be interested.

In between dates, your son needs to consider how he feels about the girl. You could say: "After you go out with a girl you'll naturally think about her and determine how you felt when you were with her. It's usually a good idea to wait a couple of days before calling her again so you can decide if you really do want to see her again."

You might think some of these ideas are game-playing (not calling boys, waiting to call, not showing too much interest). But I've found that it's human nature to appreciate a challenge. I think we've all experienced pain and humiliation by coming on too strong too early in the dating process. It's better to be cautious and protect ourselves until real feelings develop.

Dos and Don'ts for Dating

The following list of dos and don'ts is based on my own dating experiences over the years, as well as the conversations I've had with men, women, and teenagers. I've separated them by gender. Although some of the points apply to both boys and girls, there are many points that apply to one or the other sex.

Dos for Dating—Girls

Go over this list of Dos and Dont's for dating with your daughter. If you don't agree with some of these points, you can create your own list with your child. You can teach these points even if she isn't old enough to date seriously. You can always say, "This is training for the future!"

- Slowly reveal who you are to him over time. You don't want to share everything about yourself on the first date or two—be mysterious!
- Be interested in your own life rather than focusing too much on the relationship and where it's going.
- Be selective. There's always someone else out there for you, and he'll probably be even better!
- Be confident that the relationship will evolve if it's meant to be.
- Look for things in him to admire, appreciate, and respect.
- Get to know him better to determine if he's someone you can accept exactly as he is.
- Set the sexual standard whenever a sexual advance is made.
- Let him lead in the relationship (the calling, the asking out, suggesting where to go).
- Be lighthearted and fun.
- Be interested in him and what he thinks.

Don'ts for Dating—Girls

- Don't try too hard to impress him.
- Don't talk too much. (A large number of boys and single men complained that girls often talk too much.)
- Don't wait by the phone for his call or break plans to be with him—enjoy your life with or without him!
- Don't tell him how you feel about him until he shares his feelings for you first. You don't want to scare him away!
- Don't chase him. Remember, he chases you until you catch him.
- Don't constantly bring up "the relationship."
- Don't criticize him in any way. If his behavior is inappropriate,

say something. But don't criticize his interests, the way he dresses, or his goals in life.

- Don't take him for granted. Always appreciate whatever he does for you.
- Don't constantly try to compete with him; this can be a turnoff for guys.
- Don't be physically aggressive.
- Don't call him (except to return his call) or ask him out. Remember, he's the natural pursuer.
- Don't dwell on your problems too much.
- Don't be alone for too long where sexual advances could occur.
- Don't talk about past boyfriends.
- Don't assume you're an item too early.
- Don't hint or tell your friends about your interest in him. This could backfire and get back to him, and you could scare him away if he thinks you're too interested.

Dos for Dating—Boys

- Be respectful.
- Be confident.
- Ask her out after getting some sign that she's interested, then follow through as promised.
- Have the date planned. Decide where to go, have money, clean the car, dress nicely.
- Be a gentleman: Open doors for her, pay her way, walk her to her door.
- Get to know her—ask questions about her family, her interests, hobbies.
- Take the lead. Make suggestions, and always ask her how she feels about the situation. Make things happen.
- Set the sexual standard if she makes a sexual advance.
- Make sure she's having a good time. Does she like her food? Is it too cold outside for her—would she like to wear your jacket? Be considerate.
- Compliment her. You look nice tonight. You have such pretty eyes. Be sincere, but don't overdo it.

DON'TS FOR DATING—BOYS

- Don't seem too interested at first. Be cool and take things slowly—but not so cool that you seem disinterested.
- Don't be too focused on making out. Never pressure a girl to be physically intimate.
- Don't say you'll call, then not do it.
- Don't act immature on dates.
- Don't act aloof or bored on dates—be interested in her and in what the two of you are doing.
- Don't show up with no money or ask her to pitch in. Don't accept money from her, even if she offers. But it's okay to let her treat after several dates if she offers.
- Don't talk about past girlfriends, except briefly if she asks.
- Don't be preoccupied with the ball game on television.

Hopefully, your child will have many positive, memorable dating experiences that she can reflect on throughout her life. If she truly understands the purpose of dating, as well as how to behave on dates, she will develop the skills necessary to build a great relationship when the time is right. But another important aspect of dating is understanding what attracts the opposite sex. This will be covered in the following chapter.

❖ 15 ❖
Attracting the Opposite Sex

One thing I've learned over the years is that dating is largely about being attractive to the opposite sex. Of course, there's almost always someone for everyone, but I've learned that if you want to date a lot it's helpful to know what traits are appealing to the opposite sex. But where and when do we learn about this? We usually go through years of confusion and frustration trying to figure out what makes the opposite sex tick!

We also don't usually learn what to look for in a mate. It's easy to fall into serious relationships with people who are completely wrong for us or don't possess the character traits needed to make a relationship healthy and lasting when we haven't thought through these issues.

By discussing the information in this chapter, you can sharpen your adolescent's awareness of what to look for and help him to better understand what the other gender finds appealing while still encouraging him to be himself and maintain his own independence and interests. It isn't always enough to say, "Be yourself—someone will like you for you!" Amy, eighteen, realized that her heavy makeup turned guys off. As she toned it down, boys began to show more interest. Blake, seventeen, realized that his lack of eye contact and concern for girls' feelings alienated the girls he was interested in. He made an effort to change his behavior, and he noticed that girls were more receptive to him. Sometimes it's just a small shift in the way we interact with the opposite sex that can make all the difference.

"In Order to *Get* a Great Catch, You Have to *Be* a Great Catch!"

Well-meaning family and friends often give advice on how to find someone special. And there are countless books on the subject: how

210

to find the love of your life, how to get married, and how to get the love you want. But rarely are we taught that if we strive to be the best we can be, we'll draw to us someone who is our equal. Just as water seeks its own level, we draw to us the person we deserve! We complain about this or that, but we don't always look at ourselves or at what *we* have to offer.

The Sanders teach this principle in their family: "We talk about *being the right person,* not necessarily *looking for the right person.* If you do what's right in life, we believe everything will be okay. You may not get exactly what you want when you want it, but things will work out just fine. You'll be pleasantly surprised."

Have your teenager make a list of the qualities he would like to find in a future mate. Say, "If you really want to attract a great girl, the best way is to put your focus on being worthy of that kind of person. You'll draw to you the quality of person you are right now. Look at the character traits you listed and ask yourself if *you* possess those qualities. Does the list describe you? This list can give you important things to work on personally."

What to Look For in a Mate

As your teenager gets older, he'll need to think seriously about the kind of qualities he wants in a lifetime mate. This will help set the tone for more serious dating as he attends college.

Even though physical appearance or level of popularity is usually the highest priority in high school, teenagers need to be encouraged to look for noble *character* traits, as well as consider other important areas of compatibility. Go over these points with your child and come up with additional qualities that he might want in a mate:

Character: Character qualities include honesty, loyalty, integrity, humility, dignity, dependability, self-discipline, and unselfishness. Have your child give specific examples of what these traits look like in a person and discuss why they are important.

Love and affection: Obviously your child will want to find someone who loves him, and with whom he is in love. Discuss the importance of compatibility in the way of exchanging love and affection.

Attitudes: Attitudes relate to confidence, inner happiness and peace, a sense of humor, and one's overall outlook on life.

Values: Moral and religious values regarding money, sex, work/career, lifestyle, child rearing, political beliefs, goals, and dreams.

Health: Discuss the importance of finding someone who is healthy—emotionally, spiritually, mentally, and physically.

Friendships and extended family: Discuss the importance of appreciating and getting along with each other's family and friends.

Discovering What Is Attractive

Krista, seventeen, said, "I wish I knew what boys like in girls. I really want to date, but what is it that makes a boy want to ask you out?" Sixteen-year-old Sam has similar concerns: "My best friend John gets all the girls. I can't figure out what it is about him that makes them go crazy—I can't even get a girl to go out with me!"

You probably have your own teenage memories of how difficult it was to get someone interested in you. These concerns can be complex, and there isn't always an easy formula to follow for success. But if your teenager learns what is generally considered attractive to the opposite sex, he will have an easier, more enjoyable dating life. You don't want to hurt your child's self-esteem by suggesting that he doesn't already possess traits that are appealing—you are simply discussing the subject as a way to make your child aware of these traits. Undoubtedly, your child already possesses many attractive qualities. Be sure to point these out to him.

Margaret proudly told me that her fourteen-year-old son Derek said that he likes older girls because "they're more developed that way." She thought the comment was cute. This was a perfect opportunity for her to teach her son that girls are not just sexual objects; nor should you like someone primarily because of how they're built. Margaret could then talk to Derek about other qualities to appreciate in a girl, particularly *character* qualities.

Talk about What Attracted You to Your Partner

Teenagers love it when their parents talk about how they met and fell in love. Even if you're divorced, you can still talk about what initially attracted you to your child's father or mother, or you can share how your own parents fell in love. This is an excellent way for your child to learn about what brings two people together. Think about what you initially found appealing in your mate. Was it the way he confidently walked into the room? Was it her beautiful smile? Here are some examples of what attracted couples to each other. Share these with your adolescent during this discussion:

Bob: "She was easy to talk to."

Gunther: "I loved her amazing smile."

Phoebe: "He walked right up to me, put out his hand and said hi. I liked that."

Roderick: "She was holding a small child, and I loved the way she was interacting with her."

Farrah: "I had total respect for my husband because of his character. I knew he could cut the mustard and be responsible for our family. He exuded such confidence. I knew we wouldn't have money, but that didn't matter to me. I could see that he was a hard worker. He got up early and worked hard all day. That gave me confidence that he would take care of his end. We were pen pals for three years before we ever met. We always wrote letters; we have hundreds of them saved. I put a ribbon around the one in which he told me he loved me for the first time. Actually, he knew he loved me before we ever kissed!"

Jenica: "My husband tells me I was a lot of fun. He also liked the fact that I was genuinely interested in him, and his friends. I went to all of his ball games, and other events. He loved my musical ability. The interesting thing is, I was never very pretty. In fact I was quite plain, and I've never had the best figure. But appearance has little to do with it—it has more to do with your attitude. This is something I've taught my girls."

Ken: "I loved her beautiful eyes, and how she blushes."

The "What Boys Like in Girls and What Girls Like in Boys" Game

During your family night, over frozen yogurt or some other treat, have your child talk about what each gender finds attractive in the other. Preface the discussion with the fact that everyone is different, that we don't all like the same things, but that certain traits are generally found appealing in the opposite sex. This exercise will also help your adolescent to avoid developing a strictly physical view of the opposite sex.

The following list of qualities evolved from conversations I've had with teenagers and single adults, as well as from my own dating experiences. I've organized the information by gender because the comments I received from both sexes have consistently been different. Some traits overlap, but many relate specifically to boys *or* girls. This list isn't meant to be comprehensive, it's not etched in stone. Discuss additional traits that your child might find appealing in the opposite sex: spiritual traits and beliefs, personality traits, communication styles, mannerisms, relationships with others, and so on.

WHAT BOYS LIKE IN GIRLS

- Attractive and healthy. ("Cute" is a word boys frequently mentioned. But they usually followed that up with other attributes: sparkly eyes, shiny hair, clear skin, big smile, in shape.)
- Confident—able to just be herself
- Sense of humor (Boys rate this trait very high.)
- Intelligence
- Quiet, soft voice and laugh
- Femininity (Most boys said they don't like it when a girl tries to be "one of the guys." However, girls who are tomboys can still be attractive. A girl should be herself, but wearing a dress once in a while could do wonders for her dating life!)

WHAT BOYS DON'T LIKE IN GIRLS

- Arrogance
- Spoiled nature
- Know-it-all attitude
- Moodiness
- Flirts with other guys while on a date or when in a relationship with him
- Too serious (Boys particularly mentioned disliking it when girls always want to talk about "the relationship.")
- Whining, complaining
- Talks too much
- Too obsessed with her looks

- Unable to accept a compliment graciously
- Too much makeup
- Immodest
- Talks about past boyfriends too much

WHAT GIRLS LIKE IN BOYS

- Confidence
- Intelligence
- Masculinity (Most girls describe masculinity as being confident, aggressive, and the like. Be sensitive to boys who might not be particularly masculine.)
- Sense of humor (Girls rate this trait very high.)
- Hard worker/ambitious
- Humility
- Good communicator/listener
- Responsible—follows through with promises, makes mature life choices
- Understands girls (Girls often say they like it when a boy knows how to treat them and understands what is important to them.)
- Compassionate, kind, sensitive to the feelings of others

WHAT GIRLS DON'T LIKE IN BOYS

- Arrogance/oversized ego (This was mentioned more frequently than any other trait.)
- Teases too much
- Obsessed with sex/willing to say or do anything to get a girl to have sex with him
- Mean, heartless nature
- Cares too much about impressing his friends
- Poor communicator and listener
- Lazy
- Talks too much about past girlfriends and looks at other girls while on a date

The Importance of Being Interested in Your Own Life

It's typical for teenagers to become obsessed with the opposite sex. Will he call? Does she like me? Did I ruin the relationship? Is she interested in someone else? All of these scenarios will bring your adolescent valuable experience, but you will want to stress the importance of being interested in his own life, interests, and pursuits rather than on these concerns. You could say, "What people find really appealing is someone who has a full life and isn't obsessed with getting a date or attracting attention. Just focus on your goals, school activities, friends, and family. Eventually someone great will notice you, or you'll notice someone who's doing the same thing!" Point out to your teen that being involved and interested in his own life will also make him a more interesting person and a better conversationalist because he'll have more to talk about.

To Thine Own Self Be True

Your teenager shouldn't repress or ignore his natural personality or character traits in order to please the opposite sex. He should work with whatever traits he has. We all have little idiosyncrasies, and ideally we find someone who appreciates these traits. Teach your teenager to be true to himself—and especially never to compromise where his sexual standards are concerned.

The traits mentioned in this chapter are general guidelines that can shed light on what people typically find attractive. Be careful not to push them on your child, giving him the impression that he's inadequate if he doesn't possess them. Mention, too, that we all have moods. A girl isn't always going to have a good attitude. A boy isn't always going to be confident and a good listener. It's important that we remain true to ourselves and that our emotions and personalities are authentic. The ideas in this chapter can help your child, who may already be quite wonderful, to be even better.

An entire book could be written on the information in this chapter. Dating, learning about the opposite sex, and knowing what to look for in a mate are complex, confusing subjects. And the information cannot be covered in just one or two sittings. But if you share the points outlined here, your adolescent will be that much closer to understanding how to build a meaningful, loving relationship with the opposite sex. After all, *love* is the goal.

❖ 16 ❖
Building a Loving Relationship

Every adolescent should have a basic understanding of what falling in love is like and how it works. Eventually, we all want to create that reality for ourselves, and we shouldn't have to learn it through trial and error. Unfortunately, many adults haven't exactly figured out the process! We have already talked about dating. The information in this chapter will help you take your child to the next level.

You can discuss the information in this chapter with your child even if she isn't ready to be in a serious relationship. It takes time to teach these principles, so it's better not to wait until she's already in love or deeply infatuated with someone. But if you think your child might be falling in love and you haven't talked about it yet, do it now. Your teenager needs to know about every aspect of love: what it is, how to create it, the importance of commitment, and how to know if she is in love and if the other person is in love as well.

What Is a Loving Relationship?

Angela, eighteen, told me, "No one ever tells you that love and sex are two different things. I grew up thinking that I had to have sex in order to get love. You hear a lot about sex, but never anything about love!"

Adolescents want to know about love. They want to know what love is, how it feels to be in love, and how to get love. Parents often make the mistake of thinking, They're just kids! They're too young to even think about love or marriage. Besides, teenagers are incapable of comprehending what love really is—they simply have to experience it for themselves when they're older. This attitude robs our children of the opportunity to begin learning about how to recognize and experience feelings of love. The teen years are the best years to prepare for this part of life.

Start by asking your teenager what she thinks love is, and what she thinks is the difference between loving someone and being in love. Share this view with her: "You can love a sibling or a parent or people in general. But being *in love* is different. When you meet someone special, you sometimes experience an attraction so intense that a deep concern for that person develops. This feeling may start out being sexual in nature, but if it's really love it goes beyond that. You want to be with that person more often, you feel an overwhelming desire to give more of yourself and your emotions to that person. Eventually you want to commit to them. You don't want them to date other people. This caring and concern, this feeling of love and sexual attraction, grows out of *companionship*."

Make it clear that some of these feelings may be awakened immediately upon meeting a person, but they can only develop and deepen into true love as you spend many hours together getting to know each other. Sometimes you might think you're in love only to find out that it was only a sexual attraction. Or you didn't really get to know the person well enough. Stress that this is why it's important to take things slowly and to be sure that the love is real.

Troy, twenty-two, was considering marrying a young woman he had been dating for about a year. Everyone in his family loved her and encouraged him to marry her. On paper he knew she would make a great wife, but he couldn't help feeling that he just wasn't in love with her. His parents told him that love has more to do with commitment than with a feeling, and that love can grow over time. They were anxious for him to settle down and start a family. He wanted this too, but it was becoming obvious to him that his feelings for this person just weren't strong enough. Finally, he ended the relationship. Soon after that he met and fell in love with another young woman who captured his heart. His behavior around this new girlfriend made it obvious that he had made the right choice. Help your adolescent to recognize the difference between caring about someone and being in love. Finding a mate shouldn't be more important than finding someone you're truly in love with. You could say, "Romantic love is such a wonderful thing. It's the *feeling* you experience for another person, the *commitment* you make to this person—and it's the *action* you take in order to make this person happy."

How to Recognize Love

Teenagers often ask, "How do you know if you're in love, or if the other person is in love with you?" One mother told her son, "Love is being able to imagine growing old with that person—going through all of life's experiences together: having children, going gray together, experiencing health problems, and surviving it all."

You could say, "You know you're in love when you love thinking about that person—you feel so happy when you think of him. You're willing to make sacrifices for the person when the time is right. You feel compelled to be romantic, to do things for him in a romantic way. And you know your partner is in love when he does the same."

With your child, come up with tangible examples of what it's like to be in love. Some examples are:

- When you are completely committed to staying with that person no matter what, whether he is sick, poor, or troubled.
- When Mom goes fishing with Dad even though she doesn't like fishing.
- When Dad goes to the opera with Mom even though he doesn't like the opera.
- The fact that Aunt Sarah went to the hospital every day to see Uncle Jack when he had surgery.
- When you want to make the other person happy, and he wants to make you happy.
- When you accept each other's differences and imperfections.
- When two people open up and share intimate feelings for each other by saying "I love you" or "I only want to be with you." Two people also build intimacy when they share their fears, hopes, and dreams with each other. Be sure to point out that when two people love each other their actions match their words.
- When Mom and Dad hug, talk about their days, and show other signs of affection.

Come up with examples from your own life or from the lives of other people you know. The point is to help your child create a visual picture of what love is like.

USE POEMS, LOVE LETTERS, AND LITERATURE TO ILLUSTRATE LOVE

Poems, love letters, and literature can conjure up beautiful images of romantic love and inspire all of us to build deeper relationships with those we love. Search for letters, poems, stories, and movies that portray true love and share them with your teenager.

Elizabeth Barrett Browning and Robert Browning had an incredible love for each other. They expressed their love in many letters and poems. Here is one of Elizabeth Barrett Browning's most famous poems:

> How do I love thee? Let me count the ways.
> I love thee to the depth and breadth and height
> My soul can reach, when feeling out of sight
> For the ends of Being and ideal Grace.
> I love thee to the level of everyday's
> Most quiet need, by sun and candle-light.
> I love thee freely, as men strive for Right;
> I love thee purely, as they turn from Praise.
> I love thee with the passion put to use
> In my old griefs, and with my childhood's faith.
> I love thee with a love I seemed to lose
> With my lost saints—I love thee with the breath,
> Smiles, tears of all my life!—and, if God choose,
> I shall but love thee better after death.

The following love letter was written by Ludwig van Beethoven to his "Immortal Beloved." Even though Beethoven and his "Immortal Beloved" didn't marry, the letter paints a vivid picture of the intense love he felt for his partner. You can also use this letter to teach your teenager that strong feelings of love don't necessarily guarantee that the relationship will work out:

Good Morning—Though still in bed my thoughts go out to you, my Immortal Beloved, now and then joyfully, then sadly, waiting to learn whether or not fate will hear us. I can live only wholly with you or not at all—yes, I am resolved to wander so long away from you until I can fly to your arms and say that I am really at home, send my soul enwrapped in you into the land of spirits. Yes, unhappily it must be so—you will be the more resolved since you know my fidelity to you, no one can ever again possess my heart—none—

never—Oh, God! why is it necessary to part from one whom one so loves and yet my life in Vienna is now a wretched life—your love makes me at once the happiest and the unhappiest of men—at my age, I need a steady, quiet life—can that be under our conditions? My angel, I have just been told that the mail coach goes every day—and I must close at once so that you may receive the letter at once. Be calm, only by a calm consideration of our existence can we achieve our purpose to live together—be calm—love me—today—yesterday—what tearful longings for you—you—you—my life—my all—farewell—Oh continue to love me—never misjudge the most faithful heart of your beloved Ludwig.

> ever thine
> ever mine
> ever for each other.

In the book *Emma,* by Jane Austen, the process of falling in love is beautifully portrayed. When Mr. Knightley, the man Emma falls in love with, expresses his disappointment in her for making a hurtful remark to a woman on the outskirts of their social circle, Emma takes his criticism seriously and responds with deep regret and sorrow. She could have been indignant, finding ways to justify her behavior. She could have been angry at the nerve Mr. Knightley showed in reproving her. But she respected his opinion enough to see that he was right, and she attempted to make amends to the woman she had offended. John saw this reaction and his heart melted for Emma. He saw a certain tenderness in Emma, a vulnerable side that further encouraged him to fall deeply in love with her. In turn, Emma found herself developing deep respect for Mr. Knightley and his high standards.

These are the qualities that will enable your adolescent to eventually build a deep love that lasts. So often we settle for something less than this simply because we lack the wisdom needed to build such love. As you teach your adolescent values such as honesty, integrity, loyalty, and virtue, you can correlate these concepts with relationships. Explain to your child that by becoming a person of high standards and character, she can attain tremendous respect and trust with a lifetime mate.

TEACH BY EXAMPLE

Dr. Jay Gale, Ph.D., clinical psychologist, and the author of several books on adolescent sexuality, says, "We learn about love through the examples around us. The best way to teach your child about love and how to develop a healthy relationship is to demonstrate love in your own life. If you just explain love as some vague concept, kids probably won't get it. But if they see that Mom and Dad truly love each other and they express that love in healthy ways, kids observe those behaviors and internalize them."

A perfect example of this was shared by a friend of mine. His favorite grandfather, "Grandpa Lou," was married to his grandmother for sixty years. He told me, "My Grandpa Lou was so in love with Grandma Rose, even up until the day he died. I watched him very closely, especially in the last few years of his life. He was always so affectionate, hugging and kissing her often. That was my role model for love."

Former surgeon general C. Everett Koop observed that teens "are not so much seeking a sexual experience as they are to establish intimacy with somebody who respects them as an individual. I think one of the sad things that has happened in our culture is that with two working parents, and youngsters starting off as latch-key kids and then growing up into adolescence and being very much on their own, they lack the intimacy that they used to have with their parents and so they seek it someplace else. They mistake it for sex, so when they are given the opportunity, they say this is what I have been looking for."

How Love Is Created

When I asked eighteen-year-old Kurt if he had a girlfriend he said, "No, but I'm working on it!" Tamara makes his heart go pitter-patter, but he doesn't know how to move the relationship to a deeper level. "I'm real good at getting things started, like starting up a conversation and getting the girl interested," he said. "But to move it to the next level is a total mystery to me. I want to make Tamara my girlfriend, but I'm not sure what to do."

Kurt's mother or father can teach him how the process works. They could say, "Well, Kurt, if you think that Tamara feels the same way you do, then simply be honest with her. Tell her how you feel about her and that you'd like to date her exclusively. If she isn't ready to make a commitment you can continue dating until she's ready, or until you feel it's time to move on."

Teach your son that a woman falls in love with a man as her respect for him grows. She will respect him as his character unfolds.

Movies like *Braveheart* portray qualities of honor, integrity, confidence, unwillingness to compromise values, and so forth. You can rent videos like this and then discuss the traits and behaviors you observed in the actors. I'm not trying to portray a "real" man as someone who's always strong and confident, but these valiant qualities cause women's knees to go weak. Boys need to understand that a woman respects a man who is a combination of strength *and* gentleness.

Girls need to know that a man falls in love with a woman's *virtue* and *character*. Help your daughter understand that men typically fall in love through their *eyes,* whereas women typically fall in love through their *ears.* We like to hear loving, romantic words; men are usually inspired by a woman who is visually appealing, virtuous, and caring. She doesn't have to be beautiful, but she needs to be as attractive as she can be. Her focus shouldn't be on wearing more makeup or designer clothes, but on being healthy, active, and, above all, interesting.

Talk to your teenager about intimacy. Say, "Love develops as two people become emotionally intimate with each other. This means they share their innermost thoughts and feelings. The longer you know and trust the person, the more you will share private, personal thoughts and feelings with him. When you feel good about the relationship, you'll feel more confident about revealing who you are. True intimacy is almost like being transparent. You eventually let down your masks or walls, and you let the other person know the real you. Your partner does the same. You can create tremendous intimacy without being sexual. It has more to do with sharing your hopes, thoughts, feelings, and dreams."

Be specific as you talk about love. Lots of parents give answers like "You'll just know when it's right." But kids need more details. Dolly, fifteen, shared this with me: "My mom and I talk about love sometimes. I told her I've never really loved a guy. I ask her how she could have known for sure Dad was the one, because they married really young. She tells me that I'll just know. I told her I wished I knew what guys wanted, and my mom laughed. She said that guys don't know what they want. But I don't believe her! They have to know!"

Talk to your child about the traits the opposite sex finds especially appealing. Help her realize that she has the ability to create a relationship with depth because she herself is a person of depth. Also, teach your teenager what love *isn't.* Tell her that real love is about building a trusting, respectful, and harmonious relationship with your partner. Love isn't about being possessive, jealous, or controlling. Feelings must be mutual in order for a relationship to work. The other person needs space to determine how he really feels about you. Advise your teenager that the best way to protect herself is to have the attitude that she can and will walk away if the relationship doesn't progress naturally.

Point out that a healthy relationship is *not*:

- A wrestling match—constantly trying to get the other person to stop making sexual advances, for example.
- Plagued with fighting and arguing over every silly thing.
- Based on one person's control over the other.
- Full of tension and worry over what will happen or what the other person is thinking or feeling.
- Based on infatuation or a crush. It develops over time through intimacy-building experiences such as sharing your thoughts, dreams, feelings, and fears with each other. This takes time.
- Immature. Both parties discuss their goals, values, and so on, and decide what is best for each other and the relationship.

The Soufflé Metaphor

Share this metaphor with your teenager during family night. It goes something like this:

New love is like a soufflé. Do you know what a soufflé is? A soufflé is an exquisite dish (usually a dessert) that is creamy and delicious. But it's also extremely delicate. You have to be very careful as you prepare a soufflé so as not to ruin the texture and the outcome. You have to use the right ingredients and mix them just right. While it's baking, you must walk very softly so that it won't collapse in the oven. You have to handle it with kid gloves because of how delicate and precious it is. This is similar to what developing a relationship is like. You have to take things slowly; not come on too strongly, for example. After a couple have been in love for some time, and they've become completely committed to each other, their love becomes more sturdy and durable. Then it's more like a pound cake—still tender, but able to go through many more experiences without falling apart.

The Importance of Integrity in Building Love

Ask your adolescent what the word *integrity* means to her. Share dictionary definitions with her. The *American Heritage Dictionary* definition is: "Rigid adherence to a code or standard of values; probity. The state of being unimpaired; soundness. The quality or condition of being whole or undivided; completeness." Then say, "It is my hope that with every relationship you build—whether it is with a friend, a relative, or a partner—you will be a person of integrity. I've tried to teach you the values, standards, and morals that I believe will make you a person of integrity. Because you have embraced these values you are whole, complete, sound. You aren't going around using and hurting people. I'm proud of you, and I have respect for you because of your integrity. Others will recognize this aspect of your character, and they, too, will have respect for you."

Teach Your Child That She Is Worthy of Love

Help your teenager feel secure, confident, worthy of love, and capable of building a loving relationship with the opposite sex. One mother said, "I hope my daughters have learned that they don't have to put up with any mistreatment, and that they deserve to get back the level of love they give. I learned those lessons after many years of heartache."

Many young girls base their self-esteem on having a relationship. If they have a boyfriend, they feel they're okay. If the boyfriend loses interest, they begin to doubt their worth. Both sexes need assurance that they are worthy of love, regardless of how smart or beautiful or talented they are. Sometimes teenagers experience deep feelings of doubt and worry. One mother realized this when she came across some notes that her sixteen-year-old daughter had written. "I was surprised at how complex and serious my daughter's thoughts were," this woman said. "She wrote about being in love, and how this was the first time she had ever felt those feelings. She wrote that the feelings made her think about marriage, and how hurt she was because she didn't know what to do. I realized then that I had to talk to her about these things. I felt guilty, because I hadn't even considered talking about love or marriage with her. She's only sixteen, and I guess it just wasn't on my mind. I grew up in a family where we were expected to go to college and get a good education. Marriage wasn't something we were groomed for."

Another mother said, "I was so proud of my daughter for the way she handled a particular situation. She was really sick, and she noticed that her boyfriend wasn't attentive at all. He just didn't seem to be concerned with her well-being. She promptly broke up with him, and that was that. I would have rationalized the situation if it had been me. I would have made excuses for why he couldn't be there for me. But she knows when she's not being treated right, and she usually does the right thing."

If you notice that your child isn't being treated with love and respect, gently bring it up. Ask, "Honey, do you feel that Jared treats you in a loving and respectful way? You deserve to be cherished. I notice little things he says and does that I'm concerned might hurt your feelings. Let's talk about how you might improve the situation." You can then focus on building her self-esteem and convincing her that she's worthy of the best treatment, and of love.

The Realities of Love

Teens need to know that love isn't always what they might expect. You could say, "We've talked about what love is and how to recognize it, but there are a few realities about love that you need to know as well. Love doesn't always happen when we want it to. Sometimes it takes a while, and some people never find it. However, most people who want to do get married."

Remind your child that love isn't always mutual. Explain that sometimes a person loves someone, but the other person doesn't love them in the same way or to the same degree. That can be really painful for the person who loves the most. Tell her, "It's important that you find someone who likes you in the same way that you like him, someone who's willing to make a real commitment to you. That can take a while—sometimes you have to go out with a lot of people."

Important Issues to Consider Before Becoming Physically Intimate

This discussion applies to older teens of both sexes who are ready or are preparing for a more serious relationship. Begin by pointing out to your teenager that part of having integrity in building a relationship based on love is discussing important issues regarding the relationship. These issues particularly need to be covered before two people become physically intimate, even before they begin kissing passionately. If you're teaching your child to wait until marriage, you'll need to clarify how far she and her partner can go once they are in love and committed. (See Chapter 7.) Let your child know that she and her partner need to be comfortable talking openly and honestly about these things. You may want to ask your teen what she thinks the important issues are before going over the list:

How you feel about the person: Many times people become so obsessed with getting the other person to commit that they forget about considering whether they themselves even want to be exclusive. Suggest that your child ask herself these questions: Am I in love with this person, or could I be? Are we compatible? Would I want to marry this person and have children together? It may seem extreme to suggest to your child that she wait until she's in love before kissing someone, but explain the dangers of passionate kissing, such as quickly wanting to move to the next level of intimacy. Remind her that she may not want to passionately kiss several boys whom she may end up not being serious about.

How the other person feels about you: Ideally, the other person should express his true feelings for you before he makes any sort of sexual advance. But unfortunately, many don't. They just "go for it," because it's much easier than sorting out their feelings. Give the other person the opportunity to express his feelings in his own time. But no matter what he tells you, you should take some time to ponder what your intuition tells you.

The amount of time that you spend together: Your child needs to decide if the amount of time she and her partner spend together is adequate for her. Obviously, as a teenager, she's too young to get married, and it isn't wise to spend too much time with one person. But when she's ready for a serious relationship she needs to know in advance what issues to consider. If she feels lonely in the relationship, point out that the last thing she should do is get even more seriously involved by being physically and emotionally intimate with this person. Some girls tell me they think they will "hook" a guy by having sex, but that's not how it usually works. They may hook him for a while, but a relationship based on sex rarely lasts. Stress to your child that the goal is to build a relationship that has depth. Encourage her to wait until she's older and more mature before she enters into a serious relationship.

The Future: This is probably the most crucial area to consider, because no matter how strongly you may feel about the other person or how much time you spend together, if you're thinking marriage and the other person isn't, you've got a problem. You're stuck in a relationship that becomes stagnant. You've both arrived at a stalemate, and someone will end up getting hurt. Discuss the future and what you both want. More than anything, watch the other person's actions. Discuss these points now, because when your child goes off to college you may not have the opportunity to have this discussion.

Length of Time You Have Been Together: It's always best to date someone for a while and not rush into anything. But the length of time you've been together doesn't always determine the level of love and commitment you share. Although your feelings may seem strong, the longer you and your partner take to fully get to know each other, the better. Encourage your child to wait until she's at least out of high school (and possibly even out of college) before she gets serious with one person. Once she's in a serious relationship, urge her to date for at least a year before getting engaged.

Making a Commitment

If your daughter is at the age where she's ready to be in a committed relationship (eighteen or older), and she's been dating someone she really likes, she needs to know how a relationship moves along to the next level. Explain to her that there is very little she has to *do*—the guy will be compelled to take it to the next level as his feelings deepen. He should be the one to bring it up. Say, "If you continue to be yourself and allow the relationship to progress naturally, eventually he'll tell *you* that he doesn't want to see anyone else. He'll profess his love for you. But it's crucial that you don't go too far physically—that could frustrate the entire process. If he doesn't bring it up, you could express your concerns."

Boys, too, need guidance when it comes to moving a relationship along. If your son is at the age where he's ready to be in a committed relationship and he's seeing someone he really likes, you could say, "The best way to make a relationship a committed, exclusive one is to be direct about it. Girls love it when the guy expresses how he feels—they think it's so romantic! Take her out to a nice dinner, and later, under the moon and the stars, say, 'I really care about you. I want us to be in a committed relationship.' If she's ready, she'll love it. You have to be certain that she feels the same way. Watch her actions: Is she usually available to see you? Does she light up when she sees you? Does she include you in her activities, particularly those that involve her friends and family? Does she seem open to discussing the relationship, what she wants in life, her feelings for you? If so, what does she say?"

Marriage

So much of the information you have already shared with your child will prepare her for marriage. No doubt you have high hopes that your child will find a loving partner with whom she can share her life. Your adult child still needs wise counsel, and she'll probably be more open to it now than she was as a young teenager. The learning process isn't over once your child falls in love—it's the start of a whole new world of mystery! As your child searches for that right person, be careful not to place too much pressure on her to make it happen. Once she finds him, you can help her make sure he really is "the one."

Don't Place Too Much Pressure on Your Older Child to Get Married

I find it odd that the same parents who don't train and instruct teenagers in how to have a good relationship with the opposite sex often spend an inordinate amount of time hassling their older, unmarried children for not having one. Teenagers are too young to marry, but when they reach their twenties they need to be encouraged to enjoy their lives, to continue developing their talents, and to go on building meaning in their lives whether or not they are involved with someone. If you put pressure on your child to marry, she may begin to feel there's something wrong with her, that she's deficient in some way. Well-meaning family members further perpetuate this belief with repeated comments like "So, have you met anyone special yet?" or "I just don't understand these guys . . . a wonderful girl like you should be married."

The fact is, most people get married at least once in their lifetime (and many of them get divorced!). And for those who don't, the "old maid" image is almost a thing of the past. Some people don't get married for the first time until they're in their forties or older. Your adolescent doesn't need to worry endlessly about finding the right mate. She needs to be reassured that one day she will most likely meet someone who will make her heart skip a beat. But she also needs to know that this can take time, and that we are all on our own time-table.

The focus shouldn't be simply on getting married. It should be on finding someone with whom we are compatible, whom we love, and with whom we can see ourselves being committed for a lifetime. Pressure placed on single people to get married pushes some to make hasty, poor choices. Getting married is easy. It's *staying* married that seems to be a challenge. It seems that teaching kids how to accomplish that task should be the focus.

Before Getting Married

Your engaged son or daughter may need some guidance in building a great marriage. With the divorce rate as high as it is, it's worth the effort to at least have a discussion about important issues such as the following:

- **Money:** How do they plan to handle their finances? Who will pay the bills?

- **Sex:** If they are abstaining until marriage, have they discussed sexuality—desires, frequency, styles, and so on?

- **Children:** Do they both want children? How many? When would they like to start a family? Do they agree on how to raise children?

- **Religious beliefs:** Do they share the same beliefs? If not, how do they plan to reconcile those differences? Which beliefs will they observe in raising their children?

- **Goals:** Have they discussed their goals and dreams with each other? Are their goals compatible? Are they committed to supporting each other's goals and aspirations?

- **Expectations:** What are their expectations of each other, and of marriage in general? Both partners should be clear about what they are getting into.

- **Character flaws:** Are both partners aware of and able to accept the imperfections of the other? Are there serious problems that need to be addressed, such as alcoholism, drug abuse, a controlling nature, depression?

You don't want to pry or grill your child with these questions. Find some time when you can be alone with your child and just casually talk about these points. If you don't particularly approve of your child's partner, be careful not to sound as though you're trying to discourage her from marrying him. Instead, help her to consider these issues for herself. She may just realize on her own that they aren't compatible enough for marriage.

If your child becomes engaged, talk to her about how to maintain loving feelings within a marriage. Even if you're divorced, you've learned a lot about what works and what doesn't. What created love in the first place is exactly what keeps love alive. Also, teach fidelity within marriage. Your adolescent needs to know that the happiest marriages are those in which both partners are completely faithful to each other.

During family night, ask your child to share her thoughts on why it's important to be faithful in a marriage—and discuss why being unfaithful can destroy a marriage. Answers should include: because trust is destroyed, the relationship becomes tainted, hearts are broken. Also discuss the effects on the children of the marriage: heartache, fear of the future, self-blaming, missing the parent who leaves.

Every child deserves to eventually have an incredible relationship with depth. She can either go through a series of situations or she can create a loving, harmonious relationship that is based on real love and a solid commitment. As you teach these principles, your child will be well on her way.

The Big Talk Checklist

Under Eight

- Teach that the body is sacred, beautiful, and of great value.
- Have your child become familiar with how the body works.
- Communicate the importance of modesty.
- Answer questions regarding how babies are made, and the like.
- Keep a close eye on your child and teach what is appropriate behavior when necessary (no touching each other's private areas, or allowing others to touch you).

Between the Ages of Eight and Twelve

- Review previous discussions.
- "You are the landlord of your own body" discussion.
- Valuing privacy.
- Respecting other people's bodies.
- Discussions regarding the use of the Internet.
- Sex and reproduction: what sex is, the concept of sacredness, the fact that sex is sacred and a wonderful, powerful, and positive part of life between two people who are in love and are committed to each other.
- Puberty discussions: the physical and emotional aspects.
- Discussions regarding masturbation: practical aspects (and your religious views), as well as the fact that impulses can be controlled.
- Discussions regarding homosexuality: what it is, your views on the subject.
- Discussions regarding pornography: what it is, your views on the subject.
- The emotional effects of sex—oxytocin.
- Establish standards: when it's okay to become sexual, the consequences of sex and making out at various stages of a relationship, and the benefits of abstaining until marriage.
- Make a pledge to abstain.
- How to say no to sexual advances.

Between the Ages of Thirteen and Eighteen

- Review all previous discussions, particularly the standards your child established earlier.
- Controlling sexual impulses.
- Contraception: what it is, your views on the subject.
- Discussions regarding drugs, alcohol, and date rape. (Discussions about drugs and alcohol can begin earlier.)
- Establish priorities: discuss goals and your child's future family.
- Set dating guidelines: the age at which your child can date, curfews, and the like.
- Discuss dating issues: the purpose of dating, how to date, ideas for dates, and dating etiquette.
- Discuss the opposite sex: what the opposite sex finds attractive and what to look for in a mate.
- How to build a loving relationship: what a loving relationship is like, what being in love is like, commitment, marriage, and the like.
- What issues to discuss before becoming physically intimate on any level: feelings for each other, commitment, goals, compatibility, and so on.

If you are interested in receiving information regarding Laurie Langford's seminars, or would like to schedule Laurie for a speaking engagement, please call:

(310) 289-2133

Or write to:

Laurie Langford
264 S. La Cienega Blvd. #647
Beverly Hills, CA 90211

Index

Printed in the USA
CPSIA information can be obtained
at www.ICGtesting.com
JSHW012023140824
68134JS00033B/2843